PARTNERS

by   Stephen Housewright

Route 1, Box 240
Canton, Texas 75103

1995

BLANK FORMS EDITIONS
BROOKLYN, NY

Introduction
by Karen Finley   7

Locker Boys   17
Playmates   23
Lovers   29
Sons   33
Strangers   45
Friends   63
Commuters: Houston to Dallas   81
Commuters: Austin to Dallas   91
Companions: Dallas   97
Companions: Canton   153
Partners   227
After   279

Thank you Stephen Housewright for your generous, glorious, and scrupulous chronicle of your shared life with Jerry Hunt.

This intimate and frank memoir, *Partners*, written in 1995, is a series of stories that journey through the stages of the decades-long, enduring, romantic relationship between Stephen Housewright, an educator and librarian, and Jerry Hunt, an innovative experimental musician and composer. The forthright narrative provides cherished observations through a revisiting and recollecting of milestone events and daily entries with a sincere invitation to know their story. As readers of this testament, we witness and listen to remember and pass on the quixotic and adoring partnership of Stephen and Jerry.

This is a love story that weaves against and amidst mid-twentieth-century guidelines of American family values. In this volume we see the living resistance to labor and personal time, who can be authorized to love, undermining consumerism, the belief in faith but questions the existence of God. Meeting as children during the postwar '50s, their friendship matured and developed into romance, desire, and life partnership, while engaging with their family and community as beloved members.

Set mostly in Texas from 1957 to 1993, the book transports the ordinariness of daily living while being a dangerous time to be gay—before and during the AIDS crisis. In fact, engaging in "homosexual" sexual activity was criminal. Stephen and Jerry avoided criminalization by not attending traditional hot spots. Bar raids and arrests were routine with "cross-dressing" policing

and shakedowns. The couple navigated white south-
ern *discomfort*, the codes and formalities of gender role
expectations. Homophobia is systemic; testaments of
discrimination that is to be accepted, lived with, remains
traumatic history. Jerry and Stephen lived as an open
secret couple amidst the rural and working class and
conservative, God-fearing values. It wouldn't be until 2003
that the country would receive the groundbreaking case
Lawrence v. Texas, 539 U.S. 558—with a historic decision by the United States Supreme Court reversing laws
that criminalized private homosexual activity between
consenting adults as unconstitutional.

This book is a document in surviving. The AIDS crisis,
beginning in 1981, brought another danger to being a gay
man, and although the book only briefly includes AIDS
as part of the couple's story, it is apparent. From 1981
to 1992 there were 252,800 US deaths. By 1995, when
this book was written—another 257,262 deaths. That
December the cocktail was invented and the rate of death
would drop for people living with HIV and AIDS.

This book is also about a thirty-five-plus-year bond
before gay marriage was legalized. It is critical to recognize
the trailblazing achievement of the pair in their protection
of their same-sex union in the Lone Star State. And we
must understand this prose as a historical document
and as narrative proof of open defiance, pre-Stonewall.
The '60s remain not an obscure cultural movement but
a tour de force that challenged power, authority, white
supremacy, capitalism, women's subjugation, homophobic conventions, war, racism, and destruction of the
environment. And this story resides within this cultural
revolution. However, the events in this book are characterized by an unusual, self-selected, unique isolation,
setting the couple aside from participation in larger
organized movements to change society and policy. They
triumphed in the mundanity and routine of life—showing
up with their queer love in all the familiar places.

Their refusal to *go all downtown* to gay cultural
centers and bars removed them from art scene celebri-
ty-making or mentors to guide and support their own gay
pride joie de vivre. Before there was even the term gay
pride—they did it their way on their own terms. Theirs

was a relationship that suited them just fine in planning domestic bliss in all its eccentric and esoteric channeling of a love and bond so strong to assure the preservation of their union.

As a reader, there is a lingering, just beneath the surface, of the implicit aching incidents as a shadow to recall, the missed opportunities, erasure—targeted and routine discrimination, homophobia, or denial of marriage. Yet Jerry and Stephen still triumph. There is majesty in being able to have the wits, talent, family support, and the certain something-something to be able to retreat into the pastoral life "away" from it all. But it's excruciating that you never really do escape—the uplift, the beautiful gesture, is in the daring to try. Stephen and Jerry's priorities were noble, to each other, their work, service, their mothers, family, neighbors, friends, and coworkers. They didn't have time for dillydallying with the limelight. Their dedication to their crafts—the patience they brought to every project—gives us all a lesson in what it means to have creative determination without all the other unhealthy narcissistic trappings. And with their story we feel the couple's jubilant intention, sense of adventure, and celebration for their endeavors even when their love was illicit.

An essential part of Jerry and Stephen's story is their championing of the alternative lifestyle. As this story begins in 1957, when they meet as children during middle school—Allen Ginsberg's *Howl* had just been published the year before by City Lights Books. Beatniks and bohemians were making their mark in café society. The counterculture lifestyle by artists and the boomer generation in the '60s was collectively known as turn on, tune in and drop out. Jerry's career as an experimental composer innovated and influenced the New Music field with his use of computers and the way he performed his music with chance and ritual, was a refusal to create and perform traditional popular and classical music. Stephen provided a sustained commitment that gave Jerry a supported frame to center his artmaking. Stephen brought an awareness of wellness to the way he balanced his life, in not accepting the forty-hour workweek mandate and making sure he and Jerry spent time alone and together. His own career involved libraries, research, public information—this work was contrary from the lives of most men growing up in his neighborhood. His work challenged notions of masculinity and how men ought to make a living. The choices they both made, the way they lived their lives, were considered anti-establishment. Their priorities are inspiring with their practice of couple and self-care.

When the story reveals Stephen locking eyes with President Kennedy on November 22, 1963, on JFK's tragic last visit to Dallas, this significant traumatic event that is burned in our national memory also becomes a marker for Stephen's crisis of his own closeted life ending. He emerges determined with purpose and transcendence. Jerry is a maverick with his imaginative research process to make sure he has the time to dedicate to his artist hero's journey of cultivating his musical genius. The book allows for the process and progress of finding one's self's purpose, inside and outside of each other's orbit. The text is stirring in scenes like these, when Stephen lets us into his heartspeak, to hear all the joys and sorrows in this thing called *creativity on a shoestring*. Despite being hemmed in by heteronormative commandments, the couple maintained and sustained themselves with such genuineness and strength that this book is a profile in courage. They refused to be clandestine and lived in plain sight of good old boy politics. Their refusal to move away is both mystifying and to be heralded—we owe them our praise, appreciation, and tribute. Individually and as a couple they were trailblazers.

This tender book is crafted to document, as a journal timeline rather than a distillation offering sweeping critical assertion. Reading it works as a time capsule, where the finders discover their own meaning. Some of the recollections, in retrospect, have decidedly not given full context and cultural exploration in terms of hindsight, regret, political fallout, discrimination, or opportunities for change. And there is a haunting in the aftermath of such unresolved episodes as we try to grasp living and dying during these times, the choices made or not made or to remain in the past. We are gifted to contemplate and question our own reflections or what we could change in our own lives if given the opportunity.

One example is the section detailing Stephen's work as an English instructor at a maximum-security prison outside of Athens, Texas. The recollection expresses the *fear* that Jerry has for Stephen being in such a precarious, potentially threatening environment. This incident aligns with the pressure and alliance of expressing the "fear" that has been traditionally harnessed by heterosexuals for the fear of catching the disease of homosexuality, the criminalization of queerness, and the terror-joking that is always implied with prisons and male rape. So, at the same conjecture or *conjuncture*, the couple are both the feared, and the ones fearing to be criminalized—yet Stephen is "teaching" the men. Their status role allows them to express Stephen's *freedom* by the ability to have a choice to take or leave the position. This is important to acknowledge, that Stephen and Jerry could have easily been locked up for leading their lives as gay men.

This book, although written and self-published in a very limited run more than twenty-five years ago, is being distributed for the first time now in 2021—during the COVID-19 pandemic, amid urgent calls for police reform with the resurgence of Black Lives Matter. It would be disingenuous to separate the past from the present. This section of the text can't be cordoned off from current developments in the public's acceptance of gender fluidity and its concerns about corruption in the policing and prison systems. Jerry and Stephen presented as white cisgender men and were able to blend, when needed, into an egregious fundamentalist culture; to pass to some extent because of their gender presentation, despite their union. And so, in reading this part, we imagine the stories and lives of the inmates who Stephen taught—how I wish that Stephen could have been supported to continue teaching in prisons, as a form of advocacy. These passages bring to mind to today the untold stories of transgender women, primarily of color, who are incarcerated in male facilities and suffer sexual assaults and threats.

At times this book is simply hilarious, when the DIY madcap couple—experimental musician and nerdy librarian—decide to rough it and build their own home on property of Jerry's parents in rural East Texas. Some of these '80s scenes would be right at home alongside classic '60s comedies such as *Green Acres*, where it all comes together at the end of each episode—filled with wild antics, strange characters, and lots of innuendo; the happy couples always kiss and make up. The moments of keeping it sitcom-light—this resilient, barn-raising, help-your-neighbor subplot—become an antidote to the brutality of the system of bigoted laws and the coming explosion of the HIV/AIDS epidemic. Yet, there is something eerie in the dichotomy that subverts, largely by sidestepping them, the then-ubiquitous images of the terrorized, dying bodies of gay men. In this light, the chapter offers an escape valve from the gravity of the AIDS crisis era that we never really healed from. Wacky never felt so good.

Jerry and Stephen were dedicated to and passionate about the protection of animals and loving their pets. This was before emotional support animals or the term vegan were in vogue. They didn't need to verify or selfie pose their love of animals. Their joy and compassion for all creatures great and small endears us with their caring and tenderness. We understand their priorities of family, or chosen family, and that pets are part of their immediate circle too.

As many readers do, I read multiple books at one time. As I was reading this book, I was also reading Joyce's *Ulysses*—and coincidentally, while I was reading *Partners*, at the same time in *Ulysses*, early in the book, there is a scene in the chapter "Calypso," written with great gusto, where Bloom starts with breakfast and moves to defecation in the outhouse. In *Partners*, there is a scene, exhaustively delivered, about the trials and tribulations of installing a toilet and putting it to good use. I thought that was rather an amusing chance-operation/synchronistic examining and thought it worth sharing with you. I think Jerry would like that, too. There are poetic moments within *Partners*, of selected subject matter that typically isn't written about with such focus. Usually it is left unsaid or assumed, but in some circumstances everything is out of the closet, and the strategy is to treat the reader as family. To get in close. There are no scruples. Everyone wipes their ass.

And everyone dies. Yes, I can assure you everyone dies. And in this past year of the pandemic, death has been all around as. Avoiding death, death too soon, coaxing, at what risk, waiting for the vaccine. We have seen death up close and at a distance. Jerry's death in 1993 was against a backdrop of another earlier pandemic of AIDS. For Jerry, suicide—with the diagnosis of terminal lung cancer—was his ultimate decision to stop the suffering. The understanding is shared with us by Stephen, who lovingly lets us know we are not alone and shouldn't feel ashamed to speak of such subjects. It is taboo to speak about the process, the dying body—and this book breaks protocol to embrace the unspeakable. It is hard and yet easy to understand. A simultaneous heartbreak and respect for dignity and agency.

Before I go, and let you read the manuscript for yourself, I would like to let you know that I had the pleasure to know Jerry and Stephen and stayed at their home. I miss Jerry deeply. We made art together—but really, we made heart together. His tenderness, whimsy, and imagination were so endearing. They were a beautiful magnetic couple. Before Jerry died in 1993, he sent me a mobile he made with two branches and stuffed handmade hearts that he had sewn. He sent it to me for my newborn daughter, Violet, with a note—that this was for her. And that he wanted to make sure, to let me know his love and thoughts. And then he was gone.

Karen Finley
New York City, June 2021

PARTNERS

We argued off and on for thirty-five years about what he played that day, his recollection tending more toward Bach, mine toward Gershwin. He'd just transferred to my school, to the eighth grade, and the chorus teacher introduced him to the class as a very talented pianist who'd agreed to play for us. Whatever it was he played had the effect of a revelation on me: to see and hear someone my age bring music to life right in front of me, with such self-confidence and skill, lifted me a little above the safe and predictable realm I inhabited. This was the beginning.

We both clearly remembered how we met. It was just after lunch when the students left the cafeteria and spent the last few minutes of their lunch period on the black-top. I walked up to him, standing apart, and formally introduced myself: "Hello, Jerry Hunt. I'm Stephen Housewright." I believe I even extended my hand. I hope I did. In later years, when we'd both begun to look back on our youthful friendship as the initial stage of the history of our love, he'd tell this story of our meeting, always with a touch of mockery about my rather stiff manner. I'd laugh a little, too, at the spectacle of it.

But now I have the time and urge and need to examine what it all meant and what it means. That he was from another world, I must have sensed right away. (Twenty years later, critics would describe his performance art as "shamanic.") With an intuitive grasp of the meeting's significance and a sense of deference, like toward a supe-rior being, I was on my best behavior, supplying full names for the record and the contract. We soon became friends, and I'd frequently go by his house after school. His stop was just before mine on the bus route, at the end of a long street of all-brick houses (ours was merely trimmed with brick). Unlike at my home, where someone was always there, there were only dogs at Jerry's house until his parents came in later from work. We'd talk, listen to music, explore the kitchen for snacks. The Hunts enjoyed a wider variety of foods than I was used to, including capers, shrimp, and the thinly sliced hard salami they ate with mustard and crackers that became a special favorite of mine. Jerry knew his way around a kitchen much better than I did; sometimes he would perform some chore or other to help his mother prepare dinner.

From time to time, I'd stay for dinner, particularly on Friday nights. His mother would come in from her job as a secretary and start cooking, her hat still on and a cigarette in her mouth.

When Mr. Hunt was not traveling (as a salesman for Pet Milk), the four of us would have steaks and baked potatoes, grilled outside in good weather. One night Jerry and I stayed on the patio long after dark, acting silly (as we often did), taking turns playing deceased and mourner, the picnic table our bier.

That memory, still so vivid (because, I suppose, it was evoked so often over the years), serves as a kind of corrective. What mattered to me most, then, about my relationship with Jerry was that he was invariably fun to be with. Above all, our silliness was a delight in language, language serving parody, and parody sometimes serving as protection. I'm too much inclined now, as I recall our past alone, to evoke the graver significances of the details I describe. He took me out of the familiar, showed me new interests, new ways of being. But he also made me—we made one another—laugh.

The blacktop became a regular meeting place, a time for talking and being silly that counterbalanced the stifling, tedious hours of the classroom. At that time, in 1957, Jim Lowe's recording of "The Green Door" was a popular song. We got worked up about it one day, on that crowded blacktop, Jerry leaning against the outer wall of one of the classrooms, pounding with his fists and entreating, then demanding the Green Door to let him in on the secret it was keeping:

Midnight——one more night without
    sleepin',
Watching——till the morning comes
    creepin',
Green door——what's that secret
    you're keepin'?

(This was a routine we were to reprise often in the next few years.) Because we were so often together, and because our behavior was sometimes so outrageous, we became somewhat notorious at school—not a good thing for teenagers to be.

We got in serious trouble once. Every Friday morning (or was it Monday?), there was a devotional given by students and broadcast over the school's PA system. I don't remember now whether Jerry and I volunteered to give one of these or if we were asked, but it was a debacle. We were huddled close together over the microphone in the vice principal's office, reading aloud some text or scripture, and one of us got tickled, setting the other one off and making it impossible for us to finish. I think someone in the office had to switch the PA off. We were chastised by several teachers and ostracized by our fellow students for days. A classmate even came up to us while we were standing in the lunch line to tell us how ashamed of ourselves we ought to be.

It has never occurred to me until now—I'm a little sorry to admit—to wonder what my mother thought about this incident. She would have been there, I'm almost sure, because she worked in the school's cafeteria. I was always eager for the A-student's praise, and I must have told her about my turn to give the devotional. What did she think when she heard us break down, tittering over Holy Scripture? And what had she been thinking in general about her son and his new fast friend?

Although I don't remember the details, I know Jerry and I suffered some abuse by other boys who found our behavior suspicious. We were always together, and they did comment on that. I'm sure our affects were somewhat "sissified," particularly when we were in the throes of some "production" or other. I used to walk around dangling a limp right wrist; Jerry got to where he'd reach over and slap it down, especially when we were going along in front of the stores in our neighborhood shopping center. (In later years, he would claim credit for having "broken" me of that habit.) It's curious, but I think true: joie de vivre can be expressed as prissiness, but this kind of camp in boys discomfits onlookers not similarly disposed. (Years earlier, I had happily greeted the arrival of one of my aunts and her family by prancing just ahead of their car coming down our driveway, exclaiming in a melodramatic tone: "But I'm not dressed!")

Our gym teacher, Mr. Gaddis, apparently recognized how hopeless Jerry and I were at sports. We didn't spend our free time playing catch, practicing dribbling, and shooting baskets. On the baseball field, we were OK—not a liability to teams or a nuisance to the teacher because we were always allowed to wander far out into the school-yard, not even coming in when our "team" (whichever it was) came up to bat. We often stood talking or being silly at the chain-link fence along the school's perimeter. I can remember gazing into the residential neighborhood, wist-fully watching the people coming and going there, wishing I were free.

It was in the gymnasium itself where I think Jerry and I must have presented a problem for Mr. Gaddis. He figured out what to do with us, though, by making us locker boys. Whenever PE was indoors and the boys had to suit up, Jerry and I took up our duties inside the wire cage that held the hundreds of numbered baskets with gym clothes in them. We issued and collected the baskets through a Dutch door at the beginning and toward the end of each PE period. The rest of the time was ours, and we studied for upcoming tests or, usually, did the homework thus far assigned to be able to take fewer books home. We had a good time together there, amid the sounds of locker doors slamming, showers running, and the smell of stale, sweaty shirts, shorts, and socks.

Thirty-five years later, during Jerry's last year of life, our locker-room memories came back to us. Shortly after his emphysema had been diagnosed and his loss of lung function measured, Jerry was prescribed a course of pulmonary rehabilitation, which we began together in a hospital in nearby Tyler. This time, though, we were suiting up. The locker room and its sounds and smells, our gym bags, and our being in such an environment again might have made us laugh had it not been for the serious purpose at hand. Actually, we did begin to laugh about it all a little later, when we'd finished the training program in Tyler and were exercising twice a week in the athletic center in Athens. If any heart or lung patients were using the center when we were, we never realized it. The young men and women we exercised with were building muscle, losing weight, and gaining tone. We'd get tickled, in the locker room, at some of the pumped-up men who'd come to look like pieces of massive furniture. But more than that, we'd be amused at ourselves, taking lifting weights, riding bikes, and walking on treadmills so seriously now, at this point in our lives.

Sometimes Jerry had breathing problems while exercising. A spell of labored breathing might subside on its own (he snapped his fingers with a steady beat to help restore the breathing cycle and to keep himself calm). At other times, and more and more often, he'd have to stop exercising and use an inhaler to administer medicine to relax his bronchial muscle. My response to these crises was to keep exercising, finishing my number of repetitions or minutes, thereby encouraging him to resume and complete as much of his as he could. Of course, I was acutely aware of his difficulties. And I do remember people coming up to him occasionally to ask if he were all right.

I never knew how closely we were being observed, though, until after Jerry died. A month or so afterward, I went back to the center alone; I wanted to be where we had been, and I hoped that a bit of exercise might help me feel better (as indeed it did and continues to do). The young man who checked me in didn't comment about my being alone (I had always gone with Jerry); I suited up and began with a little time on the treadmill. In just a few minutes, one of the fellows working out came up to me to ask where Jerry was. I told him about his passing, and the man expressed his sympathy.

Others came up, then, one by one, during the hour or so I was there. I'd never realized they'd been watching him so closely, monitoring his decline, and admiring his willpower. The last person to speak to me was one of the coaches for the community college in Athens, and I learned that it was his son who had been checking Jerry and me in at the center for the last eight months. Sometimes when Jerry didn't need a shower, and that was the case more and more frequently, he'd dress and go out front and visit with this young man. He spoke to me, then, when I left that day, telling me how much he admired Jerry's determination and how much he had enjoyed talking with him, even when they discussed, and Jerry joked about, dying.

Playmates

When we arrived at Jerry's front door after school, we were greeted by the frantic barking of the Hunts' wirehaired terriers, Hermie and Sassie. They pawed the Venetian blinds in the window near the entrance, then they pounced on us as we walked in. Jerry got busy looking for whatever damage they might have done during their long, boring day alone; he'd discover a gnawed slipper, a shredded cigarette package, or—Hermie's specialty—a long ribbon of toilet paper extending from the bathroom several yards down the hall.

I loved these afternoons in an empty house, with the freedom and space they provided. At my house, by mid-afternoon, my whole family would usually be there: Mother, Daddy, Granny, and my sister, Judy. It was also a treat to explore adult spaces in a strange house, examining the bric-a-brac, exploring Jerry's parents' rooms, admiring the new Early American furniture in the living room and den (we'd never had suites at home).

We'd soon settle in Jerry's room, though, with its blonde desk, bench, and double bed (items I still use). Jerry had quite a few records, and we'd listen to Jacques Ibert, Béla Bartók, Maurice Ravel, and Sergei Rachmaninoff on his monaural Webcor with its simulated leather case. I had only just begun collecting records, but it was already apparent to us both that our musical tastes were different. As a pianist, Jerry was interested in music for the keyboard. He was also fascinated by orchestral tone color. I was listening to symphonies, to Richard Wagner, and still to musicals. We'd play things for one another, but it was more a matter of taking turns using the record player.

Bach was the exception. One afternoon, Jerry played a couple of keyboard concertos, performed by Helma Eisner on the harpsichord on a disc he had checked out from the downtown library. I was entranced—hypnotized almost—by the music Colette described as a "divine sewing machine" and, at the same time, energized by the propulsion. I couldn't get enough of it and still can't (although like any potent substance, it should be taken in moderation if it's to have the maximum effect). For my fifteenth birthday, Jerry gave me Wanda Landowska's *The Art of the Harpsichord*, inscribing it "Best wishes to my closest friend—Jerry E. Hunt."

Our love for music, even as it occasionally diverged, probably was what inspired us to create The Society for Fine Arts and Sciences and its "organ," *Lachesis* (named for the Fate who measures out the thread of life—but mostly for the look and sound of the word). We spent many after-school afternoons and late Friday and Saturday evenings working on that publication. Jerry would write long articles on music and religion; I'd contribute movie reviews and a kind of gossip column about movie stars; and our friend Carol would write articles about astronomy. (A fourth member of the Society and would-be contributor to *Lachesis*, Elsie, soon dropped out of our group, having discovered horses and horseback riding.)

We enrolled as many of our relatives as we could as subscribers to *Lachesis*, and I am proud to say we delivered on the promise we made to them. There was almost a year's worth of magazines sent out before we lost momentum and found other interests. I've managed to keep a few issues all these years, and it's sweetly embarrassing to read our pretentious prose.

Squabbles among ourselves about power in the Society frequently emerge in the magazine as various administrative titles are jockeyed about from issue to issue. But what I recall most warmly are the hundreds of happy hours we spent typing our articles on Jerry's Remington Rand Portable, which had a specially inked ribbon that produced a master; using the tray of gelatin called a Hectograph, we could duplicate seventy-five copies or more. I handled all the Society's correspondence at my own house on my own Remington Rand, bought, I suspect, to have one like Jerry's. I still have a box half-full of the stationery we had printed.

Some afternoons Jerry had to practice. He studied with Dr. Paul van Katwijk and later with Silvio Scionti, and performed regularly in recitals. I hated to be around when Jerry practiced because he really worked, becoming absorbed in the music and the problems it presented to the performer, absolutely indifferent to anyone who might be nearby. And he was extremely hard on himself when he played the wrong notes, banging out the correct ones over and over with a relentlessness that frightened me (and that continued to do so through the years, a few times even driving our dog and me from our two-story house on Swiss Avenue). I often think of his mother and wonder how she stood it, coming in tired from work and a crosstown drive. Jerry probably finished most of his practicing before his father got home later.

I liked to make music, too. After a few years studying the accordion, I switched to the violin during junior high. By the time I met Jerry, I could play, or play at, a little simple chamber music. On two or three occasions, Jerry, Carol, and I tried to read through one of Carl Philipp Emanuel Bach's trios. Jerry would also accompany Carol and me as we blithely raced through the violin parts of Johann Sebastian Bach's double concerto. We knew his musicianship outclassed us; it was obvious to us both that his role in these sessions was to be patient—and he mostly succeeded. I do recall a couple of times, though, when he stubbornly continued reading for a minute or two after Carol or I or both of us had floundered among the intricate scale passages and had finally stopped playing.

We began going downtown on Saturdays quite regularly. We'd ride the bus from our East Dallas neighborhood the forty-five minutes or so it took to get there. The library was our first stop; we'd return the books and records we'd checked out earlier, then we'd start on our adventures in the city. Cokesbury Books was conveniently located just across from the library. They carried the entire Modern Library, and they often had books on sale (I bought a little pocketbook of foreign words and phrases there that I still use). It was an elegant store with fine wood paneling throughout, and no place I knew of had more atlases and globes.

We'd cross the street to Titche's to visit their book and record store on the mezzanine. There was a bakery and a very cosmopolitan luncheon café on that level as well, and sometimes we'd sit down at one of the booths served by a separated walkway for waitresses and order a sandwich and the raspberry ice we both loved. It was fun filling out our guest checks with the golf pencils provided for the purpose.

Then we'd head down the street several blocks to visit Whittle's, the music store that also sold records and instruments. I'd stay on the ground floor looking through the records (and playing some in the listening booths), and Jerry would usually head down the stairs to the sheet music department in the basement and to the piano Whittle's made available there for trying out music. We sometimes dared to ride the freight elevator up to the piano department where Jerry would audition pianos—depending on the mood the salesman was in and how busy they were.

If we hadn't eaten at Titche's, we'd now eat at the Blue Front German restaurant across from Whittle's. It had a bar-like atmosphere that intrigued me, although we were too young to have lager with our Polish sausage sandwiches and hot German potato salad. There was a German lady waiting tables there whose accent appealed to us. I suppose Jerry and I enjoyed the contrast between that European atmosphere and the less exotic ambiance of Wyatt's Cafeteria and Youngblood's Fried Chicken out in our own neighborhood. Over the years, we continued to seek out unusual places to eat downtown, including Crowder's Brass Rail, which had decorative steins on display behind the bar, and the Mayflower Coffee Shop, which served baked beans in individual cassoulets and had a kitschy elf on the back wall that quoted the rhyme about keeping your eye on the donut and not on the hole as you ramble on through life.

When my fascination with Montgomery Clift began to possess me, we added another stop along our route: Harper's Bookstore. This was a tiny hole-in-the-wall that sold used books and magazines. Mrs. Harper was a huge woman who never left the easy chair in the front of the store; after her death, the tall and thin Mr. Harper kept the store open a few years, boasting a nationally famous collection of postcards. Finding things there always meant searching through shifting piles of magazines and sorting them to make a selection. I'd be working with issues of *Photoplay* and *Modern Screen*, and Jerry would be riffling through electronics magazines looking for circuit diagrams that he could use to build sound-making devices for electronic music. He also bought the odd occult book when he ran across something intriguing.

Sometimes we'd walk back uptown to the library, checking out more books or playing records in the listening rooms there (or using the desk headphones), filling our green canvas library bags with items for the days and weeks to come. Or we'd stay downtown, waiting there for the bus home, gazing up Commerce Street at the lights of the hotels and restaurants that had just come on.

Fifteen years later, we were living in that two-story house on Swiss, replicating our version of middle-class suburban life, teaching at a prep school and a college, furnishing rooms, and entertaining friends, but we had largely stopped sharing our explorations and discoveries with one another. Circumstances certainly affected our behavior, but we, too, were at fault for relaxing our vigilance and for allowing ourselves gradually to stop playing together, having adventures. In due course, I'll get into all that, but what strikes me now is that our early years were some of our best and that the better times we were later able to create were good because they were so much like those in the beginning.

"I think I like boys," I told him one night at the drive-in movie where Mother had taken Judy and us. Jerry and I had little interest in the movie, apparently, and had wandered to the very back of the lot. We were standing (as it seems now we often were) beside a chain-link fence, looking out into the nearby neighborhood.

"There's a word for it," he replied: "*Homosexual*—you know, like in homogenized milk. 'Homo' means 'same.'"

A couple of years earlier, I had experienced my first ejaculation while riding my bike. I used to coast down hills using my muscles to balance myself on the handlebars, and one day the strain resulted in that surprising, intensely pleasurable sensation. Over the next few months, I kept a tally on the garage wall above where I leaned my bike, marking each time that that wonderful feeling had occurred—rather proud of myself, I suppose, that I had managed to achieve such a "breakthrough," or receive such a gift.

I also learned that I could cause the same sensation by wearing two pairs of jeans, thus constricting the genitals. I'd walk down to the shopping center and soon have an orgasm as I passed along in front of the stores. This became my preferred technique, probably because of the challenge not to reveal anything to the people on the sidewalk about the pleasure I was experiencing and added an element of titillation to the event. I must have spent a lot of time spot-washing my clothes; I was always throwing shorts or jeans with a wet place on them into the dirty clothes hamper in the bathroom. Did Mother or Granny ever wonder about that?

In winter, though, I switched to a new procedure. I'd light the gas fire, strip, and lie on my stomach on the cool tile floor, gently moving my legs and hips to achieve the by-now familiar sensation. The five of us shared one bathroom, and although I'd abandoned my tallying when the weather got cooler, I'm sure I hadn't tried to cut back on the number of times I experienced the good feeling. I learned to pretend to be bathing; that gave me the time I needed, though I had the bother of filling the tub.

Jerry was way ahead of me, of course. His giving me a term for my confessed predilection no doubt reassured me that there were others like me, but it also established him as a sexual mentor. He showed me how to masturbate with soap and water, the two of us standing naked in front of the big mirror in his father's bathroom. Naturally, the pleasure I experienced was even more intense than what I was used to, and that was in part because I was sharing it with another boy.

Our friendship had entered a new phase. We masturbated together as often as we could, and we soon began masturbating one another. We moved to the bed one day and discovered intercrural intercourse and frottage. Fellatio followed. We experimented with positions and places, often lying on the carpet in the living room (off-limits to the dogs) between the sofa and the coffee table. I remember how amusing it was to look over at the delicate china figurines representing English gentry on the lower shelf of the coffee table while we were in flagrante. We also lay under the grand piano, which became a regular trysting place for us in later years, both when the piano was moved to the Green Shack and when we were visiting Bob in Houston and took advantage of the space under his seven-foot Steinway.

It was always a worry that Mr. Hunt would come in unexpectedly, and we did have a couple of close calls (even on Swiss Avenue, many years later). As a salesman, he might call on stores in the neighborhood and drop by the house for a bite to eat or to use the phone or the bathroom. We knew better than to lock the front door—that would be suspicious.

Establishing what at any given time others knew—or even what oneself knew—is always difficult where sensitive matters are concerned. I think now that the Hunts did suspect early on that Jerry and I were "messing around," but they chose not to think too much about it—until they later confronted Jerry with his homosexuality, at a time when I was out of the picture. However, I never felt unwelcome; as best I can remember, neither Jerry's parents nor mine ever exerted the slightest pressure on us to be together less or spend more time with others.

One of my earliest fascinations with Jerry concerned the almost adultlike relationship he had with his parents. They involved him in making decisions and gave him responsibilities to a degree that was much beyond what I was used to. When he was headstrong, they seemed to loosen the reins. I realized a few years ago that they knew all along they were rearing an exceptional child, perhaps a genius. That was, indeed, what they had always heard from their son's teachers.

Perhaps Jerry's awareness of the special regard, apart from love, in which his parents held him strengthened his sense of identity. He was very comfortable as an independent thinker even as a young boy, which had a mixed effect on me. We enjoyed sex together, keeping our secret, of course, but never questioning the implications of that facet of our friendship for ourselves and our families. It goes without saying that in the late '50s and early '60s, we had no notion of political identity as homosexuals of "gay rights."

Of this much I am sure: what Jerry knew was that he had a friend with whom he could be completely himself, someone with whom he could "play" with increasingly higher stakes. What I knew is more problematic. Even as a very little boy, I realized that other boys and men mattered to me in an unusual and suspect way. All the subtle and overt promptings I felt to care, especially for girls, meant nothing to me—except later when they became goads to what I soon realized would be an inevitable failure. Jerry and I were almost too successful in insulating ourselves from the censure that would have forced us to examine our natures and our behavior, asking the questions that would have led to self-affirmation or, perhaps, to a cry for help. In my case, that cry and that affirmation were to come almost twenty years down the road, a delayed climacteric that, today, is referred to as "coming out."

But Jerry never really needed that self-examination; he never really needed to "come out." He was cast as an eccentric early on, and it was a role he enjoyed and cultivated throughout his life. His musical talent, his genius—they dazzled people and kept him on a protective dais from which he could look down at those who dared not look up to examine his manner or his motives too closely. In a sense, he was able—freer—to love me more deeply than I was him. I was even a little afraid of him at times, afraid of his self-assurance and of the demands he made on me.

Whatever it was that got shoved aside to be resolved later, in my case, was no obstacle to our enjoying ourselves together. I began spending the night with him more and more often. His parents respected his room as his private domain. We'd shut the door, and when we heard his parents go to their bedrooms, I'd jump in bed with him, abandoning for a while the single bed that was there for a couch during the day or a guest at night. We were always careful to make our clean-up trips to the bathroom separately and at some time apart.

Afterward, I did go to my own bed. That, as I look back on it now, tells the tale. We were kids, after all, effortlessly capable of arousal and orgasm, not so capable of romantic love. It's probably just as well that that was so; had it not been, we'd have been caught for sure.

"Different—he's so different." My mother had a way of saying this, referring to Jerry, that conveyed a mixture of amusement, bafflement, and suspicion. The friends I'd had before were unremarkable as individuals: John, a boy I rode bikes with; Skipper, whom I visited in his home; and Vonnie, whom I walked with to school. Jerry would come home with me and command everyone's attention with his self-possessed manner and politeness. He was always capable of conversing with adults as an equal.

He'd play our spinet piano if Mother or Granny asked him to, but he never really enjoyed playing for people casually. Music was too important to him. When he did play at our house, it was usually something like "Autumn Leaves," "Deep Purple," or "Mood Indigo"—tunes he'd style à la Art Tatum, his keyboard hero at that time. His mother and father especially enjoyed this music—and boogie-woogie. Hearing Jerry play these songs was a good part of their return on the investment they'd made in paying for expensive lessons (and providing the transportation to them) and for the pianos themselves. Whenever the Hunts entertained and Jerry agreed to play, it wasn't Bartók or Erik Satie that their friends really wanted to hear.

We'd go back to my room (the Society's administrative headquarters) to work on projects, talk, and play with my cats, Melissa, Matilda, and Minerva. He'd have dinner with us at the relatively early hour that we'd eat to accommodate my father's schedule. As a produce shipping clerk, he had to be at work by four in the morning, and he would be home by two or three in the afternoon and ready for a meal by five. We always had a wonderful variety of vegetables and fruits from the market where

Daddy worked or from his backyard garden, but we didn't attempt gourmet cooking at our house. From her job as an assistant food preparer in the junior high cafeteria, Mother learned to serve Jello in cubes and a mound of cottage cheese atop a pineapple ring on a bed of lettuce (sometimes crowned with a maraschino cherry)—dishes Jerry would remember, and mock, for years. Over the years, he also teased me regularly about the amount of starchy food we always ate: navy beans, potatoes, macaroni and cheese, and rolls or cornbread—all in the same meal (with fried pork chops and baked apples for dessert).

Whatever the culture shock Jerry felt, and however much he exaggerated that feeling for its entertainment value, he always seemed to enjoy coming over. For one thing, everyone in my family so obviously liked him. When he hadn't been by in a while, Granny would ask, "Where's your partner? How's he doing?" (I remember being a little amused at her choice of that word, evoking, as it did at that time, Tonto and the Lone Ranger, Pancho and the Cisco Kid, or, a little later, Chester and Matt Dillon.)

Jerry and my sister, Judy, became good friends. Whenever the subject of being an only child came up, he always congratulated himself on being unhampered by sibling rivalry and able to enjoy his parents' undivided attention and support. He claimed not to understand what it's like having a brother or a sister, and he asserted his gratitude to fate for not having to know.

Judy and I argued (I often bullied her), and we competed (I usually won), and, in those early years, I suppose Jerry didn't see much advantage to having a family any larger than three people.

What happened that began to alter his thinking about siblings was that I went away for a week, during two summers, to visit my Aunt Grace in Kilgore. Jerry must have felt lonely, and he came over to visit my sister and watch TV with her while I was gone. I always think of her at that time with her hair in rollers, and I see the two of them sitting there on that sectional couch watching sitcoms and movies, snacking and laughing, and—I like to think—missing me. A sister could be good company.

Later, Judy and Jerry had another day together, their first extended visit in thirty years when she came down from Idaho to spend a week with us. They reminisced, I understand, about their childhood friendship while I was in Dallas at work. They also talked about me, about what Judy could do to help me when I was to be alone. Knowing that I had Judy was the single greatest solace Jerry had when he thought about what was just ahead for me.

*
**

No two men could have been more unlike, at least in personality, as Jerry's father and mine. Daddy had had a difficult childhood, eventually running away from home from an indifferent stepfather to live with an older sister and her husband. He worked in the fields, had little formal education, and became a fun-loving, somewhat reckless youth with an undeniable appeal to my romantic mother. He spent his early married years driving a fuel truck for Gulf Oil when he and Mother lived in Mexia. The Depression brought them to Dallas, where Daddy found a job driving a truck for Ben E. Keith, a wholesale produce company. He was later promoted to shipping clerk, and when he was more or less forced to retire due to disability, he had spent twenty-seven years in their employ.

Daddy enjoyed working in his garden more than anything else—except listening to baseball games on the radio. He worked hard on the job, and he'd come home in the early afternoon, lie down for a while, and then work outside until dinner, after which he'd watch a little TV (*Gunsmoke* was a favorite program), bathe, and go to bed. Judy and I learned early to keep quiet in the evenings.

I never really felt I knew my father until I began to work with him during my last summer in high school. I was hired to fill short orders from the huge warehouse, and I had a good time pushing my dolly from one cold storage room to another, gathering the produce and sundries to be loaded onto trucks for delivery. I'd collect the called-in orders from the front office and take them to my father; he'd shortlist the items for me to retrieve and then arrange the orders in the sequence that would represent stops on the various delivery routes. What impressed me most was his skill in working with the drivers whose trucks we'd load after our early lunch. With the greatest tact and his usual gentle humor, my father would let them know what needed to be done: make the Circle Grill before Brownie's because "Old Lady Coombs is hot again today"; be sure to hand-deliver the strawberries to the cook himself at the Golden Pheasant; pick up the crate of cukes that the Magnolia Tea Room claims arrived damaged, and replace them with two new ones.

He joked with these men, guiding them in their work and smoothing over the quarrels that arose from imagined unequal treatment or personal differences or boredom. I began to see who my father was through the reflection of him in their eyes: a considerate, fair man who was as good as his word. He even had a way of handling his frequently headstrong son—the one who, almost ten years earlier, insisted on taking his cat to Kentucky on the family vacation until he'd shown it wouldn't work by subjecting us all to a few blocks of frantic scratching and caterwauling. "Let him see," he'd say, sometimes to himself. He knew I liked to think most good ideas were my own.

Daddy enjoyed his job, enjoyed socializing with the drivers and office clerks, and even some regular customers. And everyone was fond of him, respecting him and liking to be with him at the same time. For as long as he had his health, he was in his element at Keith's, a fact that I appreciated even more when I worked there full-time after leaving high school at midyear and before starting college. I am grateful for having been able to work with him so closely, for having been able to see him, to see anyone, derive satisfaction and pleasure from a demanding job, day after day, year after year.

But I am sorry he didn't get to know me, and much of the blame for that is mine. For whatever reason, I couldn't really talk with him about my concerns, my hopes and fears. Perhaps it didn't seem too important to me then that he knew them: he was so unlike me, how could he understand, and what could he do? Jerry and I had this in common, a sad distance between our fathers and us— men whom we sometimes feared and even resented, but whom we did come to like, and love, in later years. We sometimes talked about it. We surmised that our fathers sensed their sons were homosexual early on, that they felt threatened by this fact and utterly helpless to deal with it.

Jerry's father had the personality suited to selling and enjoyed his job as much as Daddy did his. "Mike"—as his customers, colleagues, and friends referred to Clarence (a name he hated)—called on grocery stores, pushing new Pet Milk products, checking displays, and taking orders. He was a tall, invariably well-dressed man who commanded attention wherever he went, and he didn't like to stay in one place long. He was proud of his talented son, never more so than when Jerry played at the country club where the Hunts belonged. As Jerry's musical interests led him into the avant-garde, Mr. Hunt grew more and more impatient with what he saw as an irresponsible career move. Why would Jerry perversely practice John Cage and Karlheinz Stockhausen when he could so easily have renown as a classical pianist or even as a jazz pianist? He and Jerry often argued about the subject, and one day, after what had no doubt been a long siege of Jerry practicing some prepared piano piece, Mr. Hunt marched into the living room and snatched the oversized score off the piano, tearing it in half.

This volatility was a trait Jerry inherited from his father; they were an even match, and Mrs. Hunt never really succeeded in defusing their fits or confrontations. Eventually, she seemed just to stand back and let them have their heads—although failing to remain unaffected by their anger and violence, of course.

After the explosion, everything would quickly return to normal. I inherited from my father a tendency to withdraw and sulk, sometimes even making plans to get even. Jerry's house was a noisy one, mine quiet—he, his parents, and their two high-strung dogs, accompanied by the piano and TV, were always right together in the thick of things; at our house, we were all in separate rooms, pursuing our individual aims, only vaguely aware of what the others were up to. I think Jerry enjoyed coming over sometimes just to get a little relief from the highly charged atmosphere in his own home.

The surface calm at my house was misleading, though. In several ways, we were all plotting, nursing wounds, seeking vindication, keeping secrets, and longing for escape. Judy married right after high school and flew to Germany with her Army husband. I had already gone off to college, to East Texas State in Commerce, mainly to be with Kirby.

Daddy, now retired and ill with arteriosclerosis and emphysema, finally persuaded Mother that Granny had to go. He'd put up with her annoying habits, her continual cleaning and faultfinding, for almost twenty years, and he couldn't take it anymore. Mother found rooms for her in state-subsidized private residences until Granny finally had to go to a nursing home. When I went back to visit, I'd find Mother sitting in the yard under the trees reading magazines, and Daddy would be inside asleep in his recliner, the TV on. These were Mother's hardest, loneliest years, and they weren't to end until Judy's husband, Paul, was sent to Vietnam and Judy returned to Dallas.

As younger men, our fathers had in common a certain rakish, high-spirited manner that apparently attracted their future wives. From looking at pictures of them in their twenties, one can see that these men knew how to have fun—sometimes, maybe, reckless fun. My father with his hat on at a jaunty angle, Jerry's in the photobooth pictures he had taken for a lark—it is easy to look at them now and see how young women like our mothers might have been captivated by the prospect of adventure they suggested.

Shortly after they were married, my mother and father moved to Mexia. Mother had had a term at a teachers college, but she postponed her plans to teach for the sake of her husband's job. Uncle Henry told me many years later, when he and Hazel and I drove through Mexia on a road trip, how unhappy Mother had been to leave her family and settle in such a strange, distant place. We drove by the building where their second-floor apartment had been fifty years before; I imagined Mother up there listening to the radio, waiting for Daddy to come home, thinking from time to time with an excess of pleasure about the imminent change of bill at the movies.

When I think of Mother now, I often picture her in a theater seat next to me, tapping her fingers on my hand or arm to the rhythm of some song in a film or concert-music melody. She gave me and Judy music—or at least made it easy for us to partake of it, whenever we cared to—just as her mother had given it to her. Until her arthritis disabled her, Granny would sit down regularly at the spinet (her chores all done) and play hymns and boogie-woogie by ear. Mother played by ear, too, as did I before I learned to read music to play the accordion. We had a console phonograph from the time I was ten or so, and I can still hear the clunky fall of a seventy-eight "platter" onto the one just played. We listened to the big bands, the crooners, Johann Strauss waltzes, and Spike Jones. (I recall how even Daddy liked "Golden Slippers.") Show tunes and music from movie soundtracks gradually replaced these singles.

Mother also gave me the movies. When we lived in Urbandale, we were just five or six blocks from the Urban Theater. Mother and I would go there often, probably with every change of program, leaving Judy with Granny until she was old enough to go, too.

Movies with love stories and music were our favorites. We'd walk home after dark, vaguely aware of having sojourned in another realm, savoring the bittersweet return to the familiar. We were crazy about Doris Day.

A special treat was to go on the bus to downtown Dallas to one of the grand motion picture houses—the Palace, the Majestic, the Melba, and the Tower—that premiered the first-run films before moving out to the neighborhood theaters. We'd do a little shopping, then have lunch at Dunton's Cafeteria, where Judy and I always insisted on eating on the mezzanine (making all those trips up and down the stairs was part of the fun). After the film, we'd go to H.L. Green's for toys—most of their basement was devoted to toys, all displayed without their packaging and within easy reach of children's hands.

We had a drugstore in Urbandale with a soda fountain and a magazine rack. When she had a day off from her job as a sales clerk at Titche's, Mother would take us there (until I was old enough to go alone, sometimes taking Judy with me). I'd buy movie books and books with song lyrics and sit looking through them while drinking a soda. I still bought comic books as well.

By the time we moved to Casa View, I was old enough to ride the bus to town alone. I remember seeing *Oklahoma* at the Tower Theater. I bought a souvenir program and pored over it on my way home. And I still remember that bittersweet sensation of being poised between two planes of existence. It was like having just been released from a kind of spell and rediscovering with gratitude the things at hand, but with a longing for the other realm, which had already been rising in me at that age.

This romantic predisposition became a bond between my mother and me. As a child, I sensed something in her that I later realized I also owned—an underlying unhappiness arising, I suppose, from our disappointment that what we so easily imagined could, by so much, eclipse reality. Over the years, I'd find Mother crying and ask, alarmed, what the matter was. She never really told me, and I'm not sure she always could have.

As Daddy put in year after year at Keith's, growing older and less and less fit, Mother had to reconcile herself to the distance that had come between them, to the loneliness she felt. "He's a good provider . . . he'd do anything for the kids . . . he's a good man." How often we heard her say these things as she faced Daddy's growing unwillingness to go anywhere or do anything that might vary the routine or risk change.

With the birth of her grandchildren, though, Mother was herself reborn; her imagination stirred to life again as she held them and watched them grow. The companionship she enjoyed with Judy as they shared the challenges and joys of motherhood put a sparkle in her eyes that hadn't been there for a while, and it remained there up until a few weeks before her death. I look every few days at the photograph of her holding Paul Michael, just weeks old. That sparkle, that merriness, it radiates from the print: "Remember me like this."

Mother was a whistler, but you couldn't always recognize the tune she had in mind. Although my father whistled, too, I picked up that habit from her, I suppose. (Jerry pointed out frequently over the years that I tended to whistle when things were not going well. Sometimes, he'd demand that I stop, insisting that my "manic whistling" was making him nervous.) Now, fifteen years after her death, I can still hear her whistling. One of her "tunes" I recall note-perfect and whistle myself. Doing so brings me a sweet, comforting pleasure.

*
**

"If you remain calm amidst all this confusion, it's simply because you do not understand the situation." So reads the text of a picture Mrs. Hunt embroidered the year Jerry and I met. He and his mother had a great deal in common: limitless nervous energy, which they usually channeled into making something, a pleasure in entertaining people, and a love of talking. Even after what must have been a stressful day as secretary to one or more VPs at Atlantic Richfield, Mrs. Hunt would come home, fix dinner, clear up the dishes, and then work on some sewing or craft project until after midnight. Like Jerry, she was a night person; just as we had to at my house, she and Jerry had to be quiet after the early riser in their family had gone to bed. Earphones were a common sight at the Hunt house: they dangled from every radio and TV, ready to be called into service as soon as Mr. Hunt slammed his bedroom door.

Another interest Jerry and his mother shared was cooking. They'd read cookbooks, discuss recipes, and plan meals. (I'd never heard anyone read a recipe to someone else, sometimes with the manner appropriate to a narrative, until I began going home with Jerry.) Even as a teenager, Jerry was occasionally preparing whole meals for his parents and helping his mother cook when they had company. He was interested in gourmet dishes and, later, the foods of other countries: France, Italy, China, Japan, and India, to list the ones he studied most thoroughly.

Jerry and his mother were friends—good friends. They stayed up late together talking, watching TV, and playing with the dogs.

When Jerry and I moved into our house on Swiss Avenue in 1970, Mrs. Hunt would call every day or so. Sometimes she would come by on her way home from work to see him, to bring him some little gift: a cooking gadget, something for the house, or some sheet music he'd asked her to pick up at Whittle's.

I was always struck by the fact that their closeness had so few outward signs of a mother-son relationship. They talked about food and cooking, current events, programs they'd seen on TV, wildlife and animal lore, and how to do things—sharing discoveries and enthusiasms, complaints and exasperations. They'd argue, too, but rarely about personal matters. I would ask Jerry from time to time in the years to come how his mother felt about various issues or people that were affecting her or us in some important way, and he'd usually tell me he had no idea. There was a deep reserve behind her vivacity, and it was never easy to tell what might have upset her when it was clear that she was upset. And later, when the three of us were living on the farm in Canton, she'd sometimes ask me, when I'd go over to her house on the far side of the property to visit, how Jerry felt about something important and what I thought he planned to do about it.

Mrs. Hunt's mother was widowed early and soon married the man who'd been a roomer in her house, a man Mrs. Hunt never liked.

Dan worked for the railroad and drank. As a young boy, Jerry would go to Mart (near Waco) to spend part of the summer with his grandparents. He'd tell me often about the good times he had there. His grandmother was a large woman who loved to eat; every morning, she and Jerry would carry a platter of biscuits and a bowl of bacon drippings to dip them into on the front porch swing.

They'd go to the Red and White grocery store and buy an assortment of the new box cakes, which she called "little farts," and come back and immediately stir one up and bake it.

Once Dan ran out of liquor shortly before it was time for the nearest liquor store, several miles away, to close. He was too far gone to be able to drive, so he asked Jerry instead. I expect that was Jerry's first driving lesson. And I expect Jerry told his mother all about it, thus confirming her low opinion of her stepfather.

Dan sometimes took Jerry with him to the train yard where they'd climb aboard, and Jerry would explore. The self-contained, compact world of the caboose appealed to

Jerry, and he talked about it often over the years. In fact, when we were trying to figure out a way to expand our house on the farm before Mrs. Hunt died, Jerry proposed buying an old caboose, hauling it home, and fixing it up as a bedroom-and-study combination.

In Mart, Jerry played with his cousin Ronnie. Their favorite game was to sneak at night into an abandoned two-story house on Mart's main street, wait for a car to approach, then, using flashlights for illumination, enact some wild scene or strike a pose that would cause the motorist passing by to slam on his brakes, or at least slow down. This must have been a preliminary exercise for the haunted house Jerry would construct, with my help, in his parents' garage one Halloween several years later. We invited neighborhood kids in—and scared them so badly they ran home crying. When their parents began calling, we were forced to shut it down. All I specifically remember were the planks we rigged up to fall in the visitors' path.

Mrs. Hunt left Mart for Waco right after high school. She took a few courses at Baylor University; she loved biology and kept her textbook all her life. She met Mr. Hunt in college, and by the time he was drafted, she was working as a clerk for an insurance company. She often told the story of Jerry's first Christmas—of how disheartened she was that her husband was away in Europe somewhere and that she was alone with their baby at such an important time. She had resolved to let the holiday pass uncelebrated, but her mother and cousins convinced her that that wouldn't be right, so she did buy presents and decorate after all. Jerry was almost a year old before his father returned from the war.

Circumstances made Jerry's mother independent, and he inherited her self-reliance. Along with this came an enterprising spirit that they shared with Mr. Hunt. Jerry's parents were always making plans to improve their fortunes and their lives. An early project was to make decorative, playful "Butt Buckets" out of small metal pails (Mr. Hunt asked me to correspond with Mexican factories about sizes and prices). Later, Petty Enterprises (named for Mrs. Hunt's father, with no acknowledgment of humor I ever saw) acquired thousands of tiny gold-capped bottles to manufacture and distribute a new perfume. The bottles were never used and remain in storage.

Gradually the product catalogs and entrepreneurial magazines were replaced by gardening manuals, seed catalogs, and books of house plans as the Hunts made their plans to retire to the country. They couldn't wait to leave their jobs and the city, to be able to do, finally, all the things they'd always wanted to do.

When I think of the interest Jerry always had in religion and magic, I sometimes recall the story his mother used to tell about how, as a baby, he loved to stare at light bulbs. She was worried enough about it to ask the pediatrician what, if anything, she should do. He advised her to do nothing and not to worry—Jerry wouldn't hurt his eyes, and he'd soon grow out of it.

He never grew out of his fascination for other realms, other states of being, ritual magic, revealed languages, arcane knowledge. When I met him, he was already a member of the Ancient Mystical Order Rosae Crucis, and he was working his way through the lessons that arrived regularly from San Jose. I used to leaf through the beautifully bound and printed volumes he received from the Rosicrucians, occupying myself while he finished typing answers to the questions that were promised to lead to the "Mastery of Life."

As was the case with everything he set out to do, Jerry excelled as he worked his way up the Rosicrucian ladder. At some point, even before I got to know him, he had felt called to disseminate some of the ideas, the wisdom he had acquired. Years later, he told the story of how he tried to start a church to a Canadian interviewer (and fellow composer), Gordon Monahan:

> I just began putting notices up: "All Truth Seekers Write to Post Office Box Blah-blah and Receive Further Information." And I would carry them around and put them in libraries and in community centers and stuff like that, and pretty soon I had a

mail order church going. I had a group
of people who were sending me between five
and fifteen dollars a month . . . Here I
was, thirteen years old, living in the
suburbs of Dallas, Texas, with my mother
and father out in the front on weekends in Bermuda shorts doing the lawn,
while I was in the back in my bedroom
at my typewriter answering letters from
the devotees. And the funny thing was, I
think I was of help to people.

One day, an elderly couple showed up to meet the
"Master." How they traced Jerry to his house always
remained a mystery, but Mr. and Mrs. Hunt were alarmed
to be confronted by these earnest seekers of their teen-
aged son and soon put a halt to his missionary activities.

I think Jerry's parents were pleased, perhaps even a
little relieved, to see Jerry make friends with such a nice,
ordinary boy as I must have seemed. They made me feel
like one of the family, inviting me to stay for dinner many
more times than I was able to, or wanted to. And I had—
still have—scant interest in religion or the occult. They
saw the typewriter in Jerry's bedroom be put to use in
producing our little magazine, *Lachesis*, as the mail from
unknown people and distant places gradually stopped
coming for Jerry. I was *obviously* a good influence on him.

Perhaps, in some small way, I did "regularize" Jerry's
life during our early years, but, of course, I was the one
being influenced. The music and ideas, the food, the play,
the sex—I was being led, and following with delight, into
a world of greater possibilities, of heightened imagination.

We'd ride to school with Mother, who had to be at
work in the cafeteria almost an hour before the school
bell rang. We'd sit in the car until then, finishing homework, studying for tests, and making plans for things to
do after school or on Saturday—talking, arguing, being
silly. School itself was pretty much something to be
gotten through, one way or another . . . and that often
meant making "cheat sheets" for Coach Mitchell's World
History tests—the great, stapled clumps of mimeographed
sheets asking for names and dates, and culminating in

the bonus-points scrambled word, which the coach would reveal on the blackboard by jerking up the rolled-down map that hid it (e.g., LEASH UP CUB = BUCEPHALUS, Alexander the Great's favorite horse).

Good boys making good grades, growing more and more adept at duplicity. If we hadn't known how much our parents loved us, we would surely have felt contempt for them—we got away with so much for so long. Later, in high school, we imagined ourselves quite the sophisticates, Jerry reading Sartre, me smoking pastel-colored Egyptian cigarettes.

By the eleventh grade, our cheating had reached a high pitch of refinement. We shared only one class that year, Mrs. Worsham's English. We both liked her a lot and would get to her classroom as soon as we could to have a few minutes' private chat with her as she stood in the classroom door. She had a wry sense of humor, an appreciation of irony that struck us as cynical, if not world-weary, and that was quite alluring. (I later learned that her husband had just abandoned her, leaving her with a mountain of bills and a mortgage on their new home.)

It must have been that one day we happened to notice a copy of the College Outline Series volume *American Literature* on her lectern, so when we ran across that same book (indeed, two copies of it) at Harper's Book Shop downtown, the solution to the tedium of note-taking seemed obvious. And she stuck pretty close to the text. We got away with it for weeks, sitting near the back of the room (where we always liked to be so we could pass notes to one another), underlining precisely what Mrs. Worsham read. "The Transcendentalists were noted for their high thinking and plain living—isn't that what your book says, Jerry?" she asked with a mischievous grin one day. So we went back to note-taking.

This was one of our last shared experiences in school. Something was happening to us, something that we did discuss in later years but never really understood or agreed on. We were growing apart, making other friends, seeing one another less often.

By the last years of high school, Jerry's piano playing had become exceptionally good. Mr. Hunt arranged occasional gigs for him at the country club, and Jerry continued performing in classical recitals. But what really took off, and made Jerry quite a bit of money, was the playing Jerry did for Dick and Patty Hill, a musical duo that performed in clubs around town, he on trumpet, she on drums, both singing as Jerry accompanied them.

Before Jerry was old enough to get his driver's license, they'd come by the house to pick him up. Jerry also performed from time to time in a combo made up of his peers. They played rock and roll at young hangouts, and Jerry quickly developed a reputation for being a wild man, in addition to being a dazzling pianist. When he began to drive, he'd take his mother's old Country Squire station wagon, which Jerry called The Brown Goose, to various gigs across town. As word spread about how well he played and how keen he was at discerning what made both the other performers and the audiences happy, he began to get more offers than he could handle.

The most lucrative gigs were at the strip joints, notably the Montmartre Club. Jerry enjoyed these—with their eager-to-be-pleased clientele and the strippers who fawned over him—much more than he did the hotel ballroom or veterans' groups dates with the drunks hanging around the piano, making the boozy requests that they were barely able to sing along with.

His origins as a performance artist are in these club experiences, as Jerry himself acknowledged. Almost thirty years later, he gave a concert with our longtime friend, the dancer Sally Bowden at Roulette in New York City. His demeanor toward her, as she moved about the space, was reminiscent of the subtle but domineering role the accompanist can play when working with a stripper, as he becomes a kind of Stromboli who urges and exploits, all the while remaining in the background, pulling the marionette's strings. (There was an element of all this, I believe, in Jerry's work with Karen Finley at the Kitchen.)

His interest in magic had by now led him to Aleister Crowley. As he told Monahan:

> I really went full speed, full blast
> for a couple of years on magical prac-
> tice of the arcane kind, where you do
> the ritual of the pentagram, you cut

the pentagram in blood. I used to make
beetle cakes—compounds of ground wheat
and raw honey and butter and just chok-
ing spices. I used to do invocations to
planetary intelligences for example,
and stuff like that.

And it may have been Crowley, or Aldous Huxley, or
both, who piqued Jerry's interest in drugs. He had money
in his pocket, and he ran in the circles where they were
easy to come by, so he experimented with peyote, hashish,
marijuana, and amphetamines. Although he certainly got
high on occasion, I don't believe Jerry ever had a problem
with drugs. He explored with them, under their influence,
but he never depended on them, unlike some of the people
he ran around with at that time.

In addition to taking him to gigs, The Brown Goose
also took him cruising. He visited the places where boys
used to hang out, waiting to be picked up. And I heard
later that he became notorious, for a while, in that huge
car of his, speeding down the streets and talking a mile
a minute.

I never knew who, exactly, blew the whistle on him.
We didn't often talk about those years; they were pain-
ful for both of us to recall. It may have been some boy's
parents who called Mr. and Mrs. Hunt—that story has a
familiar ring—but they had to confront the fact that their
son was homosexual, and flagrantly so.

This was a time when serious family problems had to
be hidden. Just as a good friend of mine's parents were
soon to send her away to a "home" to have an "illegitimate" baby to be put up for adoption, so Jerry's parents
prevailed upon him to undergo an evaluation at a psychi-
atric hospital in Galveston. Jerry always loved to tell the
story of how the attractive young psychologist questioned
him and tested him and concluded that if Jerry was
determined to lead that kind of life, there wasn't really
anything to be done about it—especially since Jerry
himself didn't seem to have a problem with it (or to be
"conflicted," as we'd say today). The psychologist, whom
Jerry remembered liking quite a bit, relayed all this to
Jerry's parents, and he returned home if not "cured," at

least not pronounced "ill." As far as I know, nothing more was ever said to Jerry about the subject.

It wasn't long before Jerry went away to college. He had one semester only at University of North Texas in Denton, where he studied music, partied, and missed classes—even a recital he was supposed to play. (When his teacher ran into him in the hall later, she squeezed his cheek hard, and said, "You're good, honey, but you're not that good.")

In Denton, he made friends with a young lady who was to become very close to us both. Peggy was studying music, too, and was quite an accomplished pianist herself—she and Jerry performed Béla Bartók's *Sonata for Two Pianos and Percussion* in a couple of recitals. Peggy came from a Catholic background in Wisconsin, and she could be as intense as Jerry, whether in practicing or partying; they also had a similar taste in boys. Peggy was probably there the night Jerry chased the naked boy through the neighborhood, the acolyte who'd been in on the magic around the altar Jerry had built in his apartment and who'd partaken of the drugs, but who'd apparently experienced a sudden fit of apostasy. The police were called, and Jerry was evicted the next day. He always said the police had tried to run him out of Denton, but I suspect he exaggerated that for effect.

*
**

I had begun to feel that I couldn't keep up with Jerry, although I'm sure I never quite put it to myself that way. Playing violin in the high school orchestra and French horn in the band gave me the opportunity to make new friends, and I began going to Dinah's house, or Robert's, in addition to Carol's. I saw Jerry more and more infrequently.

Dinah soon became my new playmate, and she remains a very close friend. We have a similar sense of humor, streaked broadly with a capacity for silliness that has kept us exchanging mad, Rube Goldbergian invention ideas over the decades. Today, being with Dinah recalls the simple good times we had in our last years of school and evokes the wholesome, supportive feeling I always had in her and her family's presence. We tooled around town in her jalopy, taking popcorn to the outside terrace of the Love Field Airport to watch the planes land, visiting restaurants with only change in our pockets and making a meal off the complimentary tortilla chips and hot sauce and, perhaps, one order of guacamole—always laughing and singing and probably commanding attention (and, if so, loving it).

Our restlessness and boredom with the life of a teenager in the late '50s and early '60s, with the rounds of the fast food places like Charco's, Princess, and the Pig Stand (all with carhops), led us away on two remote adventures that I remember. We drove (Dinah drove us) to a little town about thirty miles east for dinner, and we returned without anyone knowing how far we'd been. And that excursion emboldened us to drive to Houston, over 250 miles away, to spend the night. Each of us had an alibi, and we might have gotten away with it had we not received a speeding ticket in New Waverly, just north of Houston.

I used to love to go to Dinah's house, sit in the butterfly chairs in the living room, talk about books with Dinah's mother, or go to Dinah and her sister Leslie's bedroom and play board games and listen to music and talk. Dinah had a party at her house one night, and she invited Jerry and Diane, the girl he was running around with then. They put in an appearance, and I remember feeling very awkward around them—embarrassed, almost, for them to see me there, enjoying what was probably a fairly typical teenage get-together for the times.

Diane took me aside and asked, "What are you doing here with these people?" She and Jerry left soon after.

I would run into Jerry from time to time at school, and he was almost always with Diane. Although I don't remember actually thinking the word to myself, I believe I felt jealous of her. Even then, she was a striking girl, poised and self-confident, tantalizingly aloof, almost arrogant, in fact. As far as I know, she was the only female Jerry ever had sex with—at a wild party, I believe. Jerry used to tell how he once prevented her and another boy, both drunk, from having sex because they were not using condoms.

Ten years later, I re-encountered Diane in graduate school at the University of Texas at Austin. She was working on her PhD in Old English, riding a motorcycle, and in love with a bookstore manager, British by birth. We shared camembert and apples and hot chocolate at the house she was renting. At school, I stood in the doorway of her cubicle, marveling at the piled-high clutter of books and papers on her desk that forced her to work on her lap. She later married the bookman and moved to Houston with him.

Jerry and I stayed in fairly close contact with her for several years. We once went by to see her at home in Houston.

She had taught English briefly at the University of Houston, but something had happened—I gathered at the time that her liberal ideas and her candor had won her enemies. She had just recently had a child, and she showed us the detailed charts she was keeping to record the infant's feedings and bowel movements. The three of us sat at a cluttered table drinking Constant Comment tea, Jerry and I no doubt taking it all in: Diane domesticated. "I imagine the two of you find all of this rather squalid," she said. We laughed about that statement for years, long after we stopped hearing from her altogether.

As much as I enjoyed being with Dinah, we never became romantically involved. She had her boyfriends, her "dates," and a quality of independence that took her, alone, to the World's Fair in Flushing, New York, as a resident employee. But I did find love with a girl, and I still look upon this experience as one of my life's saddest and most shameful.

The question as to whether I had a girlfriend came up more often in my young years than it ever did in Jerry's, I'm sure. He already had an eccentric's reputation among his parents' friends and relatives. But my aunts and uncle and cousins did bring the subject up, and I was embarrassed by their doing so and by Mother's uneasiness about it—an uneasiness she tried to disguise or dispel with comments like, "Oh, the right girl will come along someday."

There was certainly no doubt in my mind that I was attracted to boys and men. Jerry and I had demonstrated that to our mutual satisfaction over and over. My Monty Clift scrapbook had grown huge, and I had seriously thought of contacting his sister, who lived in Houston at that time, to try to get some insider information about his private life. (I had no idea then that he himself was homosexual.) I think, though, that my sexual orientation, my sexual identity, was so closely associated with my relationship with Jerry, as my erotic mentor, that I believed if he were not intimate in my life, then I had the space, the freedom, to explore alternatives. And I wonder yet whether my efforts to do so weren't really a kind of defiance of him, an "I'll show you" that might release me from an emotional and intellectual dependency on him that had come to trouble me.

In self-defense, I hasten to say that none of what happened was planned. I was eighteen and being propelled through life by feelings. And I discovered a fellow romantic, Carol—a friend from junior high school days—who, for her own reasons, was eager to have a special friend, and who shared my love of music (she, too, played violin in the orchestra and French horn in the band).

We lived only a few blocks apart and began visiting one another regularly. I got to know her mother well (the two of us went to a travel lecture once at SMU); her father was a stiff, taciturn man who sat in their living room in his recliner behind an oriental screen—removed from the lives of Carol and her sister and mother, or so it appeared to me then. Even though there was often tension in their home, I enjoyed visiting Carol there, eating delicacies like smoked oysters, and withdrawing to her room to talk and . . . neck.

Carol visited me more than I did her, perhaps because the atmosphere in my home was a more relaxed one. My parents, grandmother, and sister were quite fond of her, and I know they were all very much interested in this girl I was taking so seriously. We'd go to my bedroom and talk, listen to music, and neck.

With the money I received from graduation and some I'd saved, I decided to buy a stereo. Carol went with me to Titche's downtown, and we auditioned several consoles using the record I'd brought along for the purpose (Bach's two- and three-keyboard concerti, played on harpsichords). We selected a Magnavox: two separate cherry wood cabinets, each with a woofer and a tweeter—a superb unit for the time that was to see over thirty years of continual use and transported to eight locales, including Houston.

Carol and I also wrote letters to one another, spinning a web of words around our relationship and our feelings for one another.

We analyzed our moods in close detail, typing to the music of Wagner or Tchaikovsky, enjoying the highs and lows of our adolescent affairs. And we began to talk of marriage, talk my parents heard and rather liked, although they wondered if perhaps we might be a little young.

As this growing intimacy with Carol acquired a life of its own, I cared less and less how much Jerry knew about it. In the beginning, however, it was important to me that he be aware of the new direction my life was taking. I even admit to myself, now, that a part of me sought his guidance. I remember two disturbing incidents involving Jerry that happened at my house at about the time Carol and I had begun "seeing" one another. Jerry had come by after school, and we began arguing in my room. I left to go to the bathroom, and when I returned, he wasn't there: he had crawled out a window (opening the screen to do so) and gone home a few blocks away. It was embarrassing to try to explain his flight to my mother and grandmother, who naturally expected that he'd stay for dinner.

And another time, he told me he'd be by one Saturday night. I waited for him for hours, too proud to call his house, listening resolutely to all six sides of Bach's *Art of Fugue*, the volume low enough to let me hear the phone. He never came, or called, or explained what might have happened. We didn't see each other after that, except by accident, for some time.

Despite all the years that have passed since then, it hurts me still to think of that night. Hearing any exercise from the *Art of Fugue* brings back the feelings of wounded pride, anger, and desolation that Jerry's not coming caused. I must have also felt that I was really on my own then, and it isn't surprising that that incident, with my stubborn, hopeless waiting, would haunt me during the nights immediately following Jerry's death.

However much I liked—loved—Carol, I was using her, and this fact shames me even now. I am also angry to think that unrealistic expectations and prejudice are capable of driving people to such deceit and such self-deception. She was a bright, gentle, sensitive girl from a family whose affection for one another wasn't much in evidence (unless toward Carol's younger sister, who wore braces from polio). I took control of her emotions, of her imagination—yet I withheld much of myself, my true feelings.

I had begun working full-time with my father at the produce company after leaving school at midterm of my senior year. I needed two courses to have enough credits to graduate, and I took those (English and Commercial Geography) at a night school in downtown Dallas. There was a Sheraton Hotel near the school.

My plan was to have Carol meet me at work and then go to classes with me later—after we had spent a few hours together in the hotel.

She met me at Ben E. Keith's, having taken the bus to town. I remember walking with her through the warehouse where she caught the attention of the dockhands and drivers—much to my delighted satisfaction. We walked to the hotel, nervously checked in as a married couple, and went to our room and drew the curtains. We necked, as we so often had, and I was quickly aroused. I thought of the men who had looked at her with so much interest at work. I thought of my new friend Kirby, with whom I had gone roller skating and to the movies a few times. And I thought of Montgomery Clift in *Raintree County*. But nothing worked; I couldn't do it.

Carol and I pretended to have been satisfied—she even seemed to buy my excuse that I hadn't wanted to take advantage of her before our marriage (and she was wearing the engagement ring I'd given her). But I knew incontestably then that it was hopeless, that I simply wasn't attracted to girls—and not for want of trying to be.

With good fortune for all of us—for Carol and me and our families—her father was soon transferred to Tulsa. She and I corresponded a while, trying at first to sustain the commitment to one another but eventually giving up the pretense. I wrote to her, telling her a little about Kirby.

She returned the ring. I didn't see her for six years or so, until we ran into one another on the campus of the University of Houston, where she had just come from a French language lab conducted by a man who was soon to become her first husband and, later, my best friend.

*
**

Kirby and I had known one another in high school, but we didn't really become close until the summer after graduation. He liked movies as much as I did—more so, I think now—and we'd get together for dinner and a film almost every weekend. We also enjoyed roller skating and shopping (he had a job at a department store near his house, working to save money for college the following fall). My parents liked him (as they liked everyone I brought home), and I felt very welcome at Kirby's house, where we'd go back to his room to talk, his younger brother sticking close by.

In contrast to Jerry and Carol, Kirby must have seemed refreshingly uncomplicated to me then. He was also a good-looking young man with an ingenuousness about him that I found very appealing. In all the time we were friends—a little over a year—I never sought any kind of physical intimacy with him, although I certainly wanted it. (One day, we were about to cross a street in downtown Dallas, and a gust of wind blew the top of his shirt open, revealing a hairless upper chest. "Your top button's undone," I helpfully pointed out. "Who cares?" he replied.)

Kirby's parents had bought him a little Nash Metropolitan to take to college—a junior college in Paris, about one hundred miles northeast of Dallas. I got a kick out of going places with him in that tiny two-seater, our legs almost touching, his face so close to mine. When the school year began, I missed him violently, waiting impatiently for the next weekend when he'd be home, stealing moments in the stairwell at Keith's to moon over the picture I carried in my wallet.

I took a couple of courses at Dallas College (SMU's downtown night school) and began thinking about enrolling somewhere full-time in the coming spring. Paris

Junior College didn't at all appeal to me. From everything Kirby had told me about it, it seemed to be a close
version of high school. But East Texas State University in
Commerce, which is on the way to Paris, looked better,
and I decided to go there.

About the school itself or the teachers, I recall very
little: piano lessons with a young woman who was determined to make me read the notes, dictionary drills with
Dr. Tarpley, an American history text with musical illus-
trations, slide identification on a botany exam, and the
delicious hamburgers (with lots of mayonnaise) that I ate
almost every day while reading the *Dallas Times Herald*
to keep up with the movies in Dallas and plan Kirby's and
my next weekend home.

I lived in a dorm with three other boys; my roommate
was an Ag major with whom I had nothing in common. I
began to long for the Dallas weekends when Kirby would
come by for me in the Metropolitan and take me compactly
away to the big city. The Sundays of our return to school
were depressing, relieved only by the nighttime ride back
and the forced intimacy the little car provided; I can still
see the reflection of the dashboard lights in Kirby's eyes,
accompanied on the radio by the slow ballads he liked, the
country roads leading us relentlessly on toward parting.

There came a time when I wanted Kirby to know how
I felt about him. I had already decided not to go back to
East Texas. I wanted to work, to get a car and some nice
clothes. We were home for the summer, going to movies,
and skating still, I think, but I remember feeling that
Kirby was pulling away from me somehow; he sometimes
had made other plans when I called to arrange a date.

It was on one of those occasions when he wasn't available that I decided to act. I wrote him a letter telling him
that I'd come to love him and took it to his house, leaving
it with his brother to give to him. Kirby's parents inter-
cepted the letter—I realize now that they had had their
suspicions about me, and I also think they had begun to
worry about Kirby—and I heard nothing for several days.

Finally, a letter came for me from Kirby in the mail.
He told me how upset they had all been to read what
I'd written, that his father had actually cried—which he'd
never before seen him do.

He also urged me to go to my parents with my "problem": "That's what they're for."

Thirty years later, a librarian from my old high school
visited the downtown Dallas Public Library where I work
part-time. I reminisced a while with her about my years
at the school, and when I asked about my favorite English
teacher, she told me about Mrs. Worsham's failed marriage
and her eventual death from cancer. I had learned a few
years earlier that Kirby was teaching English (and coach-
ing drama) at the school. The librarian told me he was
still there, and when I inquired, added that *no, he had
never married.* After she left, I looked his name up in
the phone book and discovered that he was living in an
apartment complex near my family's old home. I hope he
doesn't live alone.

While continuing to work with my father on the
produce market, I began looking for an office job with the
aid of an employment agency. After a few weeks, I found
one in the mailroom of Fidelity Union Life in downtown
Dallas. I enjoyed delivering the mail to various offices
on several floors, often stopping to chat with people and
make friends. One of my favorites was Ellen Puckett, an
older lady who loved music, especially the violin, and who
often traveled to Houston to hear symphony concerts
there, especially when Zino Francescatti performed.

One office was always intriguing to visit. Carr P.
Collins, Jr. was a vice president of the Fidelity Life
Insurance Company and a consul for Italy, and his suite
was filled with paintings and sculpture and had an altogether unbusinesslike atmosphere. I'd pick up the letters
his secretary had typed for him, the envelopes unsealed
for subsequent closing and stamping by our machine
in the mailroom. Sometimes I'd read the more interest-
ing-looking letters, those that didn't seem to pertain to the
insurance business. I always read his letters to his son at
one of the Ivy League colleges; Mr. Collins regularly felt
the need to exhort his son to study harder, to do better.

One day during the Christmas season, this young man
came down to his father's office. I met him on the elevator

and rode a few floors with him, closely observing his corduroy jacket and reading matter (*David Copperfield*, in the fat Penguin paperback).

I remember wondering what it would be like to be him, to live in his world. And I resolved, on the spot, to go back to college as soon as I could.

I saw Dinah fairly regularly during that period, and she introduced me to a fellow I'd seen (and admired) in school, a clarinet player in the marching band who looked like a choirboy. Robert and I became friends, and before long, I was well into the most emotionally turbulent period of my life. I became obsessed with him over the next year or so, reaching a point where I thought about little except the ups and downs of our relationship.

Robert came from Mississippi. He lived with his mother and younger sister (who wasn't always at home) in the same neighborhood as I did. He loved to have fun, and I remember with pleasure how I could make him laugh, his deep-set eyes twinkling beneath the fringe of hair that hung low over his forehead.

He wasn't at all moody, and he was a dependable son and brother who frequently called on to help his younger sister out of some kind of trouble (she was on probation at one time). He had learned his way around the kitchen (out of necessity, I see now), and he had furnished his bedroom in Early American style, buying items piece by piece from a neighborhood store.

He liked clothes and liked to be seen, and we often went out to fashionable restaurants like Ports o' Call and then to a movie in one of the downtown theaters. He drove a sporty car with a "champagne" finish and a black interior, always sitting up perfectly straight behind the wheel, his eyes fixed on the road ahead to avoid accidents and the hikes in insurance premiums they brought.

On occasion, we went to gay bars (the Mercy Mary— or was it just Mary's?), and he loved to dance and to be admired while doing so. He might have looked the naif, but he could "get down dirty" in such a way as to command the floor's attention. I stood back captivated and probably basking a little in the indirect attention.

Because he had his own car, we were able to take two trips together. We went to Turner Falls, Oklahoma, where

my family and I had sometimes gone when Judy and I
were kids (and where I later took Mother and my older
niece Jenny). After spending a few hours at the falls, we
rented a modest cabin in the woods. I was looking forward
to having him alone for the whole evening, a welcome
change from the hurried sex we were used to having at
his house before his mother or sister arrived.

We didn't have much money to spend, so our meal
was probably hamburgers. I think we must have had a
few beers, though, because at one point after we'd gone
to bed, I conceived the notion of carrying him, nude as
we both were, into the woods. I didn't make it far before
falling—and badly skinning my knees on the rocky
ground. And to that injury was added the embarrass-
ment we suffered the following morning when we found
we didn't have quite enough money to pay for the cabin
(we'd forgotten the tax), and I had to leave my watch as a
surety bond.

Robert and I also went to New Orleans, where we
drank Hurricanes at Pat O'Brien's to the accompaniment of "Roll Me Over In the Clover." At a gay bar we
visited, I remember standing by the piano and watching
Robert dance, drinking more than I really wanted to.
By the time we finally got back to the Monteleone, I was
too drunk to negotiate the revolving door: someone (why
wasn't it Robert?) had to stop the thing and lead me out.
Quite stupidly, I wove my way over to the Carousel Bar
for another go-around. We took a short cruise into the
Gulf the next afternoon, and I fought hangover-induced
nausea the whole trip.

As much as I hated to be separated from Robert, I
attended the University of Houston in the spring of 1963,
renting an apartment within tolerable walking distance
of the campus and rushing home each day to check my
mail, hoping for a letter from him. Those I received I
carried around with me in my texts and notebooks, and I
often took them out to reread during dull lectures or the
bus ride to and from my downtown class at the university
night school.

Robert drove down to visit me once, and I took him
with me to that downtown English class. I remember
looking down at my book and letting my eyes wander over

to his legs, seductively close in their tight white jeans. We were reading Milton that night, and I expect I contributed more than my usual share of comments and answers just to impress Robert. On our way home, he said, "You really like that stuff, don't you?"

The semester grew long, and I managed to work myself up into quite a state, thinking night and day about Robert—even going to stand from time to time on a nearby street that happened to have the same name as his did in Dallas. I wrote a sonnet to him, an acrostic that began: "Robb'd of Nature's transcendent Gold" (I had his hair in mind, I think), and I sent it off to the gay *Der Kreis* (who published it, to my delight).

I became more and more miserable, finding it almost impossible to concentrate on my studies, desperate for help in dealing with the anxiety our separation and my growing uncertainty about Robert's feelings for me were causing. I made an appointment with a psychologist in the University's Office of Counseling and Testing.

Mr. Browning was a man in his thirties who, after putting his feet up on the edge of his desk, asked me what the matter was. I stared at his pink socks and told him about Robert, asking him—tearfully, I imagine—what I should do about him, about dealing with the problem that he had become in my life. Mr. Browning wanted to talk more about my being homosexual than about Robert.

I remember clearly perceiving a distinct distaste on his part for the details of my "affair." After all, he wasn't an advisor for the lovelorn but a trained professional, and the problem was my being queer. And so it may have been— but not in the way Mr. Browning understood, and not at that moment, with my notebooks stuffed with Robert's ragged letters. I never went back, calling to cancel the appointment they had set up for me the following week.

Friends

By the time I had returned from college that next summer, my father had been talked into retiring from Keith's. He had missed work due to various health problems, but it wasn't long before the doctor was able to lower his blood pressure with medication and generally build him up with vitamins. The better he felt, the more he resented how he had been treated by the company he had worked for so long. He was also very deeply hurt. Just as had Kirby his, I saw my father cry for the first time in my life during an episode of *Gunsmoke* that dealt with the situation of an old man denied work due to age and imagined inability.

Friends and relatives rallied to his need for work and asked Daddy to paint their houses (or agreed to let him). Over the next year or so, he stayed fairly busy with a succession of jobs that he enjoyed and paid him well. I was able to help him during that summer, and we worked well together—he handling the larger painting surfaces, I doing the windows, eaves, ceilings, and woodwork.

Spending that time together, we grew closer than we had ever been. We talked some, although never about our deepest feelings and concerns. What I remember most is just our enjoying being together. We'd sit eating our Vienna sausages, cheese, and crackers at lunchtime, planning the afternoon's work, and calculating the duration of the job. Then I'd get back up on my ladder, turn on my radio, and do detail work with my narrow brush while he remained below, somewhere near me, laying on paint in broad strokes.

Since I had no immediate plans to return to college, I was looking for a job. Finding permanent, full-time work is never easy for young people just returned—but not graduated—from college: businesses are afraid that their newly trained employees will soon return to school, and they frequently do. By early fall, though, I had gotten a job as an actuarial clerk with an insurance company, and Daddy had lost his painting partner.

Working downtown enabled me to visit the several bookstores there on my lunch hour, and I stopped by the Doubleday store one day and ran into Steve, a fellow I knew from high school. He told me that he and Jerry were renting a house near downtown and added that they were looking for a third person to help with the rent.

He suggested that I drop by.

The house on Bennett Street was an old frame structure that had three bedrooms on the ground floor, a fourth bedroom upstairs in a back corner of the house, and a long living room with a hardwood floor, ideal for Jerry's grand piano. My bedroom would be just behind the kitchen—third choice, but adequate. I moved in, bringing my cat, Petit Chou, from home.

I hadn't seen Jerry for a while. Being with him made me feel awkward at first, and I was somewhat of an outsider on Bennett because I was either at work or off somewhere with Robert most of the time. Steve had been a member of Jerry's high-school clique, along with Diane, and he, his girlfriend, Elizabeth (who was soon to move in with us), and Peggy all seemed rather wild to me.

There were regular parties, loud and long, that I left and returned to; I preferred going to dinner and the movies with Robert, cruising around in my new red MG Midget, the top down and rock and roll on the radio.

I had moved my Magnavox stereo to Bennett, and it sounded great in that spacious living room, bare of furniture other than the piano. Music of some kind was always coming from that room: Édith Piaf (Steve's favorite), Rachmaninoff's *Second Symphony* (a recent discovery of mine), and Stockhausen's *Gesang der Jünglinge* (that Jerry introduced us to).

The Beatles were just becoming known, thanks to Ed Sullivan, and their music came to supplant everything else on the Magnavox. The single "I Want to Hold Your Hand" could be heard around the clock; we were all crazy about it. One night after a party I'd come in on earlier, Jerry and I had sex again, after more than two years, while that song played over and over, thanks to the automatic changer. Our sexual relations had resumed, and they continued for the next three decades, only interrupted when I was away at college.

We were friends again, then, but I still thought of myself as being in love with Robert. I was also becoming more and more aware that that love was unreciprocated. Our sex was always at my instigation; he was embarrassed at any talk of deep feelings. I preferred being with him in intimate circumstances, just us two; he always wanted to be with crowds of people, to be seen. I figured out that I could keep his attention better by letting him sit facing the entrance at restaurants so he wouldn't have to keep turning around to see who was coming in.

On the day of Kennedy's assassination, Robert and I had planned to have dinner at a steak house downtown and then walk over to a movie. I had gone out at lunchtime to see the presidential motorcade, and it seemed as though Kennedy had met my eyes as I waved to him from the sidewalk. When I got back to work, the office had already heard the news. We were sent home, tearful.

I followed the afternoon's events on TV, but my main concern was that nothing would happen to ruin my date with Robert. The entire city was in mourning: everything was closed or closing, the streets were empty, people were sitting stunned in front of their TVs. Robert and I did, in fact, go back downtown to Cattleman's restaurant, but before we had finished our meal, the waitress came over to tell us that the restaurant was closing (we were the only diners remaining at that point). We left and learned that the theaters were closed as well. The evening was ruined.

Although I had certainly realized by that time that the differences between Robert and me would eventually come between us, I couldn't accept the fact that he was obviously pulling away. He would have other plans when I'd call, and he called me less and less often. I remember working myself into a deep depression one afternoon, listening over and over to the Adagio of Johannes Brahms's

D Minor Piano Concerto (a piece I had been introduced to by the film *The L-Shaped Room*).

But a new element had been added (or perhaps it had just surfaced): when I left Bennett to go somewhere to meet Robert, I was showing Jerry that he didn't matter as much. Since our reunion in bed, he later told me, he'd come to realize how important I was to him. I wasn't willing, or able, to see either how he felt or to return the feeling. To lose Robert would not only hurt me but would compromise me in some way, I must have felt, where Jerry was concerned.

There were always drugs around Bennett, and I found a bottle of tranquilizers late one afternoon when I had heard one time too many that Robert had made other plans. As soon as I swallowed the pills, I began to think of how much my death would hurt my family, my mother especially. Even if I might not have wanted to live just then, I didn't really want to die, and I was suddenly ashamed of what I'd done. I walked down the street to a medical clinic and showed them the empty prescription bottle, and they sent me in an ambulance to a hospital to have my stomach pumped. The hospital called my parents.

As a result of this deed, everyone began to see that I was in trouble emotionally. The hospital referred me to a mental health clinic where I attended group sessions (and sat speechless at the stories of drug dependency and parental sexual abuse, an outsider more than ever). My parents were alarmed to have to face what they had been afraid of acknowledging. Still, although my mother must have talked with the psychologists at the clinic, neither she nor my father ever discussed with me what the underlying causes of my emotional turmoil might have been. And Jerry, at this time, began referring to me, with a mocking affection, as the bird my mother had that was born with a broken wing. After this incident, he became both more tender and more aloof, concerned for me yet put off by the weakness my desperate act revealed—not to mention the statement it made about the extent of my feelings for Robert.

While I was foundering emotionally, Jerry was experiencing the intellectual and artistic changes that would head him in the direction he was to follow for the rest of his life. He had always been an independent thinker and an independent learner; the only thing he ever really needed to be taught was how to read—which he had to be able to do to begin studying piano (or so the teacher said).

As a child in Waco, Jerry found his way into the adult section of the public library and selected a few books of interest to him, but the librarian refused to let him check them out since he only had a juvenile library card. Mrs. Hunt always enjoyed telling the story of how she "marched right down" to the library and demanded that Jerry be given whatever kind of card it took to grant him access to any book in the library he might want.

Another story I often heard was about Mrs. Quay's abortive Latin class, an after-school group of fifth graders that was able to meet only a few times before the principal disbanded it, claiming that it showed partiality toward the children involved. Mrs. Quay was one of Jerry's favorite teachers. That she must have appreciated Jerry's special qualities is illustrated, I think, by what happened one day in class when she said to him, "Jerry, you may go now," and he gathered up his books, retrieved his coat from the cloakroom, and walked outside the building—only to discover that there were no waiting cars. He returned to the classroom, hung his coat back up, and sat down again. In a few minutes, Mrs. Quay said, "Jerry, you may go to the board now," and so he did.

I often look at a picture of Jerry in his homeroom class, taken when he was in the sixth grade. It's an eloquent portrait, reflecting the white, middle-class schools in the '50s, the uniformity of dress, pose, and expression—except that the self-possession and in-his-element happiness so evident in Jerry's eyes do make him stand out, at least to me. He must have been every teacher's favorite student in those early grades.

Even so, he was by nature an autodidact. One can trace his work with electronic musical instruments back to the electronics correspondence course his grandfather ordered but lost interest in. Jerry, at age ten, finished it. And when he stayed with his Aunt Maudie and Uncle Raby, he used to hang out at a neighborhood radio and TV repair shop (he took me by the place in 1991, when we drove to Waco to have his mother's ashes interred). I imagine him digging through the bins of surplus resistors and capacitors, looking for what he needed to build a circuit—just as I would watch him do fifteen years later when I went with him to Crabtree's or Texas Electronics Supply. I was amazed at his patience, impressed by his knowledge, and tickled at the salesman's incredulity when they heard him identify himself as a composer.

By the early '60s, he was wiring his own circuits, and he would later modify every synthesizer or sound-altering device he acquired. In fact, on several occasions, he worked as a consultant for electronic instrument manufacturers—a musician with sufficient knowledge of electronics that could recommend specific adaptations to enhance the product's musical appeal and value. (Some of Jerry's early ideas for simulating the piano pedals' role in electronic keyboards were rejected as unimportant and too expensive, only to be adopted later by the more successful companies.)

On Bennett, Jerry had just begun exploring the relationship between machines and music that was to fascinate him so much in later years. He was still practicing the piano, learning the music of Stockhausen, Mauricio Kagel, Sylvano Bussotti, and Cage, whom Jerry had met in 1964, riding a bus to Texas Tech in Lubbock to do so. Jerry always said this encounter redirected his musical career from classical music to the avant-garde and the chance operations that Cage employed.

I often wonder how our neighbors stood the noise, what with Jerry's impassioned practicing, the Magnavox in around-the-clock use, and the loud parties and frequent brawls. We were a high-spirited bunch, set on living *la dolce vita* as we saw it depicted by Fellini, eager to *épater le bourgeois*. We could also get into petty, vindictive snits that resulted in Elizabeth's breaking my kitty bowls because I'd left them on the sink, my hiding Steve's classification notice from the draft board under the ice tray in the freezer, and Jerry's and my tearing in half one of Steve's long paintings over a disagreement about where to hang it.

Jerry was our unacknowledged leader, influencing our lives in subtle and not-so-subtle ways, overseeing the decoration of the house (which was rented in his name), bringing in exotic foods for us to try like baby octopus and squid, preparing dishes from *The Escoffier Cookbook* and the *Larousse Gastronomique*, and planning parties and inviting guests. One of these was Jerry Howing, an astrologer who recently arrived from South America who became such a nuisance that Jerry and I hid in the closet one day so he would think no one was at home. Howing, by the way, cast Jerry's horoscope, telling him that his lungs would be a problem in years to come but that he would not die of them directly. That turned out to be the case.

Because Jerry was earning his living playing in clubs, he would get home quite late. We all became habitues of the corner coffee shop, Anderson's, which never closed. Jerry would be hungry after work, and he was particularly fond of their pancakes and waffles, which he would eat while smoking his Chesterfields, a "bottomless" cup of coffee at his side. Since we kept late hours, mornings on Bennett were invariably quiet, so at least the neighbors had that.

I thrived in this environment for a while, enjoying being friends with Jerry again, exploring the world at his side, impelled by his enthusiasms and his energy. However, something happened that ultimately forced me to get serious about doing something with my life.

I was still working as an actuarial clerk, but the job was becoming tedious and boring. The cycles of songs pumped into the office by Muzak had become odiously predictable, and the conversations on break and at lunch were all about TV (*The Fugitive* was popular then), which I rarely cared to watch. Even the money I was making didn't matter so much to me now that I wasn't trying to keep up with Robert's interest in fancy restaurants and expensive clothes.

Although I didn't really make friends at work, there was one young lady in my department I chatted with regularly, often talking, as I remember, about the squabbles she and her husband were having at the time. Since they lived just a few blocks away from our house on Bennett, I invited them to attend one of our Saturday night parties. Jayne came alone, mixed with the crowd, and drank too much.

At one point, she had to be brought back from the bushes in a neighbor's front yard where she had passed out. In a little while, she was able to go home on her own. I remember this occurrence as being very tangential to the party. None of us really knew her, and, I suppose, we didn't really care what she was thinking.

At work next week, I received an anonymous hate letter in the inter-office mail, insulting me for being a person of despicably low morals, for being—in a word— queer. I couldn't imagine anyone sending such a letter except Jayne, and it occurred to me that she might have thought there was more between us than there was. In any case, I was furious and naively took the note to the personnel department, which I foolishly expected would be interested in helping me find out for sure who had written it. Their concern was rather more with my being homosexual, and when I refused to deny it (that wasn't the issue, I maintained), the head of the department explained that he thought I'd be better off working elsewhere. The company would give me two weeks of severance pay if I would resign on the spot; I could come back later to pick up whatever personal items I might have left in my desk. There wasn't anything worth going back for.

I drove home stunned, and I surprised Jerry by arriving in the middle of the day. He met me in my room, where I was standing in front of a chest of drawers. I told him what had just happened to me, and, as I cried, my head down now on top of the furniture, he came up behind me and embraced me and cried too.

By the time we learned that the house on Bennett was to be torn down to make room for an apartment building, we had all begun to think of moving. Steve left Dallas, and Jerry and I returned to our homes, both of us hoping to save money in order to realize as-yet-undetermined goals.

While I was looking for another job, I helped my father with house painting. It had felt funny—wrong, somehow—to go back home, and I was happy to take up an older friend's offer to move in with him. Jay was completing his last years before retirement as an engineer for a large oil company, and he had a comfortable house with a spare back bedroom (that doubled as a darkroom). He loved music, and we spent many happy hours in his den listening to Jerome Kern, Georges Bizet's *The Pearl Fishers*, Sergei Prokofiev, and Gerard Hoffnung's Festival music. On July 4th, Jay coordinated the annual fireworks display at Fair Park with the Dallas Symphony Orchestra's performance of Pyotr Tchaikovsky's *1812 Overture*, and I helped him follow the score in the control booth. Jay and I became friends, getting to know one another surprisingly well, I think, given the difference in our ages.

Jay had never had a longtime companion. He liked to be around young boys, and he entertained (and helped financially) two or three of his friends' children without, I am certain, taking advantage of them. Jay did have one close friend nearer his own age, a partially deaf fellow by the name of Quinn who often joined us for dinner. It gives me pleasure to recall those evenings, the three of us (or four, when our friend Bill joined us) sitting on Jay's patio, "nursing"—Jay's habitual term—our drinks, Quinn laughing and blushing at the gentle teasing Jay always treated him to, probably giving him more attention than he received elsewhere.

Jay was the first older gay man I had ever known, and I learned a lot from him about getting by in a homophobic world. I also saw (and see even more clearly now) the unhappy side of subterfuge: Jay drank steadily, buying Canadian Club by the case, and he had gotten into the habit of keeping his innermost feelings, even his convictions, entirely to himself.

A few weeks before the presidential election of 1964, I came home and noticed a Goldwater bumper sticker on the back of Jay's car. I was outraged, peeled it off, and strode into the house to tell Jay what some Republican at work had done. When we later watched the election returns, Bill and I became more and more jubilant as Johnson's landslide became apparent. Jay sat quietly, drank, and retired to his bedroom before Goldwater conceded. It was only then that I realized that Jay had put the sticker on his car himself.

What he thought—to the extent that I could divine it—mattered a great deal to me. He could let drop the merest suggestion, and I would leap on it, eager to please or impress.

He rarely criticized me, but when he did, his words stung for days. I still remember the time we were washing dishes (perhaps after his favorite meal of roast lamb with mint jelly), and I was wittingly—I thought—making fun of one of my friends. "Have you always been so sarcastic?" he asked. It was a direct hit, and it still hurts.

Jay was a generous man, opening his wallet and his home to many in need. He gave my father work painting his house, and he found additional jobs for Daddy through his friends. He welcomed a girlfriend of mine who was in hiding until she could have and then give up her "illegitimate" baby. And he took me with him several times to Rockport, on the Texas Gulf Coast, where we ate redfish and sat laughing in the Adirondack chairs under the windswept trees of the Live Oak Lodge, nursing our Dos Equis.

I saw Jerry from time to time, but he was very much involved now in launching his career as a performer of avant-garde music. He had begun attending new-music concerts both in Texas and elsewhere, and he was meeting other performers and composers, making friends and contacts.

And he was still cooking. When my sister surprised us all by announcing her marriage to a young man she'd met only weeks before, Jerry offered to prepare a tray of delicacies for the reception Jay agreed to have at his house. Judy and I are still trying to figure out what some of the dishes were, but we do remember hors d'oeuvres shaped like sea horses.

For work, I had found a job "doing research" and was paid so much per "report"; what I did, of course, was to write term papers for a company that marketed its products nationwide, by topic.

I'd sit at my trusty Remington Rand typing out essays on operations research or wildlife management, consulting Jay's encyclopedias, and pillaging his library for information on subjects I barely knew anything about.

I continued to think about returning to college, and I took a correspondence course in the European novel taught by U.C. Knoepflmacher (my good luck) from the University of California at Berkeley. I threw myself into reading Thomas Mann's *The Magic Mountain*, putting my one semester of French at the University of Houston to work making a rough translation of the "Walpurgisnacht" section of that novel. During the last year of Jerry's life, I was to think often of that book, with its discussion of rales and rhonchi (rattling sounds in the lungs) and its graphic descriptions of the fatigue the tuberculosis sanatorium's patients struggled with.

Finally, I found a full-time job at another insurance company (there were, it turned out, no problems with references), and I could begin saving money in earnest. Since I had given up my MG, I borrowed my parents' Chevrolet each week, leaving them Mondays through Fridays with Daddy's truck to use for transportation. I took their sacrifice for granted, then.

Of all the jobs I had working for insurance companies (and there were five), this is the one I enjoyed the most. I worked for a company that sold health insurance primarily, but it still had quite a few life insurance policies on the books, acquired mostly through mergers and buyouts. I was the "Life Department" (and so my stamp felicitously read), and I spent many agreeable hours reviewing old policy contracts, figuring cash and loan values from rate tables, and corresponding with policyholders. I had an efficient IBM electric typewriter fitted with a font consisting entirely of capital letters, and I worked largely unsupervised, spinning out long, chatty letters to hard-up or bereaved customers. As had been the case at the other companies, though, I found the office environment stifling—but I was careful, now, to keep pretty much to myself.

While I was in Houston, I had read an article in *The Saturday Review* about St. John's College, the "Great Books School," with a uniform curriculum and no grades. I was intrigued by the concept and by the Santa Fe campus. I was eventually accepted for the fall semester of 1965, and with a combination of scholarship money, a National Defense Student Loan, and the promise of an on-campus job, I was ready to go.

But not until I'd bleached my hair and dyed it blond. Did I want a new identity? I startled everyone—I startle myself, as I think of it now, as I picture myself sitting at the seminar table, smoking my pipe (inhaling too—no one told me not to), my roots steadily darkening.

In those days, most Texans thought of northern New Mexico as we would a far-off country. None of my family or friends had ever been there. Santa Fe, in particular, we closely identified in our imaginations with its motto, "The City Different"; we pictured it snowbound most of the winter. As a farewell gift, Jerry bought me a magnificent black parka with a fringed hood and a thunderbird stitched in the white nylon lining. (Although it didn't concern us then, we were pleased to recall later that the "fur" was man-made.) I had bought a new blue suit, and I started out on what I hoped would be a real adventure, something that would change my life.

My parents hoped that for me, too, although I know it was hard for them to see me go away so far, especially since Judy had left to join her Army husband in France (and, later, Germany). I remembered how upset they had been, particularly Daddy, when we said goodbye to Judy at Love Field. (Daddy's health was by then so poor that we had to have an airport wheelchair for him.) Here they were at the airport again (commercial flights could land in Santa Fe then), seeing off their other child.

I'll never forget the altitude shock I experienced the day I arrived. Carrying my luggage (and Thunderbird coat) up the steps to the dorm on the hillside above the campus just about disabled me. I wasn't even able to speak to the fellows who had come out to welcome me. They assured me I'd get used to it—we were at over seven thousand feet elevation—and I did, but it took several weeks.

Just the other day, I was looking at photographs of the college president, Richard Weigle, and land donor John Gaw Meem surveying the yet-to-be-built campus site. There was nothing for miles around, except for the Santa Fe Preparatory School at the very bottom of the hills. Those who know only the Santa Fe of today would have a hard time imagining the remoteness, the splendid isolation, of the place in the mid-'60s. The three main college buildings and the cluster of smaller dorms were built on the side of Monte Sol in the Sangre de Cristo range. The view in every direction was of piñon trees and rocky hillsides, all under the magnificent New Mexico sky.

Santa Fe itself was a distant village. A few of us made regular treks there on Saturdays, meandering through the residential neighborhoods downward to the plaza, where we would get haircuts, do a little shopping for provisions beyond the scope of what the college store carried, and, in general, take in the exotic look and feel of the place, its adobe buildings and Native American vendors. I always stopped at the Candy Kitchen for some of the piñon brittle they made on the premises.

My freshman class was only the second on the Santa Fe campus. There was a general sense among us, both students and teachers, that we were creating the place as we went along. Although a few faculty came out from the Annapolis campus, many of the tutors I had were as new to St. John's as my classmates and I were. The feeling that we were pioneers was reinforced by the remoteness of the place and the demands that were sometimes placed on our resourcefulness. A heavy snow cut off the college's electricity one weekend; we gathered around the huge fireplace in one of the common rooms for light to study.

An older couple lived in a small apartment just back of the dorms. I assume they were monitors of some kind, but they were rarely seen (except when they came out to put more seed in their bird feeders). They missed a lot. There was steady traffic through the utility tunnels that connect the men's and women's dorms, and I knew that many students smoked marijuana. The men's dorms were noisy on weekends, the music a mixture of rock and folk; a general unwinding began immediately after the obligatory Friday night lecture.

Stress seemed to build as the weeks went by, and the closeness of a small student body studying two set curricula (one for us freshmen, one for the sophomores) intensified the pressure. Most of us cared passionately about our work. And there was no "system" to manipulate—we were always sitting right across the table from our tutors and seminar leaders and next to the people who lived with us. If you couldn't keep up, you couldn't stay. A few freshmen "disappeared" during the fall semester, chastening us all.

I learned to study at St. John's, perhaps even to think.

Where glibness had served me, a rational argument was now required. My prejudices, pretensions, and intellectual laziness were exposed in the seminars and quarterly "don rags" (where, instead of grades, individual students are examined by all their tutors, their progress evaluated and then described in detailed letters that are mailed out to parents). I struggled with Greek paradigms, sweated my turn at the board to reproduce Euclidean proofs from memory, and cursed the lab manual that defied me to treat experiments like recipes. But I was not alone, standing shaving at the row of sinks in the dorm restroom, reviewing the irregular verbs that a classmate had crayoned on the mirror.

For a few weeks, I was homesick, and I remember wondering if perhaps my going so far away, literally and figuratively, had been a big mistake. I missed Jerry, but I was also delighted to be able to write him all about the esoteric reading and studying I was doing. He could talk about Henri Pousseur, I about Herodotus. My job in the college library took several hours a week away from study time, so I was kept too busy to pine about home for long.

And I made friends: Don, with a bushy mustache and a huge capacity for silliness; Hugo, whose parents lived in Santa Fe and whose father wrote the Matt Helm detective series; and Bob Davis, who shortly became my steady companion. I lived in a dorm suite with Don, Hugo, and Henry. With only two classes on campus, there weren't very many of us, and we all knew one another, at least well enough to speak to. People got used to seeing Bob and me together; we'd be asked, when alone, where the other was.

Bob was from San Francisco and talked about being an architect someday. He was reading Henry Adams's *Mont-Saint-Michel and Chartres* in the little time he had for recreational reading, and he took thorough notes in class with his trusty Rapidograph—the notes any of us who had to be absent always asked for. He had one of the few private rooms in the dorm (had he asked for it?), and I would stop by to pick him up every morning on my way to breakfast and classes downhill. I was fascinated by the orderliness of his desk and bookshelves.

We'd go to breakfast early, as soon as they began serving, and when the weather permitted, we'd sit outside on the balcony overlooking the valley below, eating boiled eggs out of the shell, and peeling oranges with our thumbs. Bob was a relatively large-framed young man, lean and muscular, who often couldn't get enough to eat—he'd have a second stack of pancakes while I smoked my pipe.

Then we'd jimmy open the locked door to the music room and listen to Bach or Francis Poulenc for half an hour before our first tutorial. In fact, we did quite a lot that was slightly irregular; we were always going on about the "stupid" rules the college had (why keep the music room locked so much of the time?). Bob was a waiter in the dining hall at evening meals, which were rather formal. I always sat at one of his tables, and he often saved special food for me or brought me second helpings when they weren't permitted. In turn, as a library worker, I'd save new records for him. Early on, we talked the girls who prepared food in the coffee shop into letting us come behind the counter and fix our own sandwiches the way we liked them.

We got into trouble one night, and the college president himself caught us. It was late one Sunday, and we had met to play ping-pong in the dorm common room. We decided to go down to the coffee shop. We'd been studying Ptolemy and had just learned about epicycles. We undertook to demonstrate the principle as we walked through the center of the campus. Bob, being more athletically inclined, ran in a tight circle along my larger circumference. It was hilarious . . . and it may have been observed. President Weigle had been working late and was just leaving his office in the science building, but by the time he could lock up and get into the courtyard, Bob and I had helpfully begun watering the newly planted trees. "Let's let the grounds crew take care of that, fellows," Dr. Weigle said. Had he seen us dance, too?

At the time, I didn't know that Bob was gay, and it interests me now to think that I didn't wonder too much about it then. I was, of course, aware that I found him sexually attractive: he wore T-shirts, corduroy jeans, and zoris (which were expressly forbidden by college policy), and his fair good looks and swimmer's build gave me pleasure to contemplate. On warm spring days, we'd sunbathe on one of the dorm's rooftops, reading Thucydides, and the first time I saw his bare, well-defined chest, I had to catch my breath.

One spring day, a tutor took Bob and me and a couple of other students with her to her home near a wooded area. Bob and I wandered off by ourselves, discovering a stream and a hillside of dead trees, still-standing reminders of an old fire. We had been arguing about what petty things I no longer remember, but I still clearly recall the sexual tension between us that day. With some considerable effort, Bob pushed one of the huge trees over. I did the same to a nearby tree. And with increasing frenzy, we worked, sometimes together on the largest trunks, until we had flattened the whole stand. But there was no element of fun in it, and things were never quite the same between us afterward.

I realize much more clearly now how unhappy Bob was at that time. He talked every weekend with his mother—there was never any mention of his father—and these conversations always seemed to agitate or depress him. And he missed the bay and the ocean, the sailing and swimming he loved. By the middle of the spring semester, he decided to transfer to the Annapolis campus the following year; about the same time, I decided not to return to St. John's at all the next fall.

Bob and I corresponded intermittently for a year or two. I knew from the St. John's alumni directory that he had graduated from Annapolis and had returned to San Francisco. Then, in an alumni newsletter in June of 1987, I learned that Bob had died a few months earlier, at the age of 40, of a "brain infection," a common circumlocution for AIDS. He had spent two years in the Peace Corps in Nepal, received architectural training, and become a designer for the de Young Museum. He had also participated in several Transatlantic and Transpacific sailing races. The photograph in the newsletter revealed that his hair had darkened considerably.

When people would ask Jerry and me in the years to come how long we had been together, I always counted back to 1965. We had met in the eighth grade, but I didn't really think of us as a couple, committed to one another, until about the middle of my year at St. John's. Perhaps that much distance was required for me to see how I really felt.

When I came home for Christmas that year, I think I realized how important Jerry had become to me. Since he was living at home again, we could only obtain the privacy we wanted by renting motel rooms; and when we were alone together, we made love now when we'd had sex before. Our relationship was strengthened by my having gone off, I suppose, to prove something and by his having missed me.

Jerry drove to Santa Fe in his Renault to pick me up at the end of the spring semester. He'd had quite a bit of trouble with that car ever since he'd bought it (his mother eventually wrote the factory in France, to no avail), and the alternator/generator panel light had come on some-where in the Panhandle, which annoyance he removed by sticking Green Stamps over it. He called me at school from a payphone in Santa Fe, the car audibly running nearby, and he explained that he knew that once he killed the engine, he'd never get it started again. He proposed to meet me in the college parking lot, and we would then find a garage where the car could be repaired.

As it eventually was, but not without a terrible scene. I no longer remember the issue, the provocation, but at one point, Jerry had squatted down and was trying to pull the little car out of the mechanic's bay. (Twenty years later, there was a very similar scene at Sam's Warehouse Club in Tyler where Jerry, a Canadian artist friend, and I had gone for new tires. What angered Jerry was that he'd seen a customer who'd arrived after us be waited on first, and we had already waited for quite some time. While Jerry was trying to pull his Volkswagen out of the garage, I went into the store, found the manager, and he saw to it that Jerry was waited on immediately.)

A phone call to Jerry's parents satisfied the Santa Fe garage that the repair bill would be paid, and we were on our way home in a couple of days. Jerry had time to meet Bob, whom he didn't much like (he found him "arrogant" and "affected"). Moreover, given all the trouble he'd had with the garage and his car, Jerry didn't much like Santa Fe. (He was to change his opinion in the years to come, when he and his mother and I visited there, and, later, when we went up for a concert he gave at the Contemporary Arts Museum.)

We were both glad to be returning to Texas. My last don rag had been a success, and I left with a sense of accomplishment. My intention to finish college was firm, but I would go to school in Texas, nearer my family and nearer Jerry. The long drive home passed quickly, with all our talking, laughing, and lovemaking (suspended for the passing truckers)—the little Renault humming along, no warning lights visible.

We never conscientiously saved our letters to one another, but every now and then, something turned—turns—up, usually a postcard or a brief note. Jerry had little patience with record-keeping, at least when the records were correspondence and bills. And his desks and files have always been stuffed with unsorted material, left stacked and even bundled for a day when there might be time for such archival undertakings—and, of course, there never was time. He eventually came to make fun of his own sloppiness (and register his contempt for such matters at the same time) by labeling files "Important Papers" and "Mixed Bills."

A letter, either one of mine or one of his, could surface from among old bank statements and water bills. Such a likelihood serves me now as an incentive as I make my way through drawer after drawer of papers, finally sorting and discarding worthless items, a librarian weeding the collection. I sometimes feel these discovered letters are messages. What they tell me derives both from their content and from the appropriateness of their emergence at a specific time.

One of Jerry's memorial concerts in New York included a composition that Jerry had begun planning as a collaboration with Michael Schell—a piece titled *Telephone Calls to the Dead*. When Jerry realized how sick he was, he told me to ask Michael to finish and perform the work. This was done superbly, but with an interpretation that I don't think Jerry envisioned—although I am not entirely sure of that. Using videotaped images of Jerry and his work, along with sequences of mementos and artifacts manipulated by computer, *Telephone Calls* suggested a kind of high-tech seance, an evocation of Jerry's spirit using some of his own tools. I think of this piece sometimes when I run across a letter, attentive to learn both what it says and what it has to tell me now.

And so, a few days ago, I found a letter Jerry wrote to me in Houston, addressed to the house on Delafield that I had rented, located within walking distance of the University of Houston (where I re-enrolled in the fall of 1966)—a house large enough for the two of us, whenever he could join me. After filling me in on his activities, he says: "I wonder about you in Houston. This is not the best of things. But at this point, it has become quite natural. I have begun to expect you to be gone . . . each year. Do not know why you do such things, and always, but that's the trouble. We both have the various demands, six . . . one doesn't give them up." Although now I may look back with some regret on those years when my being away at college separated us, I realize, even more clearly from rereading Jerry's letter, that these were good times for us as we met our "various demands." And I am reminded of the sense of security that underlay our relationship then—finally— and that freed us, together, to live apart. However, there is still the unfortunate aspect of the separation: "This is not the best of things." Every part of that brief letter resounds today.

Jerry was working at the time with Bart Bartelmehs and his trio, playing piano in a variety of venues, including VFW halls. He was also giving new music concerts in the Dallas–Fort Worth area, playing prepared piano on a concert in Oak Cliff, doing early performance art at the Contemporary Arts Museum in Fort Worth (a piece that involved pushing a three-foot-high cigarette urn down the aisle, alarming the already incredulous audience), and performing with clarinetist Houston Higgins and his wife, Jill, a soprano.

It was a period of creativity, of receptivity to new ideas and experiments in the arts in Dallas, thanks primarily to a few SMU faculty members. The university symphony orchestra's conductor, David Ahlstrom, invited Jerry to give the southwestern premiere of Cage's *Atlas Eclipticalis*. And Toni Beck, the head of SMU's dance department, collaborated with Jerry on several innovative works (one of which was shown on CBS-TV). Jerry also earned money playing the dance piano and teaching a series of courses on music after 1950.

His real work, though, was composing works for piano—like *Sur (Doctor) John Dee* from 1966—and for piano and electronic media. He had begun identifying himself as a composer as opposed to a pianist or a musician, and the concerts he gave were to consist more and more of his own music.

Because of his association with SMU and, especially, with Toni Beck, Jerry's parents were less apprehensive about his having abandoned a career in traditional music. They were also a little more at ease, Jerry always believed, about his being homosexual and about the problems that might cause him working. In fact, it probably appeared to them in the late '60s that he was succeeding: he was obviously happy doing what he wanted to do, he was staying busy, and he was meeting and impressing influential people.

He was even making enough money to afford a studio, the Green Shack, near Inwood and Lovers Lane, splitting the rent with Houston (and a sometimes third partner, Phil Hughes). Still officially living at home, Jerry was, in fact, spending most of his time at the studio—a two-room guest house with kitchen and bath behind a private residence. (The front room was devoted to electronics, and Jerry moved his grand piano to the back room, filling it.)

He did think he might relocate to Houston for a while; that was the plan we made during the summer after I had returned from St. John's. It would have been a mistake, though, we both realized just a few weeks after school had begun. He would have had to start all over in Houston, making contacts and building a reputation. Although the larger city was later to surpass Dallas in its receptivity to new music and art, Dallas was ahead of it. Furthermore, given his inability to promote himself (or, it may have been, his distaste for doing so), it would have been foolish for Jerry to have turned his back on the extraordinary good fortune he had already had.

Nevertheless, it was hard at first for me to accept the fact that he wasn't coming. As I became more absorbed in my studies, I felt less lonely, and I made a few friends on campus to spend some of my free time with. By the middle of the fall semester, it had become clear that I was not going to find an on-campus job to supplement the scholarship and loan money I had, so I reluctantly gave up the Delafield house, with the room over the garage that I used as a study (I'll never forget the ordeal I had shoving the Magnavox stereo cabinets up the narrow stairway—only to have to lug them down a few weeks later).

I had seen a sign in a front yard a few doors up the street advertising a room for rent, and I knocked on the door one day, introducing myself to Ola Coley, a widow with two front rooms available, the rear one equipped as a kitchen. It was all the space I needed, and I moved my things to my new apartment the next weekend, pushing the Magnavox stereo up the center of the street and using a wheelbarrow for books, clothes, and smaller possessions.

Mrs. Coley was a lonely, ill old lady, barely able to keep up her house, and really beyond dealing with a roomer and the worries having a stranger living so close by can bring. All that separated her front room from mine were French doors (that formerly opened into the dining room, where I now lived). A thin, chromespun curtain hung on each side of these doors, affording both of us a modicum of privacy.

I would often hear her calling her Christian Science practitioner when she felt particularly bad, asking for counsel and prayer support. Since I could hear every word Mrs. Coley spoke when I was in my own front room, I soon figured out that I would have to do most of my studying at the kitchen table.

From time to time, we'd visit; in fact, I believe she sometimes waited for me to come out of the bathroom we shared, having been alerted by the creaky wooden floor of the back hallway. We exchanged pleasantries—I spoke to her canary, and she offered me a Hydrox cookie from the bag. (I developed the habit of helping myself to these cookies when I knew she'd gone to bed; periodically, I'd replace the bag—and I remember doing this so often that it occurs to me now to wonder whether she might have, at some point, been able to stop buying them altogether.)

Jerry came down to see me as often as he could, and we'd make love in my front room, where the double bed was. It was a delicate situation. Since Mrs. Coley spent most of her time in her front room, we tried to be careful not to alarm her. It wasn't easy to be quiet. During one especially passionate session, Jerry and I heard her telephone her practitioner, opening the conversation with words to the effect of "Honey, I don't think I can stand much more." We stifled our laughter somehow; later, we went over for a long visit.

Since St. John's, I had come to love college. My major was English, and I had knowledgeable, stimulating teachers for literary criticism, medieval literature, and Shakespeare. The university required several interdisciplinary electives, and I enjoyed art history and a course in symphony. The time I spent reading, writing, and listening to music went quickly, and the more of it I did, the more I wanted to do.

Thanks to St. John's, again, I'd had a year of Greek and declared it my minor at UH. Dr. Moore came over from Rice University to teach the language to small groups of students. She was no longer needed when UH hired Dora Pozzi, a South American native who had studied Greek at Oxford and had come to Houston with her husband, who taught in the Philosophy Department. With this brilliant, hard-working teacher's guidance and encouragement, I was able to read Attic drama by the time I graduated. My memories of the two years I spent in Houston are illustrated by images of myself riffling vocabulary cards, memorizing paradigms, and adding syntactical aids, with the sharpest of pencils, to the Greek texts that I carried to every restaurant and on every bus ride.

Sra. Pozzi recommended me to a philosophy major who had come to her searching for a Greek language tutor. Lillian began coming by for weekly lessons, often still in the white uniform she wore on her job in the Surgical Pathology Department of Hermann Hospital. I'd make us a pot of tea, and we'd read Greek, Lillian smoking her Camels and laughing loudly at her mistakes.

We became friends, often finding ourselves straying from the lesson at hand to talk about ourselves. She was forty years old, divorced, and the mother of a grown son. As she later confided, she was also a lesbian who had dutifully played a straight role but who—now that her

son was on his own—was gradually asserting her identity, allowing it to shape her life. She told me about the
lady she was seeing at the time, who would come over to
Lillian's house and sit with her in the swing on the front
porch, where they would surreptitiously hold hands. I
was fascinated by her, by her stories, and by her appetite
for learning and for life. And she was the first lesbian I
had ever known.

(But not the first I ever knew of. Jerry and I had a
math teacher in high school who rode a motorcycle to
school and wore a black leather jacket in cold weather.
She intrigued us, suggesting, I suppose, some quality of
difference that we identified with. One day we were prowl-
ing the dusty aisles of the old Aldredge Book Store, located
in a large house on McKinney Avenue. The store served
complimentary wine to browsers on Sunday afternoons
and was usually filled with people. Jerry and I suddenly
caught a glimpse of this teacher through the book stacks,
talking quietly—intimately—with another woman in a
similar biker's jacket. To our delight, our suspicions were
confirmed.)

Lillian's goal was to teach philosophy, and she went on
to receive her PhD in that subject from Tulane University.
We corresponded with one another, regularly and volu-
minously, during the thirteen years we lived in different
cities—when I was in graduate school in Austin, and she
was in New Orleans—then when I taught in Dallas, and
she did in Auburn, Alabama. Her letters were the kind
to savor, full as they were of humorous anecdotes and
thoughtful descriptions, both often illustrated by deft
pen-and-ink drawings. She loved gardening, sewing,
music, and dogs, and her letters usually touched on all
four topics.

Freed from the scrutiny of her family in Houston,
Lillian was finally able to have intimate women friends,
and she wrote me in detail about the two close relation-
ships she had before she died, at the age of fifty-five, of
lung cancer.

When I wasn't reading, I was listening to music—so
it had always been, so it is now. But, for the first time,
with the guidance of a course in the development of the
symphony, I was exploring periods and composers in a

systematic manner. I had decided, or admitted, that I am a born listener: my early violin- and horn-playing and my later attempts to play the piano were, after all, half-hearted. What I really liked to do was listen, sometimes following a score or an analysis of themes and their development. It had become hopeless to try to share this enthusiasm with Jerry, who by now had completely turned his back on "old, dead European masters." In Houston, I was to meet my ideal musical friend.

After studying piano at Centenary College in Shreveport, Louisiana, Bob (the second Bob in my life) had come to UH to major in English. He was a teaching assistant working in the French language lab when he met and married Carol in 1965. They had a daughter the following year. Then, in 1967, I ran into Carol one day on campus—the same ebullient Carol I had known years before. We visited briefly, and she invited me to come to her and Bob's apartment for dinner. That night, Bob's and my relationship began, and he remains my closest friend today. He was with me when Jerry died.

Bob and I enjoyed discussing books and ideas. He conveyed his enthusiasm for John Steinbeck and Aldous Huxley to me, and we read Milton and Shakespeare aloud together. But it was music that really stimulated us, as we shared discoveries: Carl Nielsen, Mozart's *Linz* symphony, and the piano pieces that Bob played on his old upright while I turned the pages.

He and Carol eventually moved into a two-story frame house in West University, and I would come over often to have dinner with them. Bob and I played music, went for long walks through the shady neighborhood, and talked and sometimes argued about ideas. Carol watched TV (*Mission: Impossible* and *Family Affair*), smoking, her legs tucked under her, and the baby tucked in upstairs. She usually went to bed early, exhausted from school (where she was a political science major), a part-time job, and caring for little Donna.

Jerry came down to get me at the beginning of the Christmas holidays, and he and Bob met. We made a good trio, often gathering at the piano to illustrate ideas or share discoveries. Bob recalls how much Jerry impressed him by his intelligence, wit, and musical talent. Carol had always liked Jerry, and having him with us in Houston was a happy event for all three of us.

Seeing Jerry and me together, relaxed and free in our loving relationship, may have encouraged Bob to confess to me one day during a trip to Galveston Beach that he is homosexual. He had always been attracted to boys, but he had never quite accepted that fact as one that could, or should, influence his behavior. At the urging of his cousin—and pressured by the fear of being drafted as a single man—he decided to marry and have a family. He had only begun to realize that he had made a mistake during the time we were becoming friends. In any case, the marriage was to last another few years.

The two years I spent in Houston were good ones, filled with intellectual stimulation and aesthetic pleasure. I made frequent trips to the Houston Public Library, then housed in the old Julia Ideson Building, preferring to study there and be downtown, close to restaurants, bookstores, and movies. I also subscribed to the Houston Symphony, transported by Sir John Barbirolli's Elgar and Mahler.

Sometimes, before these Monday evening concerts, I would have a meal of fried oysters at Kelley's Oyster Bar. I ran into Ellen Puckett, the elderly lady from the insurance company, having dinner there one night. She had come down for a performance of a violin concerto, even though Zino Francescatti was not the soloist on that occasion. I enjoyed visiting with her after so many years.

She had since retired, and I gathered that she was pretty much alone in the world, a long-standing widow and childless. There was a poignancy about her situation that impressed me then, and I often recalled: an old lady bravely pursuing her interests, dining at tables for one, ordering one concert ticket. A decade later, I saw her from a distance waiting for a bus in downtown Dallas. I thought, briefly, about approaching her, but she somehow didn't seem to be available—looking as though any intrusion upon her solitude would be unwelcome. I wish now that I had said *hello*, had called her back.

I had one final fling, the only affair I ever had after Jerry and I had reunited in 1966. Jim was an insurance salesman and a part-time realtor, divorced, separated from his two children in Beaumont, and very much a part of the gay scene in Houston's Montrose district. I was briefly allured by that scene, living as I did in an apartment and then in a rooming house right in the middle of the area, with its heavy cruising and its concentration of clubs and pedestrian traffic. I couldn't have had a better, more knowledgeable guide.

Lillian had just left one afternoon, and with the five dollars I had earned tutoring, I went to my favorite hamburger stand and ordered an early dinner. I was sitting at one of the picnic tables outside, eating my sandwich and reading the *Christian Science Monitor* that I subscribed to at that time for news. I noticed a man driving by several times, slowing down, staring at me, and finally parking. He introduced himself and asked if he could give me a ride somewhere.

We saw one another several times a week for the next couple of months. We went dancing (which I hadn't done since Robert), we ate out together, and we had sex, sometimes in my room, sometimes in the apartment that he shared with an ex-lover. Jim was a gentle, thoughtful man, a passionate lover, and a great deal of fun to be with, both in public and alone. He wanted a commitment from me; he was ready, he said, to settle down.

As soon as some of the newness and theatricality of what I was doing wore off, I realized—or admitted—that I didn't love Jim. We had very little in common, after all, beneath the superficial mutual attraction. Our last time together was a trip that we made to San Antonio. Although the sex was as good as ever, we both knew by then that we wouldn't be seeing one another anymore.

Jim was recovering from a bout with hepatitis when I met him—his second, he told me. I soon gathered that he had had numerous sexual partners since his move from Beaumont. As far as we know, AIDS was not yet present in the US, but I have often wondered if Jim ever contracted it, given his way of life then. I don't have the heart to try to find out.

I told Jerry about Jim one night after moving back home to work during the summer before entering graduate school in Austin that next fall. He had come over for dinner; we'd finished eating, and the two of us were

sitting on the dark patio, alone, in the huge metal chairs
my parents had had for as long as I could remember. I
suppose I felt I had to tell him that it was a problem that
had to be resolved.

He was hurt—as hurt as I had ever seen him, or as
I was ever to. I remember very clearly—now, over twenty-five years later—that for a few minutes, I was not at all
sure he and I could go on. I squatted beside him, putting
my head in his lap, and apologized, and promised that it
would never happen again.

My graduation from the University of Houston was a family event: Mother, Daddy, Judy, and Paul all came down to attend the outdoor ceremonies. Mother and Daddy stayed with me in my furnished room; Carol and Bob brought Donna by. For me, the ceremony would have been dispensable (I certainly didn't care whether Jerry attended or not), but it meant a lot to my parents, and I am especially glad now that they were there. They had done everything they were able to do to help me through college, from moving me and my things back and forth to mailing me food boxes (oatmeal cookies and canned hams) and the occasional unexpected money order.

That summer, I worked as a "destruction clerk" for another insurance company, weeding files of old credit reports and medical records that, by law, the *company* was no longer required to keep. The only entertaining part of the job was the odd narrative: I'd become intimately involved in a policyholder's life, for a brief period, reading the thicker files like a plot summary but often unable to learn the outcome.

My year in graduate school at the University of Texas at Austin was by necessity and choice devoted almost entirely to study. I lived in a graduate dorm—a two-room suite with a bathroom in the middle, each room accommodating three young men who were pretty much there only to sleep. When we weren't attending classes, we were studying in our assigned cubicles, either in the tower library or in our own departments (English, drama, philosophy, physics, astronomy, and chemistry—an interesting assortment). Most of us subscribed to a meal plan offered by a nearby cooperative house, so our getting to know one another, to the extent that we did, was accomplished over dinner. There were about ten other graduate students in our dorm (actually the second floor of what I think used to be a motel).

The operators of the dorm made a community room available to us, and we would gather there on some Saturday nights for a little socializing. The philosophy major had already begun dating one of the women in the dorm, so they were usually off on their own.

Most of the rest of us, though, would gather to listen to music, drink wine or beer, and share experiences at the university.

On one of these occasions, the astronomy major, Jos, a very good-looking fellow, told the group about an upsetting encounter he had had while sunbathing on campus. He was lying shirtless in a common area near the student union building, and another young man approached him and made some suggestive comment—an overture, perhaps. Jos was angry, he told the group, because there seemed to be so many queers on campus that a person couldn't even take his shirt off to get a little sun without being propositioned.

I might have said something had the other gay member of the dorm, the drama major, been with us that night. As it was, I coldly felt outnumbered, and I was years away from being able to meet prejudice head-on. So, without a word, I quickly finished my beer, discarded the can, and returned to my room.

Jos was there immediately, hoping he hadn't offended, asking me to return to the party. I told him that I had to do a little reading, then I was going to bed. I climbed up into my bunk, turned on the reading lamp, and opened a book. He left.

After successfully avoiding mainstream English and American literary classics for most of my undergraduate years, I was advised to read a bit more of the canon for my English major.

I enjoyed surveying the American transcendentalists in a course that went well beyond the scope of Mrs. Worsham's College Outline Series volume. I also read Milton, Dickens, Trollope, and Hardy, often sitting against a sunny wall of the English building—and not at all afraid to take my shirt off.

My Conrad seminar met at the professor's house, and I made friends with the lady who usually gave me a ride there. Anne Freeman was working on her PhD. She was a careful, sensitive reader who frequently argued her points with the forcefulness of her Irish passion, often leavened by her Irish wit. She seemed a little older than the rest of us, perhaps because she had to walk with a cane due to childhood polio.

It was the Greek minor that occupied most of my time, however. I was lucky enough to have a sequence of independent study courses offered by the classics department, and Dr. Thomas Gould was my supervising teacher. He was just finishing up his translation of *Oedipus the King* for Prentice-Hall, and he suggested that I read the play with him and, later, that I proofread and check his extensive commentary. This was an exciting project to work on, and I was flattered to have been asked—and very eager to please.

We met twice a week in his office at lunchtime (he always brought sandwiches, and sometimes we had wine). I had dinner with him once in his apartment overlooking the lake. As would William Arrowsmith and D.S. Carne-Ross (whom I had for a Milton course), Dr. Gould was very soon to leave UT to return to New England as the result of a dispute over teaching loads.

In addition to Diane, nearing the end of her doctoral program, there were two people in Austin I had known earlier. John was working on his undergraduate degree, not entirely successfully, and living in one of the first high-rise dorms Austin had. Three years younger than I, John was one of my sister's high-school friends I got to know later when I lived with Jay.

We had sex one afternoon in my room—rather suddenly, as I remember. What I do recall quite clearly, though, is Jay describing the expression on my face afterward as "diaphanous."

John didn't stay in Austin long. He wasn't ready to settle down to schoolwork, and the gay ghetto in San Francisco lured him away. He has lived there ever since, working in accounting, losing lovers and friends to AIDS, seeing the face of his beloved city cloud. A few years ago, he decided to finish his BA, and he has begun work on an MA in history. I see him once a year when he comes home to visit his family; we have a meal and a long talk and serve, I think, as a kind of milepost for one another.

Bob was now in Austin, too, having abandoned his English degree program in Houston to enter graduate school at UT in botany and work as a teaching assistant. We would meet for dinner Saturday nights, walking from our lodgings on opposite sides of the campus to a centrally-located cafe, then continuing our talks or arguments as we sauntered about the campus.

His deficiency in chemistry and a midwinter case of the flu finally did Bob in, academically—he gave up his teaching assistantship and dropped out of school, too discouraged to go on. Carol came up, found them a subsidized apartment, and worked to support the family until they eventually moved back to Houston. They invited me to dinner several times that spring semester. I played with Donna outside while Carol prepared dinner. After eating, Bob and I would sit on their tiny patio, taking turns reading *Paradise Lost* aloud, and Carol would be inside practicing her French horn for an amateur group she played in.

I continued my coursework through the two summer sessions, determined to finish the degree. To save money and be nearer the English building, I rented a room at the old YMCA just across Guadalupe for the summer. Anne had found a job teaching English at St. Mark's School in Dallas, and she encouraged me to apply to Cistercian Prep for a position. As a Catholic, she knew a priest who taught there, and she thought the school would be ideal for me.

Bob agreed to drive me to Irving, near Dallas, for the interview at the school. He waited in the car for a long time while I visited with Fr. Denis, the young Hungarian priest ("I'm thirty-three, the age Christ was when they crucified Him") who was to be the new headmaster that year. I was very much impressed by the school's demanding curriculum, by its faculty's academic backgrounds, and by the beauty and seclusion of its wooded campus, just across the hilltop from the Cistercian monastery. I couldn't wait to get started, to come back home for good, and to be with Jerry.

Jerry's Mason & Hamlin, my Magnavox stereos: their journeys draw the map of our lives. After the years on Bennett, the piano returned to the Hunts' home in Casa View; it moved again to the Green Shack, where it effectively had its own room. It had three more stops ahead of it. My stereos, after an ignominious hour on the highway shoulder somewhere between Houston and Dallas (where they had to sit while Bob and I unloaded his station wagon to get at the spare tire stored beneath the floor)— they waited for me at home while I was in Austin. Our reunion was a joyful one, lasting the two or three months that I lived at home, teaching and saving enough money to be able to make a deposit on an apartment somewhere with Jerry.

During holidays and semester breaks in Austin, I always came home, getting a ride to Dallas with my drama major roommate, who was on his way in his new hatchback to Iowa. I spent as much time at the Green Shack as I could, bringing my books and reading in the shade of the fig tree on the east of the little house.

Jerry and Houston etched circuit boards in the kitchen sink, wired interfaces, and practiced pieces for performance. When we were alone, Jerry and I made love under the piano, the only available space.

Houston's wife, Jill, met us at the shack on occasion. The four of us would go to dinner, or sometimes Houston and Jill would invite us over for dinner at their apartment. It had been on such an evening two years earlier that Houston and Jill announced their engagement, the same night that President Johnson told America that he

planned to withdraw from politics—news that added to
our celebration.

Jill had a rich, warm voice of wide range, and she
was to perform in Brahms's *German Requiem* and Gabriel
Fauré's Requiem with the SMU orchestra and chorus.
Her obliging nature and sense of fun led her two or three
times to perform with Jerry and Houston in situations
that must have baffled her: Jerry's "theatrical extensions"
of pieces by Mauricio Kagel and others, not to mention his
own compositions, might call for the unrolling of whole
boxes of aluminum foil or the use of unorthodox, primitive percussion devices. When I was able to attend Jerry's
and Houston's concerts, I would sit with Jill (when she
wasn't performing) and share her amazement.

Throughout his life as a composer and performer,
Jerry encouraged those around him to put aside their
expectations and prejudices in order to experience something different. Jill was only one of many people with
a traditional musical background whose imaginations
Jerry stimulated. Part of his success in doing this was
surely due to his rather formal dress and demeanor: his
suit and tie, his unprepossessing manner, and the seri-
ousness with which he so obviously took his work—all of
this inspired the credibility that was necessary for many
in the audience to be able to open themselves up to what
were very new ways of experiencing art.

The young, of course, don't labor under the weight
of fixed expectations and hardened categories, and they
have always been drawn to Jerry's work, predictably
gathering around him on the stage after a performance,
examining equipment, marveling at props, asking questions, and just enjoying being close to his independent
spirit. Jerry's association with SMU's dance and music
departments, formed, at first, on the basis of his piano
playing, developed in the early 1970s into guest lectur-
ing and, finally, to teaching, as the head of the electronic
music program. Jerry's courses were popular, but several
students dropped out each semester when they realized
how much work was expected of them.

We moved into our apartment (at the Court of Two
Sisters!) in the early winter of 1969—a two-bedroom,
upstairs unit with a closet-sized kitchen and a good view

of the traffic on Lemmon Avenue. The manager and his wife interviewed us, at length, in their own immaculate apartment; they wanted to be sure we wouldn't disturb the other residents with loud parties and unspecified "suspicious goings-on." Us both being teachers in a prep school and a college no doubt helped argue our case. And to be fair, we were ourselves eager to assure that we could get our work done and lead our lives undisturbed there.

The Green Shack had become too small. Jerry and Houston and Phil began sharing the rent on a house on Glencoe, a one-bedroom cottage that they soon filled with audio and electronics equipment, music and technical literature, and, of course, the Mason & Hamlin. I'd spend time there with Jerry on evenings and weekends, reading teacher manuals, preparing lesson plans, and grading papers, while Jerry worked on his own projects. He maintained a rather complete kitchen, turning out gourmet meals after a day of practicing and wiring. Gordon, an electronics engineer with Texas Instruments, became a frequent visitor, working with Jerry on electronic devices and enjoying the freewheeling conversation.

With Houston, Phil (a musicologist by training), and Gordon, Jerry conducted what might be described as a combination of a salon and boys' club. One never knew who would be there or what project might be underway, but it was always a place to have fun, to put aside for a while the pressing concerns of career and family responsibility, and to do something creative that might just count only for oneself. His dedicated hard work notwithstanding, Jerry set the example for all of us of a way of living that nourishes the imagination. But, in truth, those of us he influenced in this way were always only able to play at living like, at being like, Jerry. He had it down naturally.

The very restrictions that had at first appealed to us about the Court of Two Sisters shortly forced us to leave. Someone complained about the loud music coming from our corner apartment (I think it was the easy listening lady next door), and the manager relayed the complaint to me. I kept the stereo turned way down thereafter, and I hated it.

And one night, after a performance or gig somewhere, Jerry returned home with a stray chihuahua he had found freezing in the parking lot. The little creature took to sleeping under the covers with us. We had to take her out clandestinely, hidden under our coats. I still remember the sight of that little dog's head sticking out over the top button of Jerry's trench coat as we'd start out for our walks in the neighborhood park. (In a week or so, we were able to find a home for the dog with Phil's parents. She lived a long, happy life with them.)

After a few weeks of searching through the newspaper ads, we located a house for rent that sounded too good to be true: two stories with an attic and a basement, nine rooms, and three baths (not counting the separate garage apartment). We drove by one night, discovered that the back door was open, and went in to check it out.

The electricity had been turned off, and we had a hard time making our way through the rooms, having only the light from streetlamps and the neighbors' houses to guide us. The kitchen was our first view of the place, and it sold Jerry with its central, free-standing work counter with shelves below and its walk-in pantry. Next came a breakfast room with bay windows, followed by a formal dining room (with a chandelier and a wrought-iron gate), a spacious entry hall with a dramatic stairway, a living room with picture windows at both ends (either one of which would be perfect for the piano), and, finally, a sunroom with a tiled floor and French doors opening onto the large front porch. The four bedrooms upstairs would give us each a study, and we'd have a spare bedroom for guests. Although we couldn't get in to see the garage apartment that night, Jerry surmised that it would make an ideal electronics workroom—and indeed it did. The garage itself was small by modern standards, but it was adequate for Jerry's VW and my Austin America.

We submitted to another long interview, this time in an office downtown. It turned out that the house was owned by the family next door; they had had bad luck with the prior tenants, and the agent (who was in fact the brother of the owner of the house) was determined to find occupants who would not cause disturbances and who would maintain the property. Again, the two teachers, the serious young men, sold themselves, and we moved in almost immediately for about the same rent as we were paying in the apartment. I set up my Magnavox stereos at the back end of the long living room, and Jerry had his piano moved from Glencoe to the space near the picture window at the front. The hardwood floors made our music reverberate throughout the house, apparently bothering no one for the ten years we lived there.

As a boy, I was sometimes awakened by my grandmother's nightmares. She had her own room until my sister got to be too old to sleep in a room with me; then she shared a room with Judy—not the best arrangement, given the difference in their ages and temperaments. When the moaning started, it was enough for one of us to approach her bed and say "Granny" a time or two to awaken her.

I remember standing beside her bed one night, watching her open-mouthed breathing a while and thinking she would die someday. Perhaps I had begun to worry about losing her because my cat, Melissa, had died not long before; I had been inconsolable, crying for hours in my room, alarming even my father. Whatever prompted it, I stood that time beside my grandmother, chilled by a foreboding of loss, and grief, and the loneliness of grief (because I felt I shouldn't tell anyone about my concern). I reached down and kissed her forehead lightly—a propitiation, perhaps—and she awoke, startled and a little angry. "Just because I love you," I said, retreating.

My grandmother's family had come to Texas from Kentucky in search of the land of milk and honey that was rumored to be here. They left the hills around Greensburg to work the black gumbo near Rockwall, just east of Dallas. Maude (Granny) and her new husband, Marvin, became tenant farmers, working cotton, living in a succession of homes, and rearing two children, my mother and uncle. Marvin developed cancer of the stomach (Uncle Henry tells how he would go into the fields with nothing but a sack of Granny's soda biscuits). When he died at fifty-three, Maude sold the farm equipment and the mules and came to Dallas to live with her daughter and son-in-law, Allyne and Steve.

With Granny there to look after Judy and me, Mother was always able to work. My earliest memories of play include Granny in the background, hanging out clothes, sweeping the walk, wiping off our metal lawn chairs, but all the while watching Judy and me and our playmates. She was strong-willed and strict, and she was fastidious: Judy and I were always cleaning things up and putting things away ("so you can find it when you need it"). She spanked me harder than Mother did.

Granny never stopped missing Kentucky. She corresponded regularly with relatives there, filling her fountain pen with blue-black ink and writing long letters, conveying and asking for news. For years, she received the *Greensburg Record-Herald*, searching its pages for names she knew—the only reading I ever saw her do. She was able to make several trips back (once with our family . . . and Melissa, partway), and she always brought Judy and me souvenirs: a little cedar wishing well (my introduction to that fragrance), a paperweight from Mammoth Cave, a figurine of an old woman sweeping that she said reminded her of herself.

I've always thought I have a lot in common with my grandmother; I sensed we were special friends when I was growing up. It was important to me to make her proud. We had long talks while she did her chores: plucking a chicken for dinner, starching and ironing clothes, turning and airing beds. She taught me how to select just the right-sized twig for picking and cleaning teeth. She showed me how to put the back of a chair against the cabinet before climbing up; I learned from her to turn pot handles away from the stove's front. When she made pear preserves, I sneaked licks off the long-handled wooden spoon (once or twice burning my tongue). As her eyes began to fail, she'd call me to thread her needle. I regularly massaged her knuckles, swollen and stiff with arthritis.

When my father retired, unhappily, trouble arose between him and Granny. I was already away from home most of the time, but I knew at least that Daddy had come to resent her. In the beginning, Mother never told me much, but she did make it clear eventually that something was going to have to be done—that Granny couldn't stay there anymore.

After a long period of "visiting" various relatives, Granny finally came to live in a room Mother found in a private residence. This state-subsidized arrangement seemed to be preferable to a nursing home. I visited Granny there when I was home from college, noting the washcloth she kept drying on the windowsill and the little packages of snacks Mother had brought her sitting on top of her chest of drawers. I always found the door to her room pulled shut.

One Sunday, I took her to a harpsichord recital at the old Fine Arts Museum in Fair Park, but the music (all Bach, I expect) made her nervous, and we left at intermission. Jerry always teased me about taking her to such a concert, an outing so transparently made for myself. "Taking Granny to a concert" became our code phrase for any enterprise ostensibly undertaken for another's sake but done, mainly, because one wants to.

By the time I began teaching, Granny had had to be put in a nursing home in Rockwall. I would visit her there with Mother, bringing her ice cream in Dixie cups and finding it increasingly hard to have a conversation with her. Mother's life was sad and lonely during this period: Judy and I were away, and she was either waiting on a sick husband at home or checking on her declining mother, never knowing, as she said, what she would find at either end of the journey between them.

On one of my last visits, I tried to make Granny understand that I had become a teacher—at last. I do believe she understood, but I think the news came too late to matter much. A few weeks after that, they called us to come. I stood by her bed and watched her die, holding her hand and, then, kissing her forehead. Mother and Daddy were with her, too; Judy and Paul were in Virginia, where Paul was stationed. Jerry wasn't there, but he played "My Old Kentucky Home" on the organ at her funeral.

As busy as our jobs kept us, Jerry and I found plenty of time during our first seven or eight years on Swiss Avenue to work on the house. Our parents gave us unneeded furniture, linens, and kitchen supplies. Mrs. Hunt made fancy tasseled curtains for the bay windows in the breakfast room and slipcovers for the dining table chairs. Daddy helped me hang a gate to the backyard, and he rescreened and painted the window screens all around the house on both stories. Jerry and I painted indoors, working long hours enameling the decorative woodwork. We rented a sander and a polisher and redid the hardwood floors.

Not since living in the house on Bennett, where we tore down the wallpaper in two rooms and hung burlap, had we worked together on such extensive projects. It was fun making plans and buying supplies, and we got through the tedium of the work without too many fights. My father had taught me how to paint, and Jerry's had shown him how to refinish furniture. We got along better when applying ourselves to separate tasks like these, and we could talk and laugh without finding fault with the other's work or pace.

The yard was my private domain. Jerry cared very little for the outdoors (he always said he could take care of any unwanted growth with a generous application of salt), so I fertilized and mowed our huge yards, planted trees and shrubs, flowers and a few vegetables, and watered liberally. I uncovered a beautiful flagstone patio that the yard had overtaken, and I spent a lot of time there in our aluminum lawn chairs, reading, grading papers, and listening to the stereo or to Jerry at the piano. (He was learning Charles Ives's *Concord Sonata*, among the more traditional pieces; I was listening to Jean Sibelius's symphonies.)

One day during our first spring on Swiss, a neighbor came to the door with a puppy she'd found cowering in her shrubbery. The lady was trying to find the dog's home; she couldn't keep her, she explained, because she and her husband already had two Great Danes. Jerry and I fell in love with the dog at first sight, but we didn't want her if she belonged to someone else. We told the lady to bring her back, though, if no one claimed her. The dog was ours within the hour.

Leto was a mixed breed, spitz predominating, with long white hair, brown markings, and a gentle, sweet disposition. When she came to us, we could hold her in one hand; she grew to be a lapful. I named her after Apollo and Artemis's mother, the "fair-cheeked goddess" (according to Homer) due to the long, delicate white fur along the sides of her muzzle. And like the goddess, who had had to wander in search of a safe place to give birth to her children, our Leto had been homeless a while, too.

We housebroke her with newspapers and trained her to walk on a leash, but she seemed to require little guidance beyond that. She spent much of her time with me, lying beside my chair (or in my lap) as I read or waiting patiently nearby while I worked in the yard or somewhere in the house. Her weekdays were shared with Jerry when he was home, and he'd tell me often how she had cocked her ears at the sound of my car pulling in the driveway and run to the back door to greet me. Leto quickly learned my schedule, and we went to bed and got up at the same time for the eleven years she lived.

As companion animals so often do, Leto served as an excuse to get Jerry and me out of the house, enabling us to have the kinds of visits and talks we might not have otherwise, occupied and preoccupied as we were with our chores and pastimes indoors.

Swiss Avenue, with its broad, landscaped median strip, was an ideal place to walk. Leto trotted along in front of us, her leash comfortably slack, automatically stopping when we did, so closely attuned was she to our interests and movements. People frequently stopped to admire her, particularly after she had just had a bath and her white fur was full and cotton-like: "What kind of dog is that?" "She sure is pretty," they'd say. We once encountered the pastor of a large Baptist church, Dr. Criswell, who lived a couple of doors down the street from us. He, too, commented on her fur. "Oh, yes," I disingenuously replied, "she has angel hair."

In good weather, we'd take her to the Samuell-Grand Park a few miles away, where she could safely range through the lawns and gardens. We'd usually go after dinner, rambling at sunset along the perimeter of the putting range, picking up the odd golf ball and throwing it for Leto to retrieve. When it was muddy, we'd use the sidewalks that gave access to the tennis courts and the rose garden.

We began taking her to Fair Park, the grounds and Art Deco buildings where the Texas State Fair is held each year. We rarely met other people or animals there, and we could have an hour's walk in privacy. This was where we had our best talks—and our worst arguments. Sometimes, in our anger, we'd separate a while, and Leto would walk first with one and then the other, shuttling between us like a mediator. Our fights sometimes arose from the tensions and frustrations associated with our jobs; we often simply argued about the significance of a current event, the importance of a piece of music, the meaning of an idea. We cared about what the other thought, but we sometimes went to great trouble to disguise that fact—especially me.

When it was too cold to walk, the three of us went for car rides, usually just before bedtime. The downtown post office was a frequent destination or pretext; one of us would drive while the other held Leto in his lap, riding shotgun with her head just outside the window, the wind combing back the fur over her eyes and along her muzzle (and the car heater running full blast). Whenever we passed a street sweeper, she tried to escape from the noise by jumping into the floorboard.

However, there was a little problem with Leto when we had company: she kept them at bay whenever she could. Once I was preparing drinks for our guests in the kitchen, where Jerry was cooking. When I delivered the tray, I noticed no one had helped himself to the hors d'oeuvres on the coffee table. "She won't let us move," someone confessed. And sure enough, Leto sat on guard close to the food, the word *ours* apparent in her eyes.

The house on Swiss was made for entertaining, with its spacious rooms and professional kitchen, and we had people over for dinner every few weeks. Houston and Jill, Phil, the pianists Douglas and Avlona Taylor, Toni Beck (from SMU) and Paul Bosner, Gordon and Mary Hoffman, and Paul and Oz Srere (a professor of biochemistry and his wife, two of the earliest fans, and best patrons, of Jerry's music)—they and others were treated to the creations of whatever Jerry's latest culinary interests might be.

One of these grand meals, a Chinese banquet, began rather inauspiciously. After several trips to Jung's Oriental Foods (where Leto and I would wait in the car or walk around the neighborhood behind the parking lot), Jerry had finally secured the exotic foods he needed—including the duck feet Mr. Jung had saved especially for him. He spent two days in preliminary preparation. A couple of hours before the guests were due, he called me in from my housecleaning to see a large tray of appetiz-ers he had just finished. Using daikon radishes and food coloring, he had sculpted and painted a beautiful, edible bird garnished with other vegetables and fish and fruit. He proudly put it on top of a large can in the utility room, where we fed Leto, to get it out of his way.

And, of course, Leto found the fish. I heard Jerry's exclamation—and profanity—from the room, where I was working, and I ran in in time to see Leto's snout turning up a morsel of fish where it had lain just beneath the tip of one of the gorgeous bird's wings. Since he seemed frozen in his incredulity, I quickly moved the platter out of her reach. We had to go after more daikon to repair the damage Leto had done; naturally, she went to the store with us.

As it turned out, the banquet was a big success—actu-ally, almost too much of a good thing. Course followed course, with cries of delight modulating into protests, until finally, we all went on strike, demanding a break on the patio, where Jerry soon came to get us, calling us back to our duties as diners. I washed dishes for days.

At this meal, we got to know Rod, a young man just out of college who, like Jerry, had a radio show on the public access station KCHU. Rod had heard Jerry's programs on contemporary music and had called him to talk and share this interest.

Typically, Jerry invited Rod to dinner. Thus began a friendship that would turn out to mean more than either Jerry or I could have imagined then. Rod is now the prin-cipal curator and conservator of Jerry's work, reading (with Sharon's help) Jerry's computer files and archiving the scores of audio and videotapes that Jerry left.

In his work at KCHU, his teaching at SMU, and his own concerts, Jerry continually acquired new friends and made new fans. Most of these people came to see us regu-larly on Swiss, and many stayed in close contact with us even after we moved to the farm in 1980. A couple became colleagues of a sort: the dancer Sally Bowden, with whom Jerry collaborated in several concerts both in Dallas and New York, and David McManaway, whose work using found objects influenced Jerry's own creation of artifacts ("lightning rods of attention," as he called them). Jerry always stayed with Sally and Ted when he gave concerts in New York; I was able to join him there several times.

Ironically, we saw our older friends less frequently during the decade we lived on Swiss. Dinah had married Norman, and they'd begun raising a family. She was teaching math at a high school in Irving, and she was later to join the part-time English faculty at a local community college. Peggy had given up the study of music for medicine and, as a nurse in Fort Worth, had met and married a physician, George; they lived for a while in Majorca, then they settled in Corpus Christi.

Once, it did happen that Jerry's and my closest female friends were at the house on Swiss at the same time. Peggy had come up to attend a seminar, and Dinah had come by with her baby daughter. I introduced them, but they had remarkably little to say to one another. I remember feeling disappointed that they didn't hit it off, but as I reflect now, I am not surprised that Jerry always had his friends and I mine—with the notable exception of Bob, whom each of us grew close to over the years, though in different ways.

After their sojourn in Austin, Bob, Carol, and Donna returned to Houston. Carol taught school, and Bob worked in data processing for an area hospital. Their marriage was in trouble—had been, for several years; it was hard for Carol to accept that fact, and she made every effort to keep them together. Bob's frustrations led to violent fits of anger, and Carol avoided facing the inevitable, with the help of marijuana, for as long as she could. They both took their responsibilities to Donna seriously, and, had it not been for her, they probably would have separated long before they did.

By the end of 1972, Bob and Carol were apart permanently. Bob began living with Rany, a fellow he had known for years as a family friend. They began together the slow, gradual process of coming out, each admitting to himself his homosexual nature, at last, and taking the next step of choosing to live in such a way as to express that nature. Rany very shortly inherited a small fortune from his father, and he and Bob were able to buy a house near the Montrose district of Houston, where they live today. They also bought a Jeep and began taking trips to American West deserts and Mexico's tropical regions, where Bob indulged his longstanding passion for plants and his emerging interest in photography. They camped out as they traveled, and they stopped by our house once on their way to Canada. Jerry and I gawked at all their gear.

Our own trips were far less rustic. I had traded my Austin America for a Toyota Corona station wagon, and we traveled comfortably in that (when we didn't rent a car). We visited Bob and Rany in Houston and Peggy and George in Corpus, where they had bought a house overlooking the bay. Leto always went with us, and packing everything that the three of us needed for several nights away was a challenge and a chore.

Jerry and I had become vegetarians out of concern for animals, and we took supplies for preparing our own meals every time we traveled. We did talk about camping out, and we even bought a camp stove and used it to cook a few meals at roadside parks, but we never went as far as Bob and Rany, with their tent and water canteens and hiking boots.

I have always loved to travel, especially by car, and most of the trips Jerry and I made together were at my instigation. Jerry liked there to be a practical reason for a trip, whether to see friends or make professional contacts or fulfill an engagement somewhere. Part of this was no doubt due to the parsimony that becomes a way of life when one doesn't have a regular salary to count on. Nevertheless, there was something about leaving home that always repelled Jerry, and many of our trips began with an argument about the foolishness of the outing or our plans—or about anything at all that would serve to focus his anxiety.

However rocky the departures, we invariably had a wonderful time traveling together. I collected hundreds of photographs over the years, snapshots from trips to New York, California, and destinations in between (including Houston and Corpus). Being together on the road, with the release from habit it affords and the adventures and challenges it entails, brought us closer together by renewing our friendship. We had long talks (and good fights) riding along the back roads, one of us driving and the other with Leto in his lap.

One year, on our way to California, we spent an after-noon at the Canyon de Chelly National Monument in northeastern Arizona. We walked along the canyon rim, gazing down to the green valley below and across at the remains of the cliff dwellings—a special interest of mine since I first read "Tom Outland's Story" in Willa Cather's *The Professor's House.*

We had had difficulty getting to the canyon, making a wrong turn out of New Mexico, and underestimating how long it would take to cover what looked like a relatively short distance on the map. We bumped and rattled along a rough road, the lid of the Styrofoam cooler squeaking annoyingly, Leto tuning into and sharing our growing impatience, and Jerry yelling, "Slow down, God damn it!" every time I hit an especially deep pothole.

Finally, we arrived, left our car in the empty parking lot, and walked to the edge of the cliff to see if the view was worth all the trouble it had been getting there. To anyone who has seen it, I don't have to say it was. Even Jerry was moved by the tranquil, isolated beauty of the scene, another world there below: self-sufficient, perfected. We took it in, walking along the marked path; I made a few pictures (the one of Leto with the far wall of the canyon in the background sits on my desk at the library), and we sat down to rest awhile and watch the shadows lengthen along the canyon floor. Jerry later wrote a piece he named *De Chelly.* And I, some lucky nights, revisit the place and relive that afternoon in my dreams.

Up until the eighth or ninth grades, I couldn't wait until it was time to buy school supplies at the end of summer. I prepared my ring binder and spirals well in advance of the first day of classes, labeling everything with my name and homeroom and making dividers for each class. I took great care selecting just the right pencils and pens. The most fun I had, though, was covering my textbooks with the kraft stock imprinted with the names of businesses supporting the school (the covers had to be as tight as possible).

And I had always played school from as early as I can remember. Naturally, I was the teacher most of the time—Judy and the other children sat patiently waiting their turn, which, if it came at all, arrived just about when we were all getting tired of the game anyway. The garage made an ideal classroom, especially when I started a bicycle safety club in the neighborhood and taught the proper signals and other safety practices there.

When I finally became, officially, a teacher, I was in *my* element. Cistercian Prep is a selective day school for grades five through twelve, with an enrollment of two hundred or so boys and a faculty consisting of lay teachers and religious, a few more of the former than the latter. Juniors and seniors take several advanced placement (college-level) courses; many graduates enter Ivy League schools with almost a year's worth of credits on their transcripts. Following the European system, each class is assigned a form master, usually a priest, who stays with the group as it advances through the eight grades (diminishing by attrition as it goes).

The faculty move from one classroom to another, each teaching several grades and, frequently, more than one subject. During my nearly ten years there, I taught almost all the grades—three or four different ones a year—in English and upper-division literary criticism and music appreciation. The headmaster asked me to serve as the chair of the English department at the end of my first year, and my two colleagues and I developed a curriculum and selected texts that gave our students a good foundation for their later college work—as attested to by the advanced placement credits they earned and their regular visits back to the school to tell of us their success.

Since we used few prepared materials, lesson planning and paper grading were time-consuming processes. The upper-division readers consisted of the literature only; in our lectures and discussion leading, we used the inductive method to arrive at insights and appreciation. We also taught sentence diagramming, for which returning alumni always thanked us.

I enjoyed teaching the fifth and eleventh grades so much that I requested them every year. The eleven-year-olds reminded me of myself at that age, with their undisguised enthusiasm for every classroom activity, their love of reading (and of being read to), and their full engagement in the learning process. James Herriot's *All Creatures Great and Small* had just become popular, and, time permitting, I read a chapter aloud most Fridays, the animal stories sometimes moving us all to the point of tears.

After the hormone-induced turbulence of the middle years, something of that same ingenuousness seems to return when a boy is sixteen or seventeen, and that coupled with a questioning, often rebellious disposition makes the juniors a stimulating group to teach—doubly so since the literature is American. The better my classes went, the more work I put in preparing for them; as often as possible, I tried to simulate the kinds of lectures and seminars the students would encounter in their college English courses. Most of my time, though, was spent reading and evaluating essays and holding conferences over them.

In addition to being the faculty adviser for the school newspaper, I sponsored a literary magazine for the upper grades. I tried to involve other private schools in the area (St. Mark's for boys, Ursuline and Hockaday for girls, and Greenhill for both), but our meetings led nowhere, each school eventually developing its own product. Transportation was frequently cited as a problem, but I was also given to understand by several parents that they weren't too eager to have their sons involved that much with the other schools' students, particularly the girls from Hockaday and Greenhill.

The Cistercian parents and school board were a conservative group whose goal was (and I expect still is) to prepare their sons for college in an academically demanding environment protected from distractions and incursions from the outside. By the time the boys were in their junior year, many of them had begun to feel uneasiness about their school and how it was grooming them for a role in society (and, often, a career in the family profession or firm). It was in their English classes that they found an outlet for their concerns, a forum for their questions and criticisms. Class discussions and compositions elicited a surprising amount of discontent, particularly from those boys whose independent natures (often accompanied by creativity) had always kept them a little on the outside. Thoreau was an oracle for many.

The exacting curriculum and its strong support by the parents and the priests effectively obviated dissent. You couldn't stay if you didn't make the grades, and you wouldn't make the grades if you didn't buckle down and study most of the time. In addition, the fact that your class remained together year after year, usually with the same form master, intensified the peer pressure to succeed and conform. I did see a few students over the years who were able to thrive by playing by all the rules while nurturing, with the help of a teacher here and there, a private capacity to imagine a more variegated, richer world.

In the beginning, I saw little of the constraining narrowness of the school. I wanted us to be the best, and I wanted to be the best teacher possible. To that end, I visited the faculties of other private schools, attending their classes and inviting them to attend ours. I spent a day with my friend from Austin, Dr. Anne Freeman, who had just begun her twenty-two-year career at St. Mark's. I followed her from class to class as she walked, aided by her cane, slowing down as the afternoon wore on; with her approach, each group of boys came to quiet attention, prepared to take her as seriously as she was them and to work as hard as she did.

It was a real pleasure to renew my friendship with Anne; but I realized during the following weeks, as she continued to call me at school and at home, proposing even more classroom visits and teaching exchanges, that her interest in me had a personal dimension that was bound to cause unhappiness. I was so much in the closet then that I didn't even realize it. All I knew to do was make excuses and be a little cool to her. She finally stopped calling.

Anne and I were to meet again, twenty years later, when my sixteen-year-old niece, Jamie, came to live with Jerry and me. In January, Judy had called from Idaho explaining that Jamie was unhappy at school there and asking if I would consider having her come here and go to school in Dallas. Jerry and I discussed it and agreed that we wanted to help, and I visited with Ursuline's principal and started the process of getting Jamie accepted for her junior year there.

When the principal learned that I had taught at Cistercian for so many years, she asked if I knew Anne Freeman, formerly at St. Mark's. Anne was now on Ursuline's faculty, having been "laid off" when the school found it expedient to hire a man who could teach English as well as coach an athletic team. To his credit, the St. Mark's headmaster located the Ursuline position for Anne, and he even accompanied her on her first visit to the school.

I didn't run into Anne until I went to the school for the new parents' orientation in August. I saw her from a distance, laboring down the hallway, the grace and good humor I had always associated with her still apparent, her eyes twinkling in recognition beneath a corona of red hair. She said she had been looking for me since the principal had told her last spring about my niece.

We visited at length, enjoying the cookies the Ursuline parents' club had provided. As a development from the Conrad seminar we had shared, Anne had done some editorial work for the journal *Conradiana*. Her life had been fairly uneventful, she related; the highlight of each year was the trip she made to Princeton to grade advanced placement exams for the College Board. She lived with her mother. And she was confident that, in time, she'd get used to teaching girls.

I explained the circumstances surrounding Jamie's coming to Dallas and to Ursuline, then I told her about my work at the library. Finally, I explained my reasons for leaving Cistercian, at last righting the personal wrong I had done her years ago by not being able to tell her about my homosexuality and about Jerry. As it so often turns out, not much had to be said—always ironic, considering the importance of saying it.

*
**

Jerry's mother called him from her downtown office almost every day, usually just before lunch, and frequently woke him up. He was always a late riser, working until early in the morning, wiring, composing, reading, and writing letters. Sometimes she stopped by the house on her way home from work; she'd bring Jerry something—a shirt or a kitchen tool she'd found in one of the department stores—or she'd deliver something she had made or bought for the house. We would visit over coffee.

The Hunts were nearing retirement, and they had begun making plans to sell their Dallas home and move to Canton, a town of fewer than three thousand people fifty miles east. The town had a typical Texas courthouse square surrounded by tree-lined neighborhood streets and outlying farms and ranches. With the help of a veteran's loan, they were buying two tracts of land, each about thirty acres and located three miles apart, a few miles west of town. They intended to build a house on the smaller tract, and their hope for the larger one was that it would prove to be a good spot for some kind of business since it is at the intersection of two state highways. They began making weekend trips to Canton in the early '70s, and they built a small, two-bay barn using creosoted poles and corrugated steel. As soon as they had electricity, they bought a used refrigerator and installed it in the barn. When the weather allowed, they spent the night in the barn, alongside the tools and supplies they needed to plant an orchard of pear, peach, and plum trees and put them in a vegetable garden. When Jerry and I drove out to spend Sunday afternoons with them, we'd conclude our workday with a cookout: Mrs. Hunt and Jerry grilled chicken (Leto's favorite), and we enjoyed squash, corn, and new potatoes from the garden that they wrapped in aluminum foil and cooked over the coals. Mrs. Hunt was able to retire first, and she did most of the work involved in packing for the move. There was some delay in finishing the Canton house, so the Hunts had to rent another house in Dallas for a couple of months to have a place to store their mostly already packed things. Jerry and I helped with the temporary move and seeing them in the tiny rent house making their way among stacks of boxes. Their always looking for something they needed badly but couldn't find—sometimes even including the dogs, Hermie and Sassie—made us all think of the *I Love Lucy* episode where Lucy and Ricky have to move in with Fred and Ethel until their new home in Connecticut is ready. Jerry always said that never were people better named, and he did include himself.

Mr. Hunt came by one day to show us his new Chevrolet pickup. He would have to work on it for a few years after the move, and I expect he hoped the new truck would make the hour-long commute more pleasant (in addition to putting him a little closer to actually being a farmer). His job with Pet Milk had become onerous with its increasing paperwork (that I often saw him do at home) and the growing difficulty he had dealing with city traffic. His dream was to be free of the responsibilities of his job and be able to work outside on his own place, and perhaps go into some kind of business of his own on the corner property.

Being the outgoing, sociable people they were, the Hunts soon made friends in the Canton area. With the aid of these local contacts, Mr. Hunt began acquiring more poles and steel for a second, larger barn to house the farm and ranch implements he was gradually buying, most of them used. Over a period of several weekends one summer, Jerry and I helped him raise the new barn, laying the poles in the holes he had dug using the digging attachment on his new tractor and placing the cross members in the specially cut grooves midway up the poles and at their tops.

That post-hole digger got Mr. Hunt into trouble one day. In one part of the land, the clayey soil where he planned to erect a fence adhered to the corkscrew blade so badly that he finally got it stuck in the ground. He tried reversing the direction, but even that failed to free it. So, using the tractor's clutch, he tried to jerk the blade out of the ground by making quick lunges forward, and this, of course, caused the tractor to buck violently.

Mrs. Hunt happened to be on the phone at the time, talking with a friend she had made in the county home demonstration program. She looked out the window and saw what her husband was up to and, as she told about it later, began describing to her friend with mounting

alarm what looked liked his attempt to "break" the tractor as one would a horse. She was long used to his fits
of anger, but with heavy equipment now in the mix, the
stakes were higher—and the stories of misadventure were
ever more dramatic and entertaining. This one made its
rounds through the county for years.

Working with Jerry and his father was a hilarious
experience when it wasn't frustrating—or frightening.
Both high-strung by nature and used to working alone,
each had difficulty understanding what exactly the other
wanted to accomplish; and when he finally did understand, disagreements over how to do it invariably arose.
Each man was better at giving directions than at taking
them. Exasperation led to fits of temper, tossed tools, and
brief sulking periods—but, before long, they were back at
work as though nothing had happened.

Enlisting Mrs. Hunt's aid, we finally got the poles for
the new barn, steadied in their holes well enough to be
able to secure the horizontal supports. And before long,
the new structure, occupying almost 1,500 square feet
of space, was finished. None of us had any idea at the
time that Jerry and I would be living in that barn—after
converting it into a comfortable, seven-room home—less
than ten years later.

Building the barn was the last big chore the Hunts
undertook. After that, they were able to spend their time
in the orchard and the garden. Mr. Hunt had a tank dug,
acquired a few heads of cattle, and began salvaging telephone poles, glass insulators, and sleepers from a nearby
abandoned railroad line. Mrs. Hunt planted shrubs and
flowers around their new brick home, and she canned
tomatoes, beans, and pears and made preserves and
jellies. When Jerry and I came out for a visit, he stayed
indoors with his mother to visit and help her with her
projects; Mr. Hunt, Leto, and I, being more outdoor types,
did chores around the property. One cold fall day, we
cut firewood on a neighbor's forested acreage. Mr. Hunt
worked much as my father did, and I had no trouble
understanding his directions or taking them.

I called Mother every weekday as soon as I got home
from school and had taken Leto for a short walk up the
street and back. I'd report on my day, she on hers. It

often seemed we had little to say beyond recounting a few things we did, and I regret that, for whatever reason, we weren't able to share our worries more than we did—mine increasing with each year I taught, and hers with Daddy's physical and mental decline. Years later, one of Mother's high school friends whom I got to know and came to befriend told me she and Mother would be out shopping, and Mother would say, "Marguerite, we'd better get back. My boy'll be calling." I suppose I never realized how important that daily contact with me was to her.

While Paul was overseas, Judy managed an apartment complex in the Oak Lawn area. She and I could see how fast Daddy's health was deteriorating, and she, particularly, suffered the effects of his growing petulance and childish behavior. He expected her to come to see him and Mother every Sunday, and he'd call several times during the day to remind her and to find out when to expect her. If she were later than he thought she should be, he'd sulk. Seeing him this way, so different from his former, independent self, hurt us—and doubly so, for Mother's sake.

When he wasn't able to paint houses any longer, Daddy began repairing the wooden crates fruits and vegetables were at that time shipped in. Uncle Henry was a produce buyer for Safeway, and he found this work for Daddy, arranging for the damaged crates to be delivered to the house on Ferguson Road and for the repaired ones to be picked up whenever Daddy called. This piecemeal work kept Daddy busy year-round. He worked on the patio in hot weather, using a metal conveyor a friend had brought him from Ben E. Keith's to move the crates from the garage to where he was outside; Daddy cut a special little door in the back of the garage for the conveyor to pass through. In winter, he worked in the garage, sometimes with an electric heater nearby. Mother and I would sit visiting in the living room, listening to the sporadic hammering.

Daddy was interested in my teaching, proud that I had begun a career he knew I wanted and had worked toward, and satisfied, I believe, that I was happy. Shortly after I was hired, I took Mother and Daddy to Cistercian to see the campus and to meet the headmaster. ("Your son came to us and started teaching like he'd been here for years," Father Denis told them.)

Judy and her marriage were a concern for Daddy, though. He was skeptical, at first, that a marriage between people who had known one another only a few weeks could last. He fretted that Judy had a husband in the military, with the likelihood of having to move here and there. And he was a little put off by Paul's take-charge manner, anxious that Judy wasn't speaking up for herself. But he must have seen that they loved one another, and when Daddy died in 1972, they had been married seven years.

He had become harder and harder for Mother to manage, and one day he couldn't get up. He lived two weeks in the hospital, finally dying of pneumonia. While I was teaching that Friday, they called me to come, but he died before I could get there.

I shaved him a few days before he died. He couldn't talk (he had been intubated, the draining fluid black), and I didn't say much. But I remember being in no hurry shaving him, using his own safety razor, guiding it down his cheeks, along his jaws, up to his neck. His eyes held me in their gaze.

Many of the people who had worked with him came by the house and attended the funeral. It was very moving to see their demonstration of affection and respect. I wrote a short tribute for the minister to read, describing how hard and how well Daddy always worked and quoting the William Carlos Williams poem about the importance of a red wheelbarrow.

Mother lived alone now, and Judy and Paul were soon transferred to Illinois. I went over to see her most every Sunday, and I took her to movies and concerts whenever there was something she wanted to see. She came to Canton with us once, and I took her to Houston several times to visit two of my father's sisters who lived there and to enjoy shopping in different stores.

We had good walks whenever we could, and Leto often accompanied us ("your little friend," Mother called her). The Samuell-Grand Park was one of our favorite places to visit Sunday mornings; we'd buy a newspaper and sit reading it under the trees while Leto explored the nearby bushes. I often thought how these quiet times together hearkened back to the summer afternoons when Judy and I were children and Mother spread an old quilt, reserved for the purpose, under the shade trees in our backyard during the hottest part of the day. She always brought books out; we'd read awhile, then nap, and wake up to a snack of cheese and crackers or apples, peeled and cut into wedges.

Sometimes Mother would come by during the week, bringing us a dish of baked apples or a pot of navy beans. She'd usually whistle at the door, yelling "yoo-hoo"; I suppose she found the thought of knocking or ringing the doorbell too formal, and I'm glad she did. When she asked Jerry to play the piano, he usually would (she was luckier than most): "Deep Purple," "Autumn Leaves," and "Some of These Days" were her favorite tunes.

Her life soon came to revolve around Judy and her first grandchild, Jenny. In July of 1973, Mother rode Amtrak to Chicago to be with Judy and Paul when they had their first baby. A little later, I drove up with Mother's dog, Mr. Freckles, to join them. Judy and Paul lived in a little town near Waukegan, where Paul was an Army recruiter. We enjoyed exploring Zion and being with Judy and Paul, but the baby was long overdue and my first day of school was approaching fast. Finally, we took Judy to the hospital. Mother and I waited with a group of anxious fathers; Paul was in the delivery room with Judy, aiding her in the Lamaze method of childbirth. Jenny finally came.

Mother and I had to start back, and it was a shame she couldn't have more time with the baby. But it wouldn't be too long before Paul was transferred to Dallas, and he and Judy began buying a house just down the street from Mother's but on the other side. In the years ahead, Judy and Mother became best friends, looking after Jenny and then Jamie, shopping for them, cooking and sewing, talking and laughing and reminiscing. The special bond Mother formed with Jenny endures, now sixteen years after Mother's death; one of Jenny's first compositions in freshman English was "Remembering GaGa."

These were some of the best years of Mother's life.

*
**

Jerry had been interested in India and Buddhism since his early study of Rosicrucianism and meditation, and with our recent conversion to a vegetarian diet, he was exploring Indian cuisine. In 1975, he had a chance to visit the country, thanks to Peggy and George. They, too, had become interested in Eastern spirituality and meditation, and George was always fond of traveling (he used to write travel articles for a physicians' magazine). I don't believe Jerry would have undertaken such a trip without their practical help, and I know he took comfort in the fact that he would be traveling in a country that poses some health risk with a doctor and a nurse. As it turned out, he needed them.

> 3/20/75
> Stephen + Leto—Arrived Bombay noon Tuesday. Am as you suspect very glad to be here. We are so tired. 20 hours of airplane is almost more than you can take. Hotel very Indian, very comfortable, wonderful ceiling electric fan. The heat is a welcome relief, it was 50 in Rome and raining. Have come back from dinner (in hotel, so-so) and a walk-through area. We are next to dock, etc. I'll write you again when I've got some fancy cards and we've had a chance to sleep some and *get adjusted* to the *change*. It is Bombay, period. No *comparisons* possible. There are, though, many dogs in all places. *Some* are healthy looking and well-fed seeming. *Cows* everywhere; very healthy. Miss you & puppy. Will write more later when clearer etc. etc.
> Sleep now is best. L. Jerry.

> 3/25/75
> Not really a very good traveler—after some 300 miles through the state and

hours of going through Bombay I've sucked
up about all I can—We are going to Sri
Lanka in the morning. Possible to stay
overnight in Buddhist temple 40 m[iles]
into jungle in central Ceylon.

Miss you & Leto. Bringing back some
things, hopefully something will fit or
work out for one of us—Indian people
very friendly & overall sweetness—also
as I've mentioned beautiful, but . . . !
We will start for home c. 6th April.
Traveling to Shiva temples was very
exhausting—had mild heat stroke—don't
tell parents—wait 'til I'm back/ L. J.

3/26/75
Stephen—arrived intact—Colombo all
tropical—miserable humidity & water—
seemingly very much in pre-taint total
commercialization—food basically poor—
going to monastery for audience w/
Buddhist director of studies here—
will send card later if decide Madras
or not—some tonish Indians in city,
will see soon enough—looks pretty, like
Galveston.
J. Miss Y + Leto.

Stephen—This will probably barely reach
you, and then I'm home—I'm not sure how
fast these things are reaching you. So
thought I'd take a chance & send some
longer letter—so much has happened that
it seems I've been gone several months.
I have had heat stroke (very mild) and
also some minor intestinal trouble,
I'm sure from not sleeping and staying
in streets—Then we traveled the road
through Maharashtra and it is decep-
tively dry and so seems not hot. India is
utterly different from any place I have
ever been—As to whether it changes you,

I don't know, but it changes how you feel about Indians—and India. I'm not going to cause writer's cramp going on—We are now in Ceylon & it is different from Central India also—uniquely—Anyway as you can already expect I'll talk about it until you'll wish I had never seen India or heard of it.

After a couple of days [in Bombay] we, or I should say I, met some people, first older Hindus & toward the end of our stay, young Hindu men. Everything one hears about India is true one way or another— the complexity of their civilization here now is completely bewildering—there is a very special sweetness in Indians, a little childish and naive and yet in some way very sophisticated—! have found them really beautiful people but the complexities of their social structure make getting any sense at all out of their attitudes still very obscure.

Colombo is very much westernized and at the same time a primitive island culture and some incredible 2000 yr old statues to remind them that their culture is ancient and possessed Buddhism in its beginnings—A strange mixture again.

Today we met with Piyadassi Thera, an important Buddhist monk and teacher here. Finally tonight some excellent Ceylonese vegetable dishes—they keep trying to serve me Western food! The South Indian vegetables are all here, also a considerable S. Indian population. So rather than go to Madras, I'll probably stay here and go to Buddhist monastery next week.

I will have to come back to India next year—You could say I haven't stayed long enough, but I don't think for this trip I can take much more than 3 weeks—I'm much

more comfortable here now, & have made
several friends in India so that it will
be very easy—the cultural shock is very
real & is aggravated by the fact that I
have pushed so hard—every day was spent
in streets with as many people as possible—It has been very little problem with
George and Peggy—Only real problem is he
is a little old for the pace and stays in
hotel a lot to sleep & Peggy's lazy—They
do not have my aggressive curiosity—On
the other hand I'm exhausted already by
the constant pushing of experiences, they
are still alright—There is a good South
Indian restaurant close by for Hindus in
a hotel so there is good vegetarian food
for me always. I miss you & Leto, despite
all talk about beautiful Indians I still
think always first of you. Give goodies to
Leto for me. May not write again, mails
take at least—4 days—it took 24 hrs
flight here, it is 12,000 miles!
love Jerry

The heatstroke may have been mild, but I learned
when Jerry returned that George and Peggy had to wrap
him in wet sheets. He later told me that two of the young
Indian men Jerry met were homosexual and very much
interested in the fact that Jerry and I were living more or
less openly as a couple in the US. The "goodies" for Leto
that Jerry mentioned were carob-flavored vitaminized
treats made in England called Choco Drops, and Leto was
crazy about them.

As promised, Jerry returned with silk for his mother,
shirts for me, and a set of stainless steel *thali* dishes
that gave our dinner guests and us much pleasure over
the years. Jerry learned a great deal about South Indian
cooking when he was in Colombo after he convinced a
Hindu friend he'd made that he really did want to eat the
homestyle fare they were used to (the house cook had
gotten into trouble for serving Jerry humble breadfruit).

With the aid of cookbooks he purchased there and later in London, Jerry acquired considerable skill as a preparer of Indian food—so much skill, in fact, that he was sometimes able to recommend cooking techniques and flavor enhancements to Indians we met in groceries and restaurants in Dallas and elsewhere. During our years on Swiss, we ate Indian meals at least half the time; after our move to Canton, we ate more Mexican food than Indian, given the difficulty of finding Indian products in the rural town. For a few years, though, I grew cluster beans, bitter gourd, and doodhi in our vegetable garden, and we did manage to keep a curry plant alive for two seasons.

Peggy and George were very much impressed by the Buddhist monk Piyadassi, and they invited him to visit them in Corpus Christi.

He came several times, leading meditation sessions that George and Peggy had arranged for him. Jerry went down during one of Piyadassi's stays and returned with hilarious stories about everyone's efforts to accommodate Piyadassi's ascetic habits. Smoking for Jerry and Peggy became a real challenge. They had to take breaks from meditation to light up offstage.

Piyadassi's eating habits forced the hardest test of Peggy and Jerry's resolve and patience. The monk could eat only simple foods and in small quantities, and after noon he could have no solid food at all. This rather portly man awoke hungry and proceeded to eat a great number of small meals for as long as the clock allowed. Jerry and Peggy were at work in the kitchen before Piyadassi arose, and he kept them there until his daily fast began. When he'd go for a walk, Peggy and Jerry would whip out the cigarettes and forbidden foods, smoking and stuffing themselves and laughing while watching out for Piyadassi's saffron robe to come swinging back down the driveway.

*
**

As I sat in my upstairs study grading papers, Leto in the armchair beside my desk, I could look across our backyard to Jerry's electronics workroom above the garage. We always needed a little space between us due to our listening preferences—he with talk radio on in the background, me with classical music on the radio or on the turntable. We'd visit one another, one or the other of us crossing the yard with his coffee cup in hand, and Leto always announced our arrival, jumping up to scurry downstairs to greet Jerry or running ahead of me and up the apartment stairs to let Jerry know we'd come.

Although the garage apartment had a complete kitchen, Jerry and Houston used that space for etching circuit boards; Houston, who had gone to work for his father's metal factory, installed a couple of stainless steel sinks, and he and Jerry often worked up there late into the evening, wiring, testing, talking, and drinking coffee.

Their collaboration culminated in *Quaquaversal Transmission*, a "theater work utilizing direct audio-video synthesis and performance with interactive control," for the International Carnival of Experimental Sounds held in London in 1972. They packed the small car Houston had with electronic gear and props and a few clothes and drove to New York, where they had planned to take a budget chartered flight to London. Jerry lost his billfold (and passport) in New Jersey, and they discovered when they called to arrange for their tickets that the charter company had ceased operation and declared bankruptcy.

Mrs. Hunt and I worked frantically at this end trying to cancel Jerry's credit cards and replace his passport. Jerry and Houston managed to book another flight. Although they were late arriving, they finally did get off, and Jerry was to talk for years about the adventure—from its ill-fated beginning to the difficulties of getting suspicious-looking electronic gear through customs and then hauling it around London.

Houston's health presented yet another problem. He was a hemophiliac, and his knees gave him a lot of trouble—exacerbated, of course, by having to help move heavy equipment. Jerry was rarely comfortable leaving things in a performance space: he always preferred keeping everything with him until he could set up, and then he wanted to stay with it all until the performance was over. I expect Houston got quite a workout helping Jerry move their gear through London, in and out of taxis and the hotel room and the concert hall. He had to inject a blood-clotting factor into his knees on a regular basis, and Jerry often described the horrified amazement he felt at watching Houston do this. This, though, was always Houston's approach to his steadily deteriorating condition; he seldom allowed it to keep him from doing what he wanted to do.

Jerry and Houston made a friend in London: Jacqueline, one of the coordinators of the Congress and a teacher in the computer science department of a university there. She was fascinated by Jerry's work and personality, and they kept up a fairly steady correspondence during the rest of Jerry's life. Shortly after his death, Jacqueline sent me copies of all of Jerry's letters to her—twenty years' worth of news and updates that outlined the major events of our lives in Jerry's telegraphic, wry style. His responding letters showed affectionate concern for Jacqueline's accounts of the birth of her daughter, the separation from Emma's father, and the health problems that eventually required a kidney transplant.

Jacqueline was of considerable help to Jerry in making the technical arrangements for his 1973 trip to the International Edinburgh Festival, where he and David Dowe presented *Haramand Plane: parallel/regenerative*, a work commissioned by the Scottish Arts Council that used a "small control computer for deriving interrelationships" between synthesized video and audio. This trip, too, was beset by difficulties. David somehow got stranded for several hours in London. He and his wife, Ann, and Jerry missed a train connection to Cologne while on their way to a performance of the piece in Berlin and had to sit in a waiting room all night. Ann's disappointment at seeing the "vacation" aspect of the trip be eclipsed by the need to guard the equipment—when the three of them weren't hauling it through the streets—caused her to pretty much stop speaking to Jerry for the duration of the adventure.

I met Jacqueline in 1976 when I went to London for a couple of weeks of concerts at Christmastime. We had lunch together and talked about our teaching and about books. I think she was a little surprised to see how unlike Jerry I am in mannerisms, taste, and temperament. This was often the reaction when Jerry's friends met me; my friends were similarly surprised when they met Jerry. Perhaps such differences seem especially strange in a same-sex relationship; it's odd, though, that they should. In any case, the avant-gardist's companion regaled Jacqueline with accounts of having heard the *Kindertotenlieder* with Dietrich Fischer-Dieskau in the Royal Festival Hall, the *Messiah* at the Academy of St. Martin-in-the-Fields, and the Orchestra of St. John's Smith Square.

Jerry's video work with David led to several commissions in the States. From their studio beneath the bleachers of SMU's Ownby Stadium, they created *Procession*, an audio-video work shown on PBS's Video Visionaries series. The Rockefeller Foundation gave them a grant to serve as consultants for video-related electronic media programs in Texas universities. And David's associations with CBS and, later, Dallas's KERA resulted in his directing the thirteen-part *With Ossie and Ruby*, with supplemental music by Jerry.

As it is for so many artists, Jerry's toughest struggle was to have the time and money to do his own work. He was fortunate, as he readily acknowledged, in meeting people who were able to give him work by using him in their own. From his early piano study with Paul van Katwijk at SMU, he met the conductor David Ahlstrom (with whom Jerry performed the Cage work). Through David, Jerry met Toni, the chair of SMU's dance department; she used Jerry's music in her dance programs—including one of Dallas's first "happenings," held at the downtown Sheraton Hotel. Toni's husband, Paul, as a television producer at KERA and then for the Dallas County Community College District, hired Jerry to contribute the music to several video courses—a major source of income for Jerry all the way through the last year of his life when he wrote the music, ironically enough, for the "Living with Health" series.

Of course, people used Jerry because of his talent and skill, primarily, but they also wanted to help him and support his art. David Gibson, who did lighting for some of Toni's productions, assisted Jerry in a few performances; he made space available for one of Jerry's interactive audio-video installations in later years. The artist David McManaway created an assortment of wands and other objects for Jerry's use in performance, both live and recorded. The percussionist Ron Snider, in addition to lining up studio gigs for Jerry, assisted him in performance and loaned him exotic instruments. Ron and his wife, Joan, played in a posthumous performance of one of Jerry's chamber works.

Paul and Oz Srere found another way to appreciate Jerry's talent and help him further his own work. In the mid-1970s, they began what was to become an almost annual event, a series of Sunday afternoon recitals, with commentary, that Jerry gave in the Sreres' Highland Park home, filling their front rooms with friends and fans who came to enjoy the mostly unfamiliar music and Jerry's entertaining descriptions of it.

In 1977, one of these recitals, "The Death of the Piano," was videotaped for showing on KERA. The thirty-minute program begins with Oz and Paul setting up the folding chairs while Bill Porterfield explains what is about to happen. Jerry then walks on, talking nonstop as he makes the final adjustments to his electronic equipment; the camera catches the effect he has on the audience—how he amuses them and stimulates them and, now performing, enraptures them.

After these recitals, the guests were invited to the den in the back of the house for refreshments. Most of the audience would come forward, though, to visit with Jerry, to ask him something about the music he had played, to thank him, or just to partake of the energy he radiated. Sometimes the reception would last almost as long as the music had. When we'd finally say goodbye, Oz would force a thick envelope on Jerry, and he always protested; once she even had to give it to me. This was money Jerry scrupulously saved to apply toward his own work. After his death, I found several of these envelopes, with their thank-you notes from Oz and over a thousand dollars' worth of fifty and one-hundred dollar bills.

*
**

I always looked forward to summer vacations, having learned to do so early in life, with our annual family trips to Kilgore, or Galveston, and (once) Kentucky. Traveling

somewhere distant became, by the end of the spring
semester, a beacon that would lead me out of the dark
mine of grading essays and exams. We planned a long
trip west for the summer of 1977; Jerry's scruples about
frivolously spending money were overcome when he realized he could make a few useful contacts in Aspen and
Santa Fe.

We asked Mrs. Hunt to go with us. She and Mr. Hunt,
who had at last retired, were comfortably settled in the
country, but Jerry's mother had grown a little bored
with the routine there and welcomed a change. She had
begun to take lessons in oil painting and was keen on
photographing Colorado views for possible use as picture
subjects.

We covered quite a bit of territory on that trip, reaching Leadville, Colorado, via Aspen and returning through
Santa Fe.

To save money and better accommodate Jerry's and
my vegetarian diet, we cooked meals in our motel rooms
using the hot plate we'd brought along. Jerry and his
mother stayed with Leto while I saw a Shakespeare play
at the University of Colorado at Boulder and concerts in
Aspen and Santa Fe.

Mrs. Hunt enjoyed riding, looking at the scenery. We
would stop quite often to give Leto a little exercise and
to take pictures. By late afternoon, we'd have found our
lodging for the night. I remember sitting with Jerry on the
porch of a chalet-like motel in Ouray, Colorado, drinking
coffee and watching the sunset while our clothes turned
in the dryer of the laundromat nearby.

We drove through Pueblo, Colorado, to see what
remained of the landmarks Jerry and his mother remembered from the year the Hunts spent there shortly after
the war. Mr. Hunt was a salesman and had to cover a
large area around Pueblo, negotiating icy roads and
snowy passes. As soon as he could, he moved his family
back to Texas.

We found the hospital where his mother took Jerry
when he swallowed safety pins (closed, of course, and
harmlessly passed). Mrs. Hunt remembered the nuns
there with gratitude—both for their help in the emergency
room and for the recipe for spaghetti sauce that they

gave Mr. Hunt, who called on them regularly selling milk products.

On our way out of Pueblo, we passed the slag heap of a plant south of town. Jerry remembered how he and his parents would drive out that way sometimes to see the huge, smoldering pile glowing in the dusk. They'd pull their car into an adjacent lot and sit awhile, no doubt indulging their son, who was fascinated by the eerie, otherworldly spectacle.

Mrs. Hunt was a little uneasy leaving her husband for the three weeks we were to be gone. He worked too hard around the farm, she fretted, and he wouldn't eat right without her there to prepare balanced meals. Some heart problems had arisen; he had seen a doctor and kept nitroglycerin tablets close by. She called him several times to check on him, but he made it fine and was glad for his wife to have had the trip.

Just before that Christmas, Mrs. Hunt drove into Dallas to spend a day shopping with Jerry and to stay with us overnight. At dinner, she told us she had hated to leave that morning because Mr. Hunt didn't seem to be feeling well; he'd hung about the house a little later than usual before going out to his work salvaging telephone poles. He insisted she come in as planned.

I was writing semester exams when a Canton neighbor called to tell us that Mr. Hunt was being taken by ambulance to a hospital in Athens. He had come in from work sick, but the nitroglycerin tablet he took hadn't helped. Then he called this neighbor, a retired physician, who recognized the symptoms of a heart attack and called an ambulance. We learned later that the ambulance driver had had trouble finding the farm, and by the time they got Mr. Hunt to Athens, thirty minutes away, he was dead.

Jerry and his mother started out for the hour-and-a-half drive to Athens, not knowing what to expect when they arrived. Mrs. Hunt's feeling of guilt for having left her husband was unassuageable. Jerry talked often about that drive, about how upset his mother was and about how she couldn't believe it when she was told her husband was already gone. She came home and spent the rest of the night cleaning the house, working especially hard in the bathrooms.

After school the next day, I drove out to deliver the sheet music Jerry had asked for. Since exams were underway, I couldn't attend the funeral that was held in Mart, near Waco. One of the Hunts' longtime friends, Maydell, accompanied Jerry and his mother to the funeral home. She told me Jerry played some of Mr. Hunt's favorite songs on the organ (again, as at Granny's funeral—a public performance on an unfamiliar instrument), tears in his eyes.

Jerry stayed with his mother for over a week. When he finally left, she assured him she wouldn't be afraid of living alone on the farm. She had made a lot of friends, she said, who would surely check on her. And she had King, the German shepherd Mr. Hunt had brought home shortly after Hermie and Sassie died. Nevertheless, Jerry noted, she had gone from window to window, closing the wooden shutters at twilight—something she had never done before.

*
**

Record snow fell the winter of 1978, covering iced-over tree branches and breaking them off to fall on power lines. Some areas of the city were without electricity for almost two weeks; our side of Swiss Avenue was dark for ten days. Each morning during the unscheduled winter vacation, I'd hear from one of the priests that there would again be no school. I had to be up and ready to go, just in case—but it was a pleasure, confident as I was that I would have the morning to continue reading *Anna Karenina*, Leto in the chair beside me or on the rug in front of the gas heater.

In the early afternoon, Jerry, Leto, and I would take a long walk through the snowy landscape, where streets had become indistinguishable from yards. We tied a blue wool muffler around Leto's middle, and she trotted along in front of us, her white fur blending so well with the snow that she must have looked from a distance like a little animated scarf. We'd pick up what supplies we could (no candles, though—they were all sold out) in the few stores that were open and return home, turning up the gas furnace and trying to prepare as best we could for the dark hours ahead.

Later that winter, Jerry drove to Illinois to give a concert and fell on the icy ground, breaking his left arm— his writing arm. With painkillers, he made it through the performance and the long drive home. The months of recuperation were tedious and frustrating; he wasn't able to play the piano or wire his electronics, and even cooking was a chore with his arm in a sling. For almost two years after the break, he was to complain of aching in that arm.

Jerry had never been one to endure illness patiently, and he used to say, "I can take anything but pain." He lived with a toothache for several months, sometimes in such agony that we'd have to go to the all-night drug-store for a fresh tube of "El Numbo," as he called the oral analgesic.

When his mother and I finally persuaded him to go to the dentist, he was so frightened of what might happen there that he decided to have a few drinks before the appointment. It had been agreed that I would drive him to the dentist's office in the old Medical Arts Building in downtown Dallas. He finished his third or fourth "milk punch" (milk and vodka) on the way down. I had to give him a hand out of the car and into the building, but he needed no help talking, charming (and tickling) the dentist and his assistants with a nonstop monologue that ceased only when they got him in the chair and put the aspirator in his mouth.

As it turned out, he had to have root canals in two lower molars, a result, the dentist surmised, of the way Jerry ground his teeth when he practiced the piano. Although each of the several visits he had to make was preceded by a drink or two, he got to where he wasn't making them so strong. He actually came to like the dentist quite a bit, a rather plump young fellow Jerry always called "my tooth teddy," though never, I hope, to his face, the milk punches notwithstanding.

*
**

Mrs. Hunt's circle of friends in Canton widened and deepened; she won prizes for her oil paintings, served as secretary for a women's club, started her own informal group (the Fair and Talented—or the FAT Club, as they called it), and worked on a political campaign for the county sheriff's office.

My mother now had two granddaughters; Jamie was a year old, and there was daily visiting between Mother's and Judy's houses on Ferguson Road.

Jerry and I visited our mothers regularly, and we continued to have people over for vegetarian dinners— Indian one month, Chinese or Mexican the next. But we were fighting, more and more often, usually about the division of labor on and in the house. The newness of living in a mansion had worn off after seven or eight years, and we were rapidly losing ground in our sometimes half-hearted efforts to maintain the place. The exterior trim needed painting again, the floors needed cleaning and polishing, and the windows hadn't been washed in years.

Our rent remained the same, but we received only minimal help from the landlord: plumbing repairs and ineffectual roof patching. We finally solved the leaking roof problem by suspending giant sheets of plastic from the ceiling in the attic, taping them together in such a way as to create a huge funnel that emptied into a garden hose that led, through a vent, to the outside. Sometimes during especially heavy rains, water would collect in a lobe of the funnel—or "tit," as we referred to it—and one of us would have to go up and "milk," pressing the water over toward the drain.

Jerry was frustrated by the fact that he could get plenty of commercial work and work for academic institutions (he had begun teaching at the University of Texas at Dallas one or two nights a week), while what he really needed was more time and energy to devote to his own projects. He complained vociferously every time he had to leave the house to go to some job or other, being forced to leave his real work behind—on the piano, on his workbench, or on his desk.

I had begun to fear that I was burning myself out teaching. Planning lessons meant reading literature, listening to music, making notes, formulating discussion strategies, and devising tests, and I worked late every night. The weekends were dedicated to grading papers, usually essay tests or full-length compositions; I hated to give multiple-choice tests, trying to take advantage of every opportunity to give the students a chance to write. Free periods at school were devoted to student conferences: I was rarely ever able to get any paperwork done there.

On one occasion, I had just one or two papers left to grade before finishing a set that I had promised a class I'd have ready that day; I fled the loud talking (it was probably a Friday) in the faculty suite to finish my work in the quiet of the headmaster's outer office. (One of my colleagues saw me there and, I have always assumed, told the others.) I routinely took a set of papers to the symphony concerts I attended Saturday nights, my red-ink pen uncapped and ready to go as soon as the house lights came up for intermission.

So neither of us felt he had a lot of time to do house-keeping chores, and each, accordingly, was more than ready to blame the other for not doing his share. Jerry saw me sitting around reading; I heard him just playing the piano. When the tension led to arguments, he exploded, and I sulked. He cleaned out the utility room one day by throwing trash (and some still-usable supplies) into the backyard, shouting obscenities as he did so that I'll bet were unlike anything our neighbors the Forts—who, Jerry soon realized, were sitting on their patio—had ever heard. (And how like Jerry that shortly after he saw them, he began carrying things back in without missing a beat, continuing the epithets but toning them down a little, conducting business as usual.)

During that fit, I went off to hide just as I had over fifteen years earlier when he threw his tantrum at Jas. K. Wilson's clothes store in downtown Dallas. He had brought back a pair of recently purchased trousers to be altered, and the clerk assumed they had been worn and sniffily informed Jerry that they didn't work on "soiled" clothes. Jerry hit the roof, yelling at the poor fellow and demanding to see the manager, threatening to talk his parents into closing their account—after they'd returned everything they had ever bought from the store. I was horrified at the scene and slunk down the three flights of stairs, no time to wait for the elevator.

I wound up going into the Orange Julius restaurant next door. As I sat, still shaken, drinking the beverage I didn't want and looking out the front windows, I saw Jerry rush by, still fuming (but without the pants). I continued to sit there. He soon passed by again; this time, he looked in. On his third crossing, he entered the restaurant. He was angry with me for having abandoned him.

Over the years, we so often followed this pattern. Like his father, Jerry's temper would flare up, erupt in some violent deed, and die down. My nature, like Jerry's mother's, led me to minimize or deny the problem, then pout when I got my face pushed in it. Above all else, I had to demonstrate that I had not been affected. Eventually—almost always—Jerry would come round to apologize; then we could talk and sometimes make love. His fits served to get things out into the open. We would have been worse off without them.

My plan to stave off burnout was to ask for a year's leave of absence. Father Denis reluctantly permitted this, expressing his regret that the school could not afford to reward my eight years of teaching with a paid sabbatical. I had savings set aside, so money wasn't an issue (Jerry and I had long since gotten into the habit of living frugally). As soon as my plans were set, Jerry and I began to get along better, to spend more time with one another, and to talk without needing dramatic prologues to do so.

To make a clean break, I took a trip with Leto to New York.

Our destination was the Vegetarian Hotel in Woodridge in the Catskills. We drove up through Tennessee and the Appalachians, spending three nights on the road. We stopped at rest stops and even some cemeteries to stretch our legs. When I had to leave Leto, I always tried to park the Toyota where I could keep an eye on her. She seemed to enjoy riding, sitting in the front seat beside me and often looking ahead. In slow traffic, I'd roll the window down and she'd stick her nose out, sniffing the breeze.

One night at a stoplight, we pulled up behind a pickup with two workers sitting in the back. They saw Leto beside me, and one of them yelled, "That your woman?" Jerry loved that story.

The Vegetarian Hotel was a kind of health retreat for East Coast Jews. The same crowd, now aging, spent a good part of the summer there each year, eating sensibly, doing a little yoga-influenced exercise, and attending lectures on health and well-being under the majestic Tree of Life on the front lawn.

Lunch and dinner were social events, with an occasional night of folk dancing for entertainment. I liked the place and felt right at home, although I knew many of the guests found my being there a little odd, traveling with just a dog at my young age.

Mealtimes were especially enjoyable because of the interesting conversation at what became my regular table. I looked forward to visiting with a fellow who worked for the Educational Testing Service, and his wife, and I made friends with the octogenarian who sat on my other side (her nurse would wheel her up to the table and proceed to lay out a dozen or more pills, which the old lady scooped up and swallowed in one great gulp). I never left the dining room without a collection of scraps brought me by other guests to take back to Leto, who, I always assumed, waited patiently in our room.

I became particularly fond of a little lady who spoke seldom and very quietly but whose comments about her early life in Poland intrigued me. We visited at length one afternoon in the Adirondack chairs just outside her building, Leto lying between us. She told me a little about her childhood and her parents, and she said that what served most effectively to keep her memories fresh was music, the Yiddish songs she learned as a girl and still sang.

Because of my obvious interest in these songs, she invited me to visit her in her room where she promised to sing for me. I took my tape recorder along and recorded a lovely modal song about a fisherman who goes out early one morning to cast his net while spinning a dream of someday finding his beloved. The ocean murmurs sadly; maybe it is lonely, too. The fisherman returns home empty-handed. Ethel helped me transcribe the Yiddish words as we listened to the tape I made.

Leto and I would usually go exploring in the hills around Woodridge after lunch. One day, in a village antique store, I found a pair of ornate wrought iron bookends that I almost bought for Jerry (they were expensive) and always regretted not doing so. Sometimes I would bring back ice cream for my octogenarian friend from the little shop in town—Leto and I delivering it to her as she sat under a huge, white parasol in her accustomed chair.

I went to two or three of the folk dancing evenings, mainly for the music: Yiddish tunes played on an accordion. I noticed that I was always paired with the same young lady, an English teacher from New Jersey. I didn't think much about this until she came to my door after dinner one night, inviting me to accompany her to a small gathering in a friend's room—probably comprising the whole of the youthful contingent at the hotel at that time. I declined to go, explaining that I had letters to write, or a call to make, or whatever.

The day before I was to leave, one of the three or four young men who had come up from Brooklyn to work in the hotel kitchen for the summer approached me on the terrace and asked to borrow a dollar. He'd pay me back the following day, he said. There was something unusually aggressive about his manner, but I didn't take it personally. When I was packing my car to leave the next day, I noticed this same fellow standing with his buddies and a couple of girls in the corner of the parking lot near the kitchen door. I became aware that they were looking at me and laughing. As Leto and I drove away, I heard the word—they made sure I heard the word—queer.

Our journey home took us west to Erie, then south through Kentucky, where I drove through the area around Greensburg (Granny's birthplace) that our family had visited in 1952. I was glad to get back home and eager to get started on making my year off from teaching count. I reviewed my Greek, eventually reading *Hippolytus* and *Medea*. I practiced the violin and even tried to play the first movement of Beethoven's Spring Sonata with Jerry. And I rented an accordion, not having even held one for over twenty years, in order to learn to play Yiddish songs.

*
**

During my leave of absence from the school, Jerry and I made several trips to Houston and to Corpus. Bob and Rany had moved into a two-story house not far from Rice University and had had a swimming pool put in the backyard. Peggy and George's house in Portland, right on the shore, made you feel as though you were aboard a ship: when you looked through the windows at the back of the house, only water was visible. We waded out into the bay one afternoon, Leto paddling along behind us; we went too far for her, apparently, and Peggy noticed her struggling and helped her back to shore. I have a picture that I took of the two of them that I took on our return to land—it reminds me of how much Leto always hated water. (When wet, she looked like a "drowned rat," Jerry said, with her usually flowing hair pasted alongside her body.)

Both destinations offered music. Bob had bought a new Steinway with Jerry's help. On one of Jerry's and my trips east, he met us at the Steinway factory in Queens. Leto and I waited under a tree in the parking lot while Jerry and Bob selected an instrument. Peggy and George had acquired a Steinway, too—one once used by visiting artists and since retired.

So, in Houston and Corpus both, there was always a great deal of piano playing and a lot of talk about music. Jerry especially appreciated the contrast in action and tone those Steinways offered to his own darker and more ponderous Mason & Hamlin, but he always maintained that his piano was better to learn music on, perhaps because it made you work harder.

With the extra time, I was able to do more yard work and gardening. I planted seven kinds of hybrid tea roses in our backyard on Swiss, and during our frequent trips to Canton, I experimented with Chinese and Indian vegetables. I also enjoyed maintaining a regular exchange of letters with Lillian, now a professor of philosophy at Auburn. We wrote about books and music (she introduced me to Edward Elgar's *Sea Pictures*), and she sent me a beautiful muffler she wove by hand and dyed with pecans as well as a little teddy bear she made that had a laurel crown on his head, named "Feisty." One wintry day, a quilt arrived—a masterpiece she made out of old ties that she had collected from her colleagues at the university.

By the next midsummer, I believed I was ready to return to teaching in the fall. The school had been very good about respecting my desire to have a year away. With one or two minor exceptions, I had had no contact with anyone there. It is true, though, that I had never really socialized with the other faculty, apart from having one of the science teachers and his wife over for dinner a time or two. (On one occasion, when we were still eating meat, Norman embarrassed us by pulling a USDA inspection tag out of the chicken stew Jerry had made—a story Jerry delighted in retelling.)

Father Denis called in early August and invited me to the abbey for dinner to discuss the upcoming year. During the hour just before I was to leave to meet him, Jerry and I made love on the hideaway bed in my study, in the late afternoon sunlight that was angling in through the blinds. I remember dressing and thinking of my sports coat and slacks as a kind of uniform that I was putting on again. But it would be all right, I believed, and that belief was strengthened by the intimacy Jerry and I had just shared.

I was wrong. Nothing at school was the same because I wasn't the same. For a couple of months, I went through the motions, mechanically preparing lessons and grading papers, talking enthusiastically, and ignoring a rising sense of desperation with the aid of several stiff drinks each night before dinner and just before bedtime. I slept fitfully, awoke earlier and earlier, and began finding longer and longer alternate routes to school. I startled myself by crying on the way there one morning; I wore my sunglasses into the school to conceal my red eyes.

The crisis came while we were reading Hawthorne's *The Scarlet Letter*. In teaching literature to the upper forms, I had always stressed its relevance to daily life, to the world we live in. At my lecture, I was Arthur Dimmesdale in his pulpit; I knew it, and many of the boys knew it. One of the juniors had suspected I might be gay; word had gotten around that I lived with another man and had for years, and all it took was for this boy to raise the issue and start the rumor.

I am sure there had been some suspicion in the years past.

Two students whom I believed to be gay were frequent visitors in my office, although I tried not to show any favoritism. One of these boys, Mark, used to wait for me each morning at the top of the stairs. He was one of the brightest students I had ever had, and I enjoyed his ironic sense of humor. I never really felt threatened or compromised by the association with him; no one overhearing our conversations could have thought them in any way out of place.

In any case, Mark had graduated during the year I was away. What had changed when I returned was my own sense of who I was, and this change was pushing me toward the realization that, like Dimmesdale, I was living a lie. The closer I came to that realization, the more unstable and vulnerable I became, and that vulnerability opened the blinds far enough for some of the more sensitive students to see in.

What they saw, of course, disturbed them. One of their favorite teachers had a secret that set him apart, provided an unspoken subtext to everything he said about characters and themes in literature as well as people and events in the news. This secret also threatened their developing sense of their own masculine sexuality precisely because they were so fond of me.

From time to time, I heard a stage-whispered comment from the back of the classroom, a hurled barb meant to sting, to goad me into saying or doing something that would relieve the tension that had become intolerable for all of us.

And so, one Friday, I knew I was through. Nothing in particular precipitated my decision—"enough was just enough," as Jerry described it in a letter to Jacqueline. I went to see Father Denis in his office after school. I told him I couldn't go on teaching, that I was gay, that some of the boys knew it, and that I had become so disturbed emotionally that concentrating on my work had become impossible.

Father Denis recommended that I continue teaching. "There is no such thing as homosexuality," he said, meaning, I suppose, that one should simply deny same-sex attraction and certainly not act on it and instead, conduct business as usual—the business, in this case, of digging one's own grave. If a nonreligious person may be permitted to imagine grace, I can say now that I received something like that gift that day in Father Denis's office when I claimed the right to be who I was and who I am. We embraced tearfully, and I cleaned out my office and drove away.

For the second time, I returned home from work with important news for Jerry. On this occasion, though, the news was good. We took our usual after-dinner walk with Leto, moseying through the rose garden at Samuell-Grand, talking about what had happened to me—to us—and about what might be ahead. I remember becoming aware of a feeling that might be described as anticipated happiness, a sense of hopeful expectation borne out of relief. Although I knew that Jerry was worried about me and disturbed to realize how unhappy I had been (and how far apart we must have grown in some ways for him not to have known that I was), I also believed that he thought I had made the right decision. We had a wonderful, long talk. It was almost like exchanging vows.

I look at the pictures of us our friends took over the years and see in every one of them the bond between us. That I felt I had to hide this, the best part of my life, causes me intense regret. And I am amazed at how duplicitous I was, keeping the school world and my home life separate and, for years, doing so comfortably. As soon as I left Cistercian, I saw the damage I had done—to Jerry, to my family, and to myself.

Telling Mother was not difficult: I always suspected she knew her son was gay, and I knew it made no difference in her love for me. We both deluded ourselves by thinking it was better not discussed, and we were both relieved when I brought it out into the open. She had been concerned that I'd be alone in life, and she worried about the difficulties that my being different might cause me. Sitting on Judy's sofa that November day, I told her about my love for Jerry and my hope that it would last a lifetime. I believe I was able to reassure her that I would be happier for having left the school. Judy helped in her gentle, non-intrusive way. We talked about a couple of relatives we believed were lesbians.

Jerry soon saw how difficult being openly gay had been for me, that it had presented problems in my life that he had never had, associating as he did with musicians, dancers, and artists. He gave me all the loving support he could during the crisis and beyond, unfailingly ready to listen and urging me to take my time in planning for the future.

Leaving the school so abruptly was disorienting: I had put a lot of myself into the job, and having that world and all the habits associated with it disappear left me confused and even a little frightened, in spite of the immense relief I felt. Several faculty members and students wrote to tell me how much they had appreciated my work and to convey their best wishes. (I never really knew, but I believe Father Denis told the school community that I had experienced some kind of nervous collapse.) I did feel at times as though I had let down people who had depended on me.

Just to get away for a few days, Jerry and I went to Houston. Bob suggested a day trip to Sargent, a fishing community on the Gulf southwest of Galveston, and he and Rany and I, their dogs, and Leto drove down. I remember sitting a long time, just listening to the waves wash ashore and the seagulls cry. And I remember beginning to feel better, more in the mood to celebrate my thirty-fifth birthday. I would like to return to that special place someday; doing so would almost be a pilgrimage.

During the next few months, I set out to gain experience living and thinking as an openly gay man. I began to realize just how deeply I had internalized homophobia when I heard myself tell the owner of a gay bookstore that I didn't live in Dallas, that I was just visiting. One day I walked into a gay bar in downtown Dallas and sat nervously drinking a beer, trying not to stare at the men in business suits who had come in for cocktails after work. The point, of course, was not to see them but to have them see me, a gay man advertising that fact. I read *With Downcast Gays: Aspects of Homosexual Self-Oppression* by Britishers Andrew Hodges and David Hutter, a mathematician and an artist. And I resolved never to conceal my identity as a gay man again, a resolution I have faithfully kept.

I spent several weeks visiting the downtown library regularly. Seeing Larry Kramer's *Faggots* prominently displayed among the new books startled me one day—and challenged me: I found I could remove it, walk to a table, and peruse it without shame. As I browsed in the Humanities and Fine Arts divisions, I overheard the librarians talking among themselves and with patrons, and I began to think I might like to work in such an environment, so seemingly open and relaxed, yet quietly purposeful and filled with the books and records that I loved. After a couple of months of part-time work conducting telephone surveys, I got a job as a clerk with the Dallas Public Library, and I began a second career that has so far lasted more than sixteen years.

As I had for years, I went out to trim the trees and shrubs in Mother's front yard right around the time of my birthday, November 19th. Judy had baked a birthday cake for me, and I looked up from my work to see her walking up the street with it, Jenny and Jamie (not yet two) leading the way. I didn't particularly think it odd that Judy had baked the cake instead of Mother, but I realize now that Mother hadn't been feeling well for some time and may not have been up to it.

Mother had had a bad cold early that winter, and it had left her with a nagging cough that wouldn't go away. She finally agreed to go to the doctor, and I took her to our family physician. Dr. Hancock advised her to consult a pulmonary specialist, and he recommended a bronchoscopy. This doctor told me in the waiting room that he had indeed found cancer, inoperable, in a bronchus. He referred us to an oncologist to plan radio- and chemotherapy.

I will never forget the impression that surgeon made on me: he announced his discovery with a kind of zeal, a man aflame with the intellectual passion resulting from his having solved The Riddle (as Sherwin Nuland calls it in *How We Die*) that fascinates most specialists. I took his news like a slap in the face, and as soon as he rushed away, I retreated into a nearby phone booth and called Judy and Jerry, crying freely to both.

Mother didn't know for sure that she had cancer until I got her home late that afternoon. She was looking through the papers they had given her at the hospital and saw the word *carcinoma.* "That means cancer, doesn't it?" she asked me. I tried to equivocate, but it was no good. This was the first of several such scenes I was to be a part of—when the news suddenly comes that one has cancer and begins its work of transforming a person's life. As soon as she recovered from a severe allergic reaction she had to the codeine prescribed for her, Mother proceeded to tell family and friends, always uttering that word a little more softly than the others, as though confessing. As I listened to her, I sometimes heard myself saying "gay" in the apologetic way I used to.

We began making frequent trips to the oncologist for radiation and checkups, where the weigh-in was the critical moment. Mother had chemotherapy in pill form, and she took prednisone and an antitussive that never seemed to do much good. She was worried by her steady loss of weight (although she joked about it, saying that she could finally wear the petite sizes she had always wished she could), but the continual coughing was the worst thing she had to live with.

After a good Christmas that we all feared would be her last, I took her out to movies, plays, and concerts as often as she felt like going. Eventually, we had to give up anything that would make us a part of an audience: her cough was worse and had begun to embarrass her. We made long drives into the county, then, and sometimes went visiting.

She was able to spend time each day with Judy and the girls, and she occasionally took them to town on the bus (she and Jenny and I had lunch one day after I had started working for the library). Apart from a couple of brief hospital stays required to combat infections, she made it fairly well for six months after her diagnosis. She was able to see her third grandchild be born in March, and rocking little Paul Michael became her supreme pleasure. Jenny and Jamie doted on her, waiting patiently for their GaGa to come down each morning to take them to the store, to read to them, just to be with them. When the weather grew warm, she'd spend time with them on a quilt she'd lay beneath the trees in the backyard. Judy and I were touched to see how generous she was with her time, just as she had always been with us.

It worried Mother that she had become a burden. Judy was down the street with three young children and no transportation (when Paul had the car with him at work), and I was at the library downtown and, by summer, attending library school a couple of nights a week and on Saturdays. She hated to ask us to take her to the doctor, a three- or four-hour ordeal that involved a lot of waiting. As a new library employee, I was still on probation and received no time off without making it up.

Judy and I encouraged Mother to deal with her illness in whatever way she thought best. From the very beginning, her oncologist had made it clear that doing nothing about the cancer was an option. Mother decided to fight the growth and spread of tumors by radiation and chemotherapy, and for a while, it did appear that she had reached a plateau: there was no change. The chemotherapy had made her much weaker, however, and as she saw her ability to live as she wished diminished, she began to change her mind about the good of going on. She had a large cylinder of oxygen in the back bedroom (my old room), and she was spending more and more time in bed, lying beside a window that looked out into the shady backyard. When I came out to mow, I'd see her watching me as I pushed the mower back and forth across the grass. She got sick in late June and had to go to the hospital, where she shared a room with a lady with cancer of the tongue. There had been an accident, the doctor said: a portion of a tumor had become dislodged and was partially obstructing her airway. She was slowly dying of oxygen deprivation. Given her age (seventy-two) and the poor prognosis of her disease, the oncologist recommended that we not intervene (entailing surgery that would result in the need for mechanical assistance in breathing). In her subtle ways, Mother had already told Judy and me she was tired of struggling.

They began giving her morphine in the early afternoon. Until she went into a deep sleep, we took turns sitting with her, Judy, and me, talking a little, but mainly just looking into her eyes and holding her hand. The night before, I was sitting by her bed doing library school homework. We had been talking, then she grew silent and appeared to rest. She startled me by turning her head toward me and saying, "You're content, aren't you?" I told her yes, that I was.

She died around six, her chest gradually growing still. The nurse led us away from her bed and into an empty room across the hall where we could cry as long and as hard as we needed to, Judy in Paul's arms, I in Jerry's. Mother had been fortunate to die an easy and good death, herself up to the end. And she died knowing her children were very greatly loved and would be all right.

*
**

By the end of the 1970s, Jerry was composing more than he ever had. He began making records on his own Irida label, a name he borrowed from the Ceylonese art gallery that a high-school friend of ours was operating in Berlin at the time. With the purpose of releasing music by new composers (including himself), Jerry found a pressing plant in Dallas that did good work cheaply. He collected some money from the composers whom he'd invited to participate, and he made up the difference himself. I don't believe a lot of thought was given to royalties and residuals; the idea was to get the music out there and to supply the composers with a good stock of their own records.

The first Irida disc was devoted to Jerry's own work, "for various mechanical and electronic instrument combinations and systems." Two of the words he used in naming pieces on the disc have personal associations for me: "Cantegral" is the name of a short street near downtown Dallas that we happened to see while taking Leto for a ride one evening; and "Phalba" (pronounced "foul bee") is a little town southwest of Canton that we drove through (and nearly missed) on one of our trips out to check on Mrs. Hunt. For Jerry's 37th birthday, I had Neiman Marcus bake him a gaudy cake with the shortening-based icing that he liked and decorated with the words *Cantegral* and *Phalba* and *Lattice* (another piece) encircling a bouquet of frosting flowers. In one of my favorite pictures, he sits grinning at the camera, Leto in his lap, with that outrageous cake on the coffee table in front of him. That previous summer, in 1980, he had gone to Minneapolis to participate in New Music America, the largest experimental music series ever held in the US. Tom Johnson reviewed the concert Jerry gave in the Walker Art Center for the *Village Voice*:

> Jerry Hunt . . . presented his Haramand Plane in a performance that I found profound, skillful, completely original, and utterly baffling . . . I can't get the piece out of my mind. I recall that the light was very dim, that Hunt kept walking downstage to whack a large cardboard box with a curious stick, that he rattled some unidentifiable objects in one hand for a while, that a recording of electronic sounds sometimes accompanied him from the loudspeakers, that there seemed to be no explanation for anything that happened, and that I was simultaneously fascinated and disturbed. I think I must have dozed off during part of the performance, but I'm not really sure. The piece already existed in some strange dream world . . . All I can say for sure is that Hunt was doing something very strong and very different from anything I have ever heard from New York composers.

I quote the review at some length because it is fairly typical of so many Jerry was to receive over the years: the critic is baffled yet moved, describing what Jerry did and his own reaction to it, but is unable to say how the piece worked or what, exactly, it was about or why it impressed him so.

The trip to Minneapolis broadened Jerry's audience and resulted in concert engagements in the immediate future and beyond. Jerry had long since realized that his work would not be popular in Dallas—if, indeed, very much so anywhere. As he told our friend Jane Van Sickle in an interview she did for *Dallas Studio* in 1981:

> The fact is that a lot of people just
> don't want to take music too seriously,
> and that's fine with me. If I'm person-
> ally discontent because I make a kind
> of art which just naturally is not going
> to attract a large, overwhelming audi-
> ence, that's not the world's problem, it's
> mine. . . . Anyway, people will like what
> they like.

But he was to discover as the decade progressed that
he had a following, particularly on the East Coast, and
that that following was both dedicated and growing.

*
**

It was the West Coast, however, that was responsible
for the last road trip we were to make with Leto. Jerry was
invited to give concerts at the San Francisco Art Institute
and at Mills College in November of 1980. I arranged to
miss a couple of weeks of library school classes and take
vacation time from work to go with him. Traveling in
November always seemed a good idea to us, after the fall
tourist season and before bad weather.

Leto was the star of this trip. Many of my memories of
it are of getting her in places where dogs weren't usually
allowed and of our walks and of riding through scenic
areas with her there in the front seat of our rented Buick
Skylark, her nose sometimes out the window.

Jerry and I preferred to stay in independently owned
motels whenever we could: not only were they cheaper, but
also they were more picturesque. During the '70s and '80s,
many of these establishments were managed by foreign-
ers who were reluctant to see animals on their premises
and in their rooms, perhaps because these people had
not yet realized how much a part of the American family
dogs are. It was my job to enter the motel office and make
the arrangements while Jerry waited in the car with Leto
sitting beside him, her head clearly visible (and probably
turned toward where I'd gone).

I would lovingly describe Leto's gentle ways and offer
to leave a pet deposit, and I never once failed to get her

in, often in spite of the "No Dogs Allowed" sign above the registration desk. The motel clerk would look out at her, waiting patiently in the car, and decide it would be worth the risk. What the clerk didn't know was that Jerry was talking sweetly to her the whole time and petting her assiduously to keep her from barking and howling in her puzzlement over where I had gone.

In Berkeley, we stayed at the Golden Bear Motel and managed to get special permission to walk Leto on the terrace of the Lawrence Hall of Science high in the hills. She wandered through the University of California's botanical gardens with us, and she and I spent a morning on campus, occasionally making forays into the buildings in search of water fountains.

Leto's biggest coup came the night we went to dinner at the Pasand Madras Cuisine restaurant on Shattuck Avenue. We parked on a side street just outside the restaurant's windows, intending to go in and order a couple of Thai dinners to take out. The Indian maître d' protested that it would be difficult to prepare so many dishes to go, and we explained our situation—that we didn't want to leave Leto waiting in the car while we ate a long, leisurely meal. "Why don't you just bring her in?" he asked, in his heavy British accent. "It's a free country here, isn't it?"

We took our time enjoying the delicious food, every now and then slipping Leto a morsel of pakora or vegetable samosa, a piece of puri, and, finally, half a gulab jamun. She was quite content to be with us, lying on her leash at our feet, concealed from view under the huge table. When we had finished eating, we walked toward the door with Leto trotting along behind us. The other diners turned their heads in amazement to see a dog in the restaurant, but the faces I saw expressed startled delight, not outrage. In his San Francisco radio interview the next day, Jerry told the story—and gave the restaurant a generous plug.

She did suffer a kind of comeuppance, though, when we went to visit Jim Pomeroy in his San Francisco studio home. Jim's dog, Sorghum, was a large, protective German shepherd who apparently felt that Leto had overstepped the territorial line when she jumped onto the couch where Jerry and I were sitting. Sorghum rushed forward and

bit Leto—on her side, I think—but her teeth didn't pene-
trate the skin, thanks to Leto's heavy coat. However, it
was an affront for Leto. She had never had any trouble
with another dog, including all those we encountered on
our walks in parks everywhere and even Mrs. Hunt's own
fiercely protective shepherd. She became, for a while, a
little less self-assertive.

When Jerry went out to make preparations for his
concerts and to see people (including David Ahlstrom,
who was now a choral director in the Bay Area), Leto and
I stayed in the Golden Bear.

We had made ourselves quite at home there, with food
stored in the cooler for preparation on the hot plate later
and the clothes that I had washed in the bathroom sink
drying on hangers that had been hung on every available hinge, handle, or knob. Leto and I enjoyed walking
through the quiet residential neighborhood just behind
the motel. As we meandered, I studied for the make-up
exams I would have to take when I got home and returned
to library school.

After the spectacular drive down the coast on Route
1, we spent a couple of nights in Hollywood, where Jerry
was interviewed on LA's Pacifica station. On the morning
of our last day, Jerry met a young man at the payphone
of the motel who posed a bit of a problem for us. As many
people were, the fellow was fascinated by Jerry's friendly,
somewhat eccentric personality, and he may also have
detected a certain vulnerability that he believed would
make Jerry an easy mark. He clearly had more time than
money and was prepared, as I learned when Leto and I
joined Jerry, to tag along with us whatever our destination. I let them out, with some uneasiness, at a music
store where Jerry had an appointment to see a new
synthesizer; Leto and I visited shops and bookstores on
a busy street close by (I'd tie her leash to parking meter
poles while I dashed in).

When I went back for Jerry, he told me that he wasn't
quite ready to leave the store, that another salesman with
more knowledge of the synthesizer had just arrived, and
that he wanted another hour with him. Our new acquaintance, though, had had enough technical talk and said
that he'd wait with Leto and me in the car.

I decided something had to be done about this boy. "We've come to a parting of the ways," I said, summoning what I could recall of the disciplinary tone I used to use in teaching. "I'll take you anywhere you want to go, as long as it's not too far." After a moment's confusion, he came up with a friend's address, and I drove him there.

Jerry told this story, the story of how I'd "rescued" him many times through the years. I have no doubt that Jerry would have rid himself of this hanger-on eventually, but it might have taken him a long time to do it, and there just might have been an unpleasant confrontation.

Jerry's quality of expecting the best of people did endear him to many, but it also sometimes put him at risk. The closest call he ever received came a dozen years later when he had gone near sundown to a local arts group board meeting in a downtown Dallas office building. He was stopped on the street by a couple of boys who demanded his billfold. He told them he was sorry but that he didn't have any money. "Maybe this'll make you change your mind," one of them said as he pulled a gun out of his jacket. As Jerry told it, he looked the boy right in the eye and said, "No, I'm sorry, I really don't have any," then he turned and walked away, overhearing the other fellow say, "Come on, let's get outta here." By the time Jerry got to the meeting, he was shaking with fear at the thought of what had just happened.

All the people who ever heard this story were, of course, horrified at what Jerry had done, but most of them were not surprised by either his foolhardiness in resisting the attempted mugging or his success at having brought it off. Whether they described it as charisma or strong will or clarity of focus, they acknowledged that Jerry had something about him that could overpower people—the same quality in a slightly different form that could hold people mesmerized during his performances. When the risks were high enough, when his life or his work was on the line, this quality surfaced, and he got his way.

We received a form letter during the winter of 1981 telling us that our rent for the house on Swiss Avenue would soon be tripled. Jerry was working less (by choice), and my clerical job at the library didn't leave me much money to spare, with my travel expenses to and from library school in Denton two nights a week and every other Saturday. We were alarmed, and I called our landlord, who lived next door, and asked him to come over for a talk.

In the ten years we had lived there, we had gotten to know Mr. Topletz fairly well. I used to go over and visit with his wife before she died of cancer a year earlier (she had a statue of Saint Francis put in the flower garden and told me, "He'll protect me"). Every Christmas, the Topletzes remembered us with a bottle of fine whiskey. But, Mr. Topletz now explained, maintenance expenses had risen so much for all the rental property he and his brother owned throughout the city that they had decided to raise rents across the board—and in looking at their holdings, they realized that what Jerry and I were paying was, relatively speaking, much too low. He did tell us, though, that we could continue paying the same rent for the next few months, but if we decided to stay, we would eventually have to pay the new figure. At least we had the time to consider alternatives and make plans.

I suggested we move to the country, and Jerry liked the idea. At first, we thought we might live on the corner property Jerry's parents had bought ten miles east of Canton, either building a small house or buying a trailer to put there. So far, the land had been used only for pasturing cattle and was being rented for that purpose by a couple the Hunts knew from Dallas. There were no structures on this property other than the shed Mr. Hunt had built facing the highway intersection that he thought might someday be used to sell . . . something.

It was Jerry's idea to convert the big barn on the land where Mrs. Hunt lived into a house for us. We talked our plan over with his mother, and she seemed pleased that we would consider settling close by. Although she had many friends and kept herself busy with crafts and club activities, she was still uneasy living alone in what was then an isolated part of the county. And I knew she was happy at the prospect of having Jerry near and being able to visit with him regularly. We made it clear that we intended to pay our share of the cost for utilities.

Jerry had just finished his music for the PBS series *With Ossie and Ruby,* so he was able to spend most of his time that spring in Canton, doing what he could do without help to get things ready. I had been promoted to the reference department of the library and was in my next-to-last semester of library school, so my time for house-building was limited. I came out every weekend that I could, bringing Leto.

Before any work toward converting the barn could be done, it had to be cleaned out. Mr. Hunt had filled it with tools, fencing supplies, and farm implements, and from his salvage work, there were thousands of white and blue-green glass insulators piled in a corner. Most of what Jerry did initially was to clear these things out, saving the heavier items for me to help with when I could join him. Mrs. Hunt inveigled several of her friends into helping her move the insulators to the little barn, where they stacked them on wooden pallets.

When the barn had been emptied, we got down to the serious business—and fun—of turning it into a place to live. I brought do-it-yourself books home from the library; Jerry studied them and devised our strategies, looking always for the least expensive, most energy-efficient ways of doing things. We used Mr. Hunt's old pickup to transport supplies from Canton and Tyler, a much larger town thirty-five miles east.

It had been a cold, rainy spring. By late April, we were ready to cut windows in the corrugated steel walls, having drawn our floor plan and located where the kitchen appliances would go. Starting holes with a jigsaw and then cutting the window openings themselves with a large pair of tin snips, we made our way around the perimeter, taking turns with the tasks. Leto followed us, wondering at the sudden access of light and air. We put more windows in the south wall than in the north, and later, when we had boarded up the east and west barn doors, we installed a row of windows along the tops.

Putting the floors in was a challenge. The barn sits on a slope, and we wanted, of course, to make the house as level as possible. We used broken glass insulators to fill in the low corner of what would be our bedroom. From one of the library books, Jerry had learned about the use of a water hose filled with water as a leveling tool: You lay the hose on the floor in various places, and wherever water spills out of the hose is a low spot, requiring more concrete mix. We carried on with this technique for hours one evening, alternately laughing and cursing at one another; as she usually did when she saw Jerry and me engaged in some long, incomprehensible enterprise, Leto went off and found a quiet, isolated place to sleep.

By the time we began installing the interior walls and ceiling, it was getting hot outside. Placing strips of glass wool insulation behind the wire matrix we had made to hold them in place was the most unpleasant part of building the house. We had to wear caps, masks, gloves, and long-sleeved shirts to protect ourselves from the fiberglass, and sweated profusely as we unrolled, cut to size, and slid the strips behind the wires. We covered the insulation, both walls, and ceiling with bamboo fencing from huge rolls that we had brought in from Tyler. When nailed to the ceiling crossbeams, the bamboo screens naturally sagged a little in places and gave the house a hut-like look by its undulations.

Again consulting library books and talking with the fellows at the feed and hardware store in Canton, Jerry installed the PVC plumbing and wired the house, acquiring a separate light meter so that we could keep track of the amount of electricity we used. We dug a deep trans-evaporation pit on the low east side of the house for wastewater, and we installed a self-contained anaerobic

toilet using a fifty-gallon watering trough and a marine
commode (fitted with a hand pump). We bought a French-
made water heater that runs on propane and comes
on only when a hot-water tap is open, and we put in a
five-burner stove, which we connected to the same gas
supply—two ten-gallon bottles, to be taken to Canton and
refilled as needed. An apartment-sized refrigerator and a
compact toaster/broiler oven gave us our independence
from Mrs. Hunt's kitchen.

Moving our furniture from Dallas to Canton was a
protracted ordeal. We made many trips—fifty miles each
way—using the pickup, covering our things as best we
could with plastic sheeting and an old tarp. It often rained
on us, and high winds would lift first one corner of the
tarp and then another, forcing us to pull over and retie the
cords. Leto made every trip with us; she would often stay
in the truck as though to be sure it didn't leave without
her. She must have been a little confused and disoriented by all the changes that were taking place around
her, particularly when we began carrying the furniture
away, slowly emptying all the rooms she'd lived in for over
ten years.

We temporarily stored some of our furniture in Mrs.
Hunt's house until we could finish flooring. The large,
central area of the barn that was to become our living
room was where we put the double bed. It looked strange
sitting there in the middle of the space, a nightstand on
either side and an ornate chandelier hanging above it. It
was a good place, though, to make love to celebrate the
beginning of a new chapter in our lives.

*
**

Losing Mother had been hard for Judy—her best
friend was gone. My new job and library school kept me
busy learning new things and gave me the opportunity to
meet people, but Judy was home-bound with three young
children and all the routine chores of caring for them.
I think of her now as it must have been for her then,
waking each day to reconfront her loss, feeling guilty for
being sad around those young spirits and a stubbornly
solicitous husband. And Mother's house, our family

home, was just up the street and being rented by strangers. It was probably a good thing for them all that Paul was able to arrange a transfer to an Army recruiting office in Wisconsin, where they moved in the spring of 1980. Before they left, they gave Jerry and me a maple tree to plant in front of our new home.

When Jerry and I made the decision to move to Canton, he was still teaching a night course at the University of Texas at Dallas, and I was working full-time—although I was permitted to work a four-day week. Thanks to an imaginative and understanding professor in library school, I earned credit for three courses through independent study: writing a long paper on the founder of the British Museum, Sir Anthony Panizzi, compiling an annotated bibliography of sources of information on vegetarianism (later published in *Vegetarian Times*), and evaluating the general reference collection of the library by compiling statistics of use. I much preferred gathering data on breaks and at lunch and typing late at night to driving the forty-five miles to Denton and back, even if it did mean carrying card files with me everywhere.

We needed a place to stay in Dallas, as a pied-à-terre, and I learned from Judy's and my realtor that the family that had been renting the house we jointly owned had fallen behind on their rent and would probably be moving. They did, in fact, leave in time for Jerry and me to bring furniture and other household goods by, as we left the house on Swiss. Then, as we finished areas of our house in Canton, we would move things there. Our goal was to be together as much as possible, to spend as many nights together as we could, in either Dallas or Canton, and we struggled with our schedules each week to accomplish that.

As I sit here now looking around this house we built, I realize that what I live in is an interactive environment Jerry created: it is, in fact, a piece, a work of art. All the interior walls, cabinets, and built-in shelves are made of particleboard and utility-grade pine, much of it heated with a propane torch to emphasize the grain and knots, revealing sometimes startling patterns and odd symmetries. Lengths of chain, parts of old tools, scraps of railway salvage are displayed everywhere, dimly glistening in their coat of polyurethane varnish. Moldings of varying shapes and sizes outline geometric figures, sometimes concealing seams but often merely serving as accents. One could walk through this house as one might a museum.

And yet, for all the antic, exuberantly artistic quality of the place, it boasts a practicality that seems defiantly primitive at times. To facilitate drainage, we mounted both the toilet and the shower stall several feet above floor level. When she saw the toilet, with all its ancillary hoses and pumps and valves, my elderly friend Marguerite exclaimed, "Oh, no!"—even though Jerry had very thoughtfully mounted a shovel handle in concrete beside the steps to steady the user. (When she lived with us, my niece Jamie made an intricate origami model of this toilet "throne" as a birthday card for Jerry.) Hooks suspend storage baskets and even shelves in many places, and the tile work in the bathroom and at the front door reflects in its unusual design the use of whatever materials were at hand at the time. When we got cats, Jerry cut triangular holes in the bottoms of three interior doors to enable them to move freely throughout the house; these holes can be playfully unexpected sources of light from the next room.

Our moving to Canton not only gave Jerry an outlet for his creativity and his nervous energy, but it also made possible more freedom from having to make money. All of this is conveyed in his letters to Jacqueline at the time:

> After some looking and thought we decided a CITY was too EXPENSIVE and that left only the property my parents own . . . so we went there in May after I returned from NY and built a house there, directly by hand (Stephen and I doing ALL of the work): the result has been for $3,000 . . . a HUMAN but high-tech SLUM or DUMP . . . the utility costs have been minimized . . . this means I do not have to work any more than I want to BY NOT USING ANY MONEY: by doing a job for money for commercial television for example, I can live a year without working again . . . this means finally that the biggest

> cost is technical, the computer gadgets & so forth . . . I am including some photos I hope with this so you can see what happened here, most have a reaction of shock, misery or laughter: that depends upon their relation to us. . . .

And from a later letter, the work continuing and the costs rising:

> This house building business an endless TERROR; we have produced now a combination BARN/TENT/ SHACK/BAMBOO THATCH HUT: the toilet system was a year's work, I still have fingers crossed, it is a kindness to the soil we think but a JOB to use: many PUMPS, THUMPINGS, ETC., makes you think every time you go for it, DO I NEED TO USE THIS NOW? OR CAN I WAIT? The odd part of course is living in the middle of construction work always, I am flooring in the bath now, starting on kitchen this week, and walking over and around tools, etc., to live . . . you do a little as you can afford . . . the goal here was to KEEP ALL COSTS SMALL: the entire effort has cost only about $4,000. . . .

The toilet, by the way, is still working fifteen years later. A watery effluent is conducted to a leach field not far from the house; the solid matter is digested by bacteria while suspended in the tank along hundreds of strips of cedar paling that Jerry pounded flat by hand.

*
**

Although we moved my much-traveled Magnavox stereo to the house on Ferguson Road, I wanted my books in Canton. The two rooms on the north side of the house were to be our studies; they are separated by a bamboo screen wall, with a small wood-framed door joining them.

To house my library, we built a ceiling-to-floor wall of shelves made of composite boards and supported by ten-inch lengths of the creosoted timber that once held the insulators for power lines. This wood, needless to say, is irregularly shaped.

The shelves finished, I began organizing my books on the study floor, intending to get them up in alphabetical order. Leto, of course, was with me, lying in a corner and resting, assured that I would be there a while. I filled the top three or four twelve-foot-long shelves, making it through "K" or "L" when, very slowly but ineluctably, the books and the shelves began falling forward. I tried to stop the collapse, but there was nothing I could do. Within less than a minute, I was sitting in the middle of the floor, surrounded by books and lumber.

Leto's reaction to this calamity puzzled me. Normally she would have come up to investigate, to check on me, and to nose among the rubble, curious to see what had gone wrong and how I would react. This time, though, she watched the little avalanche without stirring; when it was over, she got up and left the room. I found her later sleeping under the bed (still in the living room).

I think it was at about this time that we began to worry about her, and to watch her. We reminded ourselves of how much she had been through during the last several months, of the seemingly never-ending hauling of goods and changing of places. It would never have done to leave her: she made every trip with us, riding in the cab of Mr. Hunt's pickup (and sometimes needing help climbing into it).

Leto was eleven years old and had never been spayed. She stayed so close to us; we always felt we could prevent her mating; we reasoned that spaying her, subjecting her to the anesthesia and the surgery, would be to make her suffer for our convenience. One of the veterinarians we used did recommend it, pointing out that it sometimes prevented problems with the reproductive organs down the line, but we put it off and eventually did nothing.

All the moving and uncertainty, the sudden changes after a decade of carefully nurtured habits, may have weakened her immune system. We began to worry for sure when she started to go off by herself more and more.

Jerry was staying with me on Ferguson Road, and we agreed one morning that he would take her to the vet if she didn't perk up that day.

In the middle of the afternoon, Jerry called me where I was working in the general reference division. He had taken her to the vet and the news wasn't good: a uterine infection had developed into peritonitis; surgery would give her a fifty-fifty chance of surviving, but without it, she would die very soon (she was already unconscious). I told my boss, Wayne, that I had to go, that this dog was very important to me, and I left the ringing telephones to rush across town.

By the time I got there, the surgery had been done. The vet took Jerry and me over to a basin to show us the infected tissue and organs he had removed. We stared at it all blindly. I think now that he had seen what losing her would mean to us, and this demonstration was his way of suggesting that the loss was likely. The question was if she'd make it through the night.

We lay in bed waiting for daybreak and drove to the clinic, arriving just as it opened. The kennel attendant went to check on Leto; she was gone too long—in fact, she never returned. In a few minutes, the vet drove up, went back, and came out to tell us that Leto had died in the night.

Jerry and I walked outside and sat on the edge of the brick planter, crying. We were there a good while. No one bothered us. Finally, we went back in, paid our bill, and asked for Leto. We took her to the house on Ferguson, where I wrapped her in a gold thermal blanket Mother had given me, and after Jerry called his mother with the news, we started out to Canton, Jerry driving the pickup and Leto in my lap.

Mrs. Hunt met us as we turned to head over toward our house. She walked in with us and helped me put Leto down on the bed beneath the chandelier. We combed her fur around the bandage as best we could and then rewrapped her in the blanket.

Jerry and I went to town to buy white pine for her coffin, asking the yardman to cut the boards in the dimensions Jerry had devised. We returned, made the coffin, put Leto in it, and nailed the top on, and then we dug the grave beneath the post oak tree where the drive-way divides. Hermie and Sassie and two of their pups had been buried there years ago.

We covered the coffin with earth and found a large, animal-shaped stone that we used to mark the grave. I later had a brass plate engraved with these lines from Hesiod's Theogony:

Leto . . . a sweet (goddess) always . . .
Sweet from the beginning, the gentlest of
    all who dwell on Olympos.

The trophy shop charged extra for all the Greek ("We usually just do fraternities," the man told me). After we had stood at her grave a while, Jerry, his mother, and I went over to her house. We began remembering incidents in Leto's life, in our life with her—how she'd howl when Jerry and I left her, how spoiled she was. Jerry reminded me of the time she bit the boot of the man who'd come to talk with Mother and me about reroofing her house. "Well, she doesn't like boots," I'd said. Then there was the famous story of how she ate a wing off Jerry's banquet bird.

And we recalled that sweltering day at Mesa Verde. This was on the trip we made with Mrs. Hunt, and we had all four arrived at the park very thirsty. We stood forever in a long line, waiting our turn to drink from the public fountain. As we got closer, we heard parents telling their drinking children to hurry up, that there were people waiting.

Our turn finally came. Mrs. Hunt drank, then Jerry, then I, and while he held the valve open, I cupped my hands and filled them with water for Leto. I heard someone say down the line, "Look! They've got a dog up there. We're waiting on a dog!"

*
**

Shortly after I received my degree in library science, I began to work for the Humanities Division of the library. I was given the responsibility of selecting materials in classical literature and literary biography, as well as literary theory and minor European and Eastern literature. This was the goal I had been working toward, and I derived a great deal of satisfaction and had a lot of fun in building and maintaining collections that had traditionally been strong in the library and that were of personal interest to me.

This was the library's golden age, we all realize now.

Generous endowments and strong municipal support meant that we could aspire to be a research library for the city, and as a selector, I was told by my new boss, Frances Bell, that I could order anything we needed. Using a bibliography on cards of Greek and Latin authors that I had prepared as a library school project, I set out to be sure that the library owned texts, commentaries, and translations for the major authors and their works, with representative critical support. The job was made for me; I was being paid to do what I would have done anyway: reading literary reviews and articles and exploring the library.

Dallas's new Central Research Library was opened in 1982, and Humanities moved onto the largest floor (an acre in size). In the old building—the building Jerry and I had grown up using—we had had to place plastic sheeting above some shelves due to a badly leaking roof. We were now in a magnificent new ten-level building, and we were eager to show it and our state-of-the-art online catalog off to the public and to other librarians. When Dallas hosted the American Library Association's annual convention, a reception was held on my floor that spilled out onto the spacious balcony overlooking the new city hall across the street. We were the envy of the profession.

I made several friends at the library who remain close today: Frances (and her friend, Drew), Marsha (later to marry Evan), and Jim (whose friend, Dick, was later to relocate to Dallas after a library career in Montana, and share a house with him). As the coordinator of the Writers Study Room in our division, I met several interesting people during the ensuing years, one of whom, Eileen (with her friend, Marie), has become very dear to me.

As active and as fulfilling as were my days in the library, my nights in the sparsely furnished house on Ferguson Road were lonely. I wanted to be in Canton, but I couldn't justify adding two hours of commuting time (not to mention the expense) to my workday. So I went home, often picking up a pizza on my way, and settled sadly into an evening of desultory reading, listening to music, and . . . drinking.

One night I listened to a recording of Hermann Prey singing Carl Loewe ballads. I had had a few glasses of sherry—one or two beyond the usual number that put me in a "mellow" mood. Unaccountably, I developed a craving for buttermilk, so I decided to run to a convenience store not far away and pick up some to have before bedtime. As I drove, I was vaguely aware about the need for me to be very careful—to be sure to come to full stops and look in every direction before going through intersections.

I suppose I was a little too careful. The officer who stopped me asked me to recite the alphabet. I got bogged down at "P" and "Q," so he took me to the station for a breathalyzer test, which I almost passed. I spent the night in jail sleeping it off.

The worst part of one's first night in jail is the morning after. I was finally allowed to call a bail bondsman, and I telephoned Frances at work to explain my absence by telling her I was sick but that I now had medicine and was getting better. In my shame, I was hoping to get through the experience without anyone knowing what I had done.

The bondsman provided transportation, and we stopped by the house on Ferguson for me to get my checkbook. Jerry drove up, Frances having called him, worried, before she'd heard from me.

(I later learned that Ron, the assistant manager of the division, had driven out that morning to check on me— had even forced the garage door open only to discover I wasn't there.) Jerry followed us to the bond office, and then he took me to get my impounded car. When I finally got to work, I arrived at a very busy time at the service desk. I immediately began helping a patron using the computer terminal. Frances walked over to me and very gently squeezed my arm. It was a while before Jerry and I talked about the incident.

I had to admit that I had had a drinking problem before, during the last year at Cistercian. He had never suspected, probably because I drank late at night and always went to bed long before he did. We realized things had to change, that our separated life wasn't good for either one of us. Living so close to his mother, just the two of them alone so often, Jerry felt that he had in a sense returned to his childhood. In the letter he wrote to Jacqueline telling her about Leto's death, he said:

> This changed so much that it is as if a block of life is over, she was so much a centralizer for this time. No more dogs for a time though, & this leaves, in theory, some freedom to travel and so forth, but then OTHER TIES, so there you are, same BUCKET, same water.

Just talking about it helped, as it always did. Until we could figure out how to solve the problem, we made an effort to spend more time together. Jerry drove in to spend the night more often, and I took vacation days here and there to give us several consecutive days together in Canton.

And Fate brought us another "centralizer"—two, in fact. I drove out one weekend to find Jerry standing at the front door of our barn house with tiny kittens sitting on each of his size-12D feet. Their mother, we surmised, had been killed on the highway, and the little creatures had made their way down the hill to our house. They had gotten his attention, Jerry said, by mewing loudly; one of them, whom Jerry later named Frances (not after my boss), had climbed the screen door to make her screams better heard.

Jerry told the story of his first few days with Frances and Mary often. He had never had cats and didn't particularly like them, and he was determined that they would stay outside. He gave them some milk and scrambled eggs, and he built a little shelter for them out of scrap lumber. It was by no means certain they could even stay.

The next day a thunderstorm passed over, and Jerry realized their shelter was leaking when he heard Frances caterwauling pitifully and climbing up the screen door again. He let them in ("little drowned rats")—and they've never left the house again, these thirteen years, except on leashes.

Living with frisky kittens is a challenge, and Jerry had to deal with it pretty much by himself. They explored their new home thoroughly, knocking things over on shelves, rummaging through drawers accidentally left open, spreading books and papers around on desks, and sometimes pushing everything off onto the floor. Jerry's electronic equipment, with its levers, knobs, and patch cords, was a special fascination for them. And feeding them turned out to be a problem: the vet told us they had probably not been weaned, so we had to mix up queen's milk for them (thereby, thankfully, putting an end to their vomiting and diarrhea).

We were lying in bed one night during their third or fourth week with us, and Mary and Frances were running wildly across the sheets, hissing at one another in play, and continually snagging the bedclothes with their scimitarlike claws. From time to time, they'd run across one of us, leaving a sharp pain in the place they'd used as a launching pad. "That's it," Jerry finally said. "I'm gonna drown 'em in the tank." And he got up to do so.

I lay there without saying a thing, thinking, "If he does it, he does it"; after all, they were mostly Jerry's burden. I don't know for sure what Jerry did. I heard noises in the kitchen among the paper sacks, and I heard yelling. In a few minutes, the cats settled down and came to bed, where they slept together at the foot. Jerry soon joined us.

When my brother-in-law retired from the Army, he and Judy returned to Dallas to live in the Ferguson Roadhouse. I rented an efficiency apartment for the nights I stayed in town, and Jerry brought Mary and Frances in with him when he came to spend a night or two with me.

The cats soon grew accustomed to our cars.

Frances, always the more adventurous, liked to ride sitting on the flat headrests of my (Mother's old) Nova; Mary's spot was on the floor in front of the passenger seat. In his VW, Jerry usually held Frances to keep her from roaming and jumping back and forth across the seats. It was hilarious to see him start out, looking so serious and with a little kitten staring out the side window, her head just visible above the sill. I expect we entertained a lot of people on the road—especially when we all four traveled together, as we preferred to do.

*
**

We invited our Dallas friends out to have dinner with us in the country, but we didn't see people as often as we had when we lived in the city. One reason for this was our ever-present need to do chores: something had to be done to the house, or it was time to do yard work. I dug a garden on the south side of the house where I planted the rose bushes I had brought from Swiss Avenue; each year, I added vegetables and herbs, and the larger the garden grew, the more time it required.

Our friends' lives were changing too. Jerry's sometimes associates were staying busy with their own work and personal lives: Phil had gone through a divorce and was seeing another person, Joyce; Gordon had taken a job in Colorado Springs, and he and Mary were later to move to Portland, Oregon, where they adopted a daughter; and David and Ann were kept occupied by two teenagers at home.

We did have dinner with Houston and Jill in Dallas on a fairly regular basis, and Douglas and Avalon almost always joined us. Houston and Jill had bought a beautiful home in North Dallas, and their son, Patrick, was attending St. Mark's. One evening in Jill's elegant dining room, Jerry embarrassed himself and amused us all by helping himself to so much soup that the tureen had to be returned to him for a refill before it could finish its journey around the table. At Douglas and Avalon's home in Garland, we were once treated to a concert after dinner on the two grand pianos in their living room—our hosts played Rachmaninoff's Suite No. 2.

Our friends Paul and Oz took us to dinner every couple of months, and they continued inviting Jerry to give concert-lectures almost every fall.

One year, Jerry offered a tribute to his mother ("At Long Last"), thanking her publicly for all her and Mr. Hunt's support over the years. She ate so many macaroons and drank so much sherry—on an empty, nervous stomach—that she was sick on the side of the road during her and Jerry's trip home.

Shortly after we had moved to Canton, my Houston friend Lillian died. She had been diagnosed with lung cancer a year earlier, and radiation and chemotherapy had not been able to prevent metastasis. I spoke with her a few times on the phone, and she asked me to send her some Westerns because she didn't feel like reading anything else. She'd spent a decade teaching philosophy at Auburn and had shared her home with a younger lady, Elizabeth, for several of those years.

When her son called me from Houston (where she had been taken to a nursing home) to let me know about her death, I told him that we had been regular correspondents for almost fifteen years and that I had hundreds of her wonderful letters I'd be happy to share with him whenever he might like. I never heard from him, and it's probably just as well. Lillian was a very private person, and I doubt she ever told her son or her mother (who outlived her) that she was gay. If I'm right, I hope she destroyed my letters to her.

*
**

As often as I could, I traveled with Jerry to the concerts he gave. In the early years, we could fill a car with all he needed to perform: speakers, monitors, amplifiers, power supplies, synthesizers, tape recorders, and various electronic keyboards and other devices—not to mention props. Technological advances in the early '80s reduced some of the weight and quantity of what he needed, and not only was traveling easier but also Jerry was better able to realize his work. He kept up with new technology and continued to serve as a consultant to audio engineers; he was one of the early owners of the Amiga computer and a big fan of its sound and image capabilities.

Never, though, did he become a techno-freak—far from it. In a letter to Jacqueline, he wrote:

> Do you still work with computing machines?
> The technical inevitable in music can and has bred hateful resentment; it has all become incredibly costly overall, in time, patience, money, etc. The more

> complicated all of it gets, the cruder
> it all seems to become, with a slick
> surface to shield this reality sense at
> the last until you see the ghost has
> gone out of it, or never was there in the
> first place . . .

I'm sure Jerry appreciated the irony of using the computer to store and manipulate the arcane magical symbols he used in his compositions. Perhaps this was his way of keeping the ghost in the machine.

The theatrical element of his work, present from the beginning, gradually narrowed in focus. A videotape of his 1982 performance in Dallas with Sally Bowden dancing records the large movements and gestures (he stomped across the space wearing the heavy wood and metal boots he had made) that characterize earlier work. In subsequent performances, he scaled down his onstage activities, calling the audience's attention to small objects he often held up on sticks. Very frequently, these objects could simultaneously be seen moving on video monitors. He began traveling with his own lights, a collection of bulbs of various sizes and colors that he mounted on poles and held by hand, often using these individual lights in a dim space to illuminate objects or gestures or even facial expressions.

What came to matter more and more, both to him and to his audiences, was Jerry's own apparent relation to what he was doing, the significance he seemed to place on his actions. He once referred to the objects he used as "lightning rods of attention."

I have seen him enthrall audiences by simple movements of his body, movements that convey some magical meaning that is heightened by the music and the video and the lighting. Reviewing a 1983 concert at the Kitchen for the *New York Times*, John Rockwell wrote that Jerry's performance "resembled that of some highly nervous witch doctor . . . The result was wearing, but curiously appealing, too."

He was invited to participate in the San Antonio Festival in the spring of 1983, where the *Express-News* critic Mike Greenberg described *Ground* as "extraordinary . . . compelling, altogether magical" in a review from May of that year:

> The music is a series of continuous tapes, variously containing roars, brutal march rhythms, chirpings and poundings, of gathering and waning intensity. While this is coming out of the loudspeakers, Hunt himself is on the dimly lighted stage going through 'an action flood of theatrical-mimetic exercise' with canes, rattles, sticks slammed against suit-cases, electric torches, an artificial hand on a stick, a tambourine and an assortment of unnameable but clearly magical instruments [implements] . . . I was bowled over by what I saw and heard.

Critics responded to 1984 performances with the same mixture of bafflement and awe. Patrick Lysaght described Jerry's appearance at the New Music America annual festival in Hartford, Connecticut, as the "one show [that] stood out among the virtuosi . . . His interplay with vibration-sensing electronic sound selection was fresh and unprecedented." And John Santos wrote of Jerry's San Antonio Festival concert that year that it was "enigmatic but powerful . . . the centerpiece of the evening."

I attended these concerts and watched the effect Jerry and his work had on people. As he finished the last-minute preparations, he would chat pleasantly with the audience, inviting people to come and go as they wished during the performance. Those who had never seen or heard him were invariably startled by the intensity of his work, coming as it did after the modest, even self-deprecating comments he made at the start. A few outraged individuals would leave early on. Most of those who stayed came up to meet him or visit with him after the concert, perhaps counting on him to bring them back to earth just as he had transported them.

His sense of humor was an integral part of his work. Although he never smiled or laughed at anything that happened during a work, audiences felt free to laugh (perhaps they simply couldn't help it) at odd coincidences or outlandish behavior. This element of fun intensified the drama, making the work even more moving.

It often appeared that Jerry had been possessed by forces beyond his control; this created tension and laughter served to relieve that tension. Jerry exhausted his audiences.

I watched Jerry just as any member of the audience would, but also as someone more closely related to him, more intimate. My own bafflement and awe had a personal dimension. When he began performing, I felt him leave me, leave that comfortable plane we dwelled on together. Of course, I was affected, was moved in much the same way others were, but I was also a little chilled, a little lonely. It was obvious to me that when he was on stage and realizing his work, Jerry was more alive and more fulfilled than he ever was elsewhere (with the possible exception of when he was making love). I would wait, on the periphery, for the people who had come up to visit with Jerry to leave the stage, and then I would help him pack his gear and load the car. It was a pleasure to share his exhilaration and sense of satisfaction to the extent I could, but, as we would drive away, I would already be looking forward to having him return to me from wherever he had been.

*
**

When the opportunity arose, in the fall of 1984, for me to take a permanent part-time job with the library, I jumped at the chance—but not because the work had become unsatisfying. In addition to seeing the Humanities collection widen and deepen, I was participating in the library's user-education program by meeting high school and college classes, orienting them to our division, and showing them how to take advantage of its research capabilities. And I very much enjoyed the people I worked with, as well as other friends I had made elsewhere in the library. I took the part-time job because I had come to love being in the country, and I wanted to spend more time there with Jerry.

Frances and I devised a regular work schedule that has remained pretty much the same for almost eleven years: I work two full days (Saturdays and Mondays) and a half-day (Sunday) each week. My selection responsibilities were reduced somewhat, but I continue reading reviews and buying materials in the subject areas that interest me most. I spend about half my time answering reference questions at the service desk.

For several years, I spent Saturday nights with Marguerite, the lady whom Mother went to school with and who lives on Ferguson Road across from our old house. I attended Dallas Symphony Orchestra concerts or went to movies or plays with friends, and thanks to Marguerite's hospitality, I was spared a long drive home. Eventually, though, as I lost interest in the symphony and its predictable scheduling of crowd-pleasers, I began driving home every night.

Jerry and I were able to travel together more due to my abbreviated schedule. With four consecutive days off each week, we could visit our friends Bob and Rany in Houston, taking Mary and Frances with us in their separate kennels for the four-hour ride each way. I had begun to teach myself how to swim, and Bob and Rany's pool was an excellent place to practice—far better, if less picturesque, than Paradise Bay of Cedar Creek Lake, on whose shores I'd lay my library books, opened to the diagram of whatever stroke I was working on that day. Bob and Jerry spent a lot of time at the piano; in addition to sharing their enthusiasm for music, Jerry was helping Bob, who had begun taking lessons again, with technique. We kept our cats and their dogs separated, although there was frequently attempted trafficking beneath the doors, particularly between Frances and their schnauzer, Battery.

The cats had the run of the living room and dining room, and Jerry and I slept together under Bob's Steinway on a pallet or in a sleeping bag I had bought for the purpose. Bob and Jerry stayed up late talking and watching television and videos in the study adjacent to the living room. The cats and I turned in around midnight, Frances in an armchair and Mary in the piano. Jerry would join me around two or three under the piano—a good time, and traditionally a good place, for lovemaking.

Sometimes we'd leave Mary and Frances with Bob and Rany and drive down the coast to spend a couple of nights with Peggy and George in Corpus. One year, Jerry kept the cats in Houston while Bob, Rany, and I and their dogs visited Big Bend National Park. Houston became a second home for us, a pleasant place to visit not only for the companionship of our friends but also for the sake of the city itself—the variety of vegetarian restaurants and ethnic food stores, the films and concerts, and the beauty of the lush landscape, with its semitropical flavor. And Bob's willingness to look after Mary and Frances meant that Jerry and I could leave them there while traveling to New York and, later, Holland. A couple of times we were able to return the favor by looking after Battery and Vinci while Bob and Rany traveled.

Our routine at home settled into a comfortable pace and rhythm. I worked outside most mornings, often taking the cats out with me on their leashes. Jerry slept late; when he awoke, we would run errands in Canton, Tyler, or (less frequently) Dallas. We'd prepare a large evening meal and go for a walk afterward, coffee mugs in hand. Then we'd return and settle into the evening's activities: reading, writing letters, or listening to music for me, and composing, making commercial music, or writing letters for Jerry. Since our studies were separated only by a bamboo screen (with a wall of bookshelves against it), we had to use headphones and earplugs—that is, *I* used earplugs.

At some point every day, Jerry would go over to visit with his mother in her house on the other side of the grove of post oak trees. We ate dinner with her one or two nights a week. She kept busy with club activities, and she regularly had several ladies she used to work with in Dallas out to spend the day. As long as she was able, she managed her own affairs and looked after her property— even mowing her own lawn with the Ford yard tractor she bought, protected from the sun by a large straw hat and skin cream.

One day when I came home from swimming in the Cedar Creek Lake, Jerry told me he had just heard on the radio that open bodies of water in Texas were no longer safe for regular swimming: "Look at your feet—they're green!" he pointed out. I wrote the state government to see just what the risk might be, and I received a letter explaining that, indeed, it was not recommended to swim more than occasionally in any Texas lake because of pollution from the chemicals used in agriculture. To tell the truth, I had begun to worry about exposure to the sun anyway.

I located an indoor pool at the Cain Center in Athens (a community athletic center with a YMCA office on the premises), and I began going there to swim one day a week. Jerry would often go with me, visiting the Radio Shack or shopping at Wal-Mart while I swam. There was never any question of his joining me: he had always hated the water ("Swimming is unnatural," he'd say time and again, as though I'd never heard it before) from the time when his parents had taken him to Galveston as a little boy and he first stuck his toes in the "slimy liquid."

In the late afternoons, I had begun riding a bike along the country roads near our house. I usually followed a circular route, taking me by several old cemeteries, a wild game preserve, and past fields of cows, sheep, and goats. Thinking I might persuade him to join me, I bought a used racing bike for Jerry. He had stopped lifting weights, and he agreed that he needed some exercise.

He made three trips out with me. We didn't go far or fast; I didn't want to discourage him. I felt certain that he would come to enjoy biking if he could just build up a little strength in his legs and a little stamina. I was wrong, decidedly—he complained of the heat and the hills, the gnats, and the mosquitoes.

Something in the air was affecting his allergies. And the farm dogs that playfully chased us alarmed him.

On our last trip, my patience wore thin with his whining, his litany of complaints. He began bitching about how his trouser cuffs (he refused to wear shorts in public) were always getting caught under the chain guard, so I offered to switch bikes. Now the seat was too hard, the handlebars too low.

I blew up. We turned around, and I pedaled home on his bike as fast as I could. When I got to our gate, I threw the racing bike over the barbed wire fence and rode it across the fields to the tank . . . where I pushed it in. It's still there today, as far as I know.

Of course, I realize now that he already had diminished lung function due to smoking; he simply couldn't breathe well enough to ride a bike for any distance. Even at that time, in the mid-'80s, he was talking about smoking less ("not quitting—that would be too extreme"), and he had begun to chew Nicorette to the point of irritating the mucous membranes in his mouth.

So nothing more was said about bike riding. I continued going out alone. But we kept up our after-dinner walks, I am glad to say. One July evening, we crossed the little creek north of the property, and when we reached the top of the rise beyond, we were surprised to see the valley to the east filled with lightning bugs. We stood a long time, marveling at the spectacle of the thousands of blinking lights. It was good to know that these insects were coming back with the reduction of the use of chemical pesticides. They reminded us both of our childhood.

There was little, generally, about the outdoor world that interested Jerry. We'd drive along, and I'd point out a field of wine-cups or prairie phlox; he'd look, dutifully, but never stop talking. He'd sometimes mock me when I was in one of my demonstrative moods by pointing this way and that with both hands (once to the amusement of the people in the car behind us). Only animals really captured his attention: the stately Brahman cattle with their odd humps, a hillside of goats, or the symmetrically marked calf or pony.

Vultures did fascinate him, though—the turkey vultures that are commonly seen circling in the Texas sky or removing roadkill from the highways. "Hell chickens," he called them. We'd drive along and startle a group gathered around the body of an armadillo or a dog, and Jerry would call out: "Tasty, girls? Dead yet?" Another bird he loved to see was the heron; he often called my attention to one flying overhead, heading back to Cedar Creek Lake at sunset, its long legs trailing behind it, feet tight together.

A goose came to live with us one summer, bringing a pair of mallards with him. We had never seen geese or ducks around the tank on our property because it is too close to the highway.

These birds came from our neighbor's tank—and, after the summer in question, we saw no more. Jerry took a serious interest in the goose, who marshaled his ducks around the yard and looked out for them when they slept.

For several weeks they spent their days with us, leaving to go to the tank only at sunset. I had just planted a Shumard oak in the backyard, and when I filled the circular bed around the base of the tree with water every other day, the ducks would hop in and swim enthusiastically. The goose strutted along the perimeter, squawking now and then and keeping an eye out for trouble. The way he lifted his head and turned it to fix a seemingly vigilant gaze in the distance conveyed a sense of concerned disapproval: "These silly ducks will swim."

Jerry caught that look and added it to his repertoire. Whenever I would say something foolish or presumptuous, he would lift and turn his head just like the goose, fixing me with one widely opened eye. It always made its point, and he kept it up for years.

As did his mother, Jerry loved meteor showers, so dramatic in the August night sky. We used to stay up late and watch them when, as boys, we'd spend the night together. As it happened, they were especially dramatic during Jerry's last August. I put a butterfly chair on the front porch for him, and we sat there together for over an hour, exclaiming at the brightness of the meteors and at the length of their incandescent trajectories.

"Not now"— "Just leave them out, I'll look at them later"— "Let me get a cigarette first": these were some of Jerry's usual responses to my suggestion that we look at pictures together. And as we traveled, he didn't try to hide his impatience whenever I stopped to take a picture. In the five large ring binders containing the hundreds of photographs I took over the years, there are more than a few of Jerry looking at me behind the camera (while he holds his glasses), his eyes saying, *Come on, get it over with.*

When I'd prevail, we'd sit for a few minutes riffling through stacks of recently made prints or turning the pages of an album, and I always realized he was indulging me. He rarely commented on individual pictures, and he had no questions about exact locations or vantage points. He'd often look away, his impatience becoming more and more apparent. When we'd gone through the lot, he'd jump up and hurry off elsewhere, his duty done.

It was the same with reminiscing. Whenever his mother or I would tell stories from the past, recalling relatives or friends and incidents, Jerry would pay little attention and change the subject as soon as his forbearance allowed him to. He shifted the conversation back to the present, to his current preoccupations, or to the immediate future, to plans for things ahead.

As much as I would like to be able to imagine him with me now looking at these pictures from the mid-'80s, I cannot do it. It may be just as well: alone, and without the tug of his resistance, I can journey so effortlessly into the black-bordered rectangles of sunlight or shadows. I can stand before a New York City bar with three names and an enormous replica of Miss Liberty's crown on its roof; or sit in Mark and Alan's Philadelphia apartment and laugh while Alan puts a pair of glasses on their dog Jake's nose; or gaze at a bundled-up Jerry standing in the courtyard of Santa Fe's Palace of the Governors as the record twenty-inch snowfall commenced.

And so it was with reviews. Jerry never made any effort to find them (I'd do that at the library). When I brought them home or when others sent them to him, Jerry would sometimes give them a cursory glance, but usually he'd put them on a shelf out of his way and comment that he'd read them later. Only when he had to collect several to include in a grant proposal or for publicity purposes would he give them any substantial attention.

Of course, favorable criticism pleased him, but he often told me even *that* failed to convey what it was he thought he was doing. I sometimes joked that he was afraid of being "nailed."

The best reviews, he agreed, were the descriptive ones. But as it was with photographs, so it was with reviews: they're all from the past and of scant relevance to today or tomorrow—time traps for the self-indulgent, the unwary.

What would he think of me now, turning the pages of a photo album or rereading the reviews I've carefully put in chronological order? Had he been left, would he have done the same with my papers and mementos? As far as I knew, he never even reread a book unless it was to review information. It is hard for me to imagine him setting out to lose himself in reverie. Come to think of it, that was always his objection to alcohol—that you lose control of yourself and your steady hold on time. I engage my imagination to evoke events, faces, and feelings; the images Jerry made were mostly in the service of his art, and for him that was more than enough.

What years these were, though. The budget crisis that was to cut funding for the library so severely had not yet come. I spent three days a week selecting books and assisting patrons joining in the life of our magnificent new research library. Judy and her family had moved back to Dallas, and they were now living in our old home on Ferguson Road. I enjoyed spending time with my nieces and nephew, taking them out for an afternoon in turns, going to playgrounds, the movies, and malls. Sometimes Jerry accompanied us as we rambled along creek beds, raided a dumpster behind a department store, and sat and swung. He intrigued the kids because he insisted on talking with them as though they were adults. They called him "Uncle Jerry."

*
**

Twice in 1985, Jerry performed in New York. In February, he appeared in the Brooklyn Academy of Music's "Meet the Moderns" series. Sharon Cucinotta described Jerry's piece for the *Brooklyn Phoenix* in a February 28, 1985 review.

> Most exciting, however, was composer Jerry Hunt's Cyra—an eye-opener of intense originality—scored for chamber

orchestra, electronics, accordion and performer.

As the musicians were ostensibly tuning up, a disoriented individual ambled into the theater stalking the space between audience and orchestra. As the orchestra began the formal piece, this person beamed lights into faces, stamped his feet, and spit hostile whispers into the audience.

Of course, this person was Jerry Hunt, gangly and spectacular in his uninhibited antics.

Because of this added dimension of participation, there was palpable energy from the orchestra. The score, dense and driving, blended well with the electronics. A coda pitted Hunt on a percussion suitcase with tambourine against accordionist Guy Klucevsek. Klucevsek succeeded in chasing the composer off the stage.

Whenever Jerry went to New York, he stayed with Sally Bowden—our dancer friend from Swiss Avenue days—and her husband, Ted. They occupied two adjacent rent-controlled apartments on the Lower East Side, within easy walking distance of both SoHo and the Village. Sally was teaching dance as a guest artist in various schools around the country. When her work brought her to Dallas, we were able to spend time with her and renew the friendship, which had now gone back a decade.

In the summer of 1985, Sally, Ted, and their little daughter Nora visited us in Canton. I had just prepared the earth beneath the gazebo (which we had built from a mail-order kit) for planting St. Augustine grass, and Nora and Ted had a good time playing in the shade, turning over the freshly dug dirt, all three of their New Yorker faces looking pale in the pictures I took.

That July, I continued a tradition I had begun several years earlier of going to Santa Fe to attend concerts in their chamber music series. I celebrated a private homecoming by visiting St. John's, walking the routes through the grounds and the buildings that brought back memories from twenty years earlier. I had long since lost touch with Bob Davis, and—with the exception of an on-again, off-again correspondence with Hugo—I had no more contact with the friends I made there.

From my lodging at the Galisteo Inn near Lamy, I drove to Las Vegas, to Chama (where I rode the Cumbres and Toltec Scenic Railway), and to Taos via the High Road. Most evenings took me into Santa Fe for music; a highlight was hearing the then relatively unknown Jean-Yves Thibaudet perform in the Dohnanyi Piano Quintet in C minor. Mornings I spent reading Paul Scott's *Raj Quartet* after a good swim in the inn's lap pool.

In an unusual symmetry, soon after our separate trips to New York and Santa Fe, we were to travel together to both destinations. Our 1985 fall vacation was planned around concerts Jerry was to give in Buffalo and at Roulette in New York City.

On our drive east, we stopped in Philadelphia to visit with my ex-student and friend Mark—the same fellow who used to stand at the head of the stairs at Cistercian, waiting for me to arrive.

Mark and I had kept up a regular correspondence ever since he graduated, the year before my last at Cistercian. Although several of my ex-students came by the library from time to time to say hello, Mark is the only one with whom I have grown close. He studied French and theology in college and, for a time, contemplated entering the priesthood. He ultimately settled on law and took his degree at NYU. After graduation, he moved to Philadelphia with his friend, Alan, who enrolled there in rabbinical school.

Spending several days with Mark and Alan in their apartment, with their dog and cat, and their bikes on the front porch, with their energy and unconcealed affection for one another, gave Jerry and me plenty to talk and think about. Of the two gay couples Jerry and I had gotten to know well, Bob and Rany had always kept pretty much to themselves. But Mark and Alan appeared to represent a new generation of homosexuals who maintained political awareness of gay rights issues and who were determined to be open and candid about their sexual orientation in their everyday lives. Moreover, each man was committed to social work to some degree: Mark, as a teacher of para-legal studies, frequently discussed the law in relation to gay issues, and Alan was preparing to be an openly gay rabbi in a synagogue welcoming homosexual Jews. We had to admit that Mark and Alan made us feel a little stodgy—and even a little selfish.

*
**

Every place we stayed on that trip east was upstairs, and that meant lugging the Emulator synthesizer, other electronic equipment, and various percussion devices (including the battered Samsonite suitcase) up narrow stairways so that we could protect them in our room. Jerry sometimes had a little work to do on the equipment, repairing or readjusting things in preparation for the next concert. We recreated a homelike environment wherever we went, setting up cooking facilities, doing our daily laundry, and each of us arranging his study corner for reading (and, in my case, writing letters).

The equipment also posed a problem en route, and this was exacerbated by the rental car we drove. There were no intermediate-sized automobiles available when we went to pick up a car for our three-week trip, so they "upgraded" us to a sporty blue Camaro with very little storage space. The car drew attention wherever we went, and Jerry and I got a kick out of the spectacle of the two of us tooling around the country in such a sexy car.

However, the amusement ended in New York City. Parking on the streets there is a challenge: for years, we had watched Sally and Ted move their car daily from one side of the street to the other to comply with the regula-tions designed to prevent long-term storage of vehicles on the street. One afternoon, I drove Jerry uptown for a meeting and let him out. We arranged to meet at The New School in the Village a few hours later. I drove back downtown and began the block-by-block search for an empty space, listening to Prokofiev's *Overture on Hebrew Themes* on the Camaro's fancy radio and thinking what a pleasure it was to be in the Big Apple again.

Finally, I found a place in front of a bodega—a little farther east than I would have liked, but still within walking distance of the Village. The men loitering in front of the store did seem to be impressed by the car, I later, embarrassingly, admitted.

After doing a little shopping in the book and record stores near NYU, I met Jerry at the New School, where we had coffee and pastries in the cafeteria. We walked across town to where I had left the car, got in, and started the engine . . . but the car wouldn't move. "We're not going anywhere," Jerry said dismally.

I got out to investigate and discovered to my eternal shame that both rear wheels had been stolen—the axle left sitting on cinder blocks. A couple of the loiterers walked over to commiserate with us.

We locked the car and walked to Sally and Ted's apartment and told them what had happened. Sally was disappointed that her careful efforts to instruct us in where you go and don't go in the Lower East Side had failed. I had, of course, to take all the blame. I said I had been lulled by Prokofiev into a false sense of security. Jerry put it more succinctly: "He left the Camaro at the corner of Rape and Dope Streets."

Finding a tow truck whose driver would even go into that area was not easy. I did all the calling while Jerry and Sally smoked and paced. I finally located a driver in Queens who agreed to help us, and he picked Jerry and me up in front of Sally and Ted's for the short ride to the wrong side of town. The driver happened to pass a police car on our way; he pulled over and asked if the officers would escort us to the Camaro, and they agreed readily. The car was towed to Queens for new wheels and tires, and while we waited, Jerry and I reminisced, a little forlornly, about our last visit to that borough when Jerry had helped Bob choose his Steinway at the factory there.

A couple of hours later, the Camaro sat parked across the street from Sally and Ted's, easily visible from their front windows. We kept it under watch and ward until Jerry's concert was over, and we could leave town. It would have been too much to have to submit a second insurance claim.

The October 5 concert at Roulette received what I consider to be one of the best reviews Jerry ever got. Linda Sanders, in her October 22 Soundings column for the *Village Voice*, wrote:

> I've only seen him perform once before, and his towering oddity knocked me out. He's got the magnetism of a Bible Belt preacher or a snake-oil salesman. With electronic music blaring in the background, he'll attach metal claws to his feet and stomp and scrape around the room. Or he'll wave a pole, to which is attached some indescribable glop that rattles.
>
> He does all this with such a serene lack of self-consciousness, it's like watching him putter around in the garage.
>
> This time, though, the lights went down and an eerie tape came on, and off to the side there was a video that showed spectral color images.
>
> It seemed like some kind of ritual. At first, he kept things merely fascinating, as he placed a crystal goblet on a table and waved around lights and wands that presumably triggered changes in the electronics. But then the music started getting louder, the room seemed darker, and the poles started looking phallic.
>
> Things got seriously spooky, and when he looked up to (through?) the ceiling and began to yell 'COME ON DOWN!' I started wondering whether I was cut out for this line of work. Fortunately, nobody or nothing showed up, and Hunt continued the performance in a more rational manner, if you call lying inside a wooden outline of a coffin normal.

*
**

I had always wanted to see Niagara Falls. There is something very appealing to me about traditional American tourist destinations that are no longer fashionable: the Borscht Belt, the Adirondacks, and Niagara Falls now serve as nostalgic links to the past, evoking by means of their dilapidated grand hotels, pokey amusement parks, and kitschy souvenirs a time when travel, and pleasure, were defined differently. The natural beauty that originally inspired these vacation spots mostly remains and is all the more prominent without crowds of tourists. Jerry and I felt quite comfortable visiting passé places in the off-season, and we were glad to have a couple of days in Niagara Falls before the Buffalo concert.

Driving north and then west through Upstate New York gave us a relaxing pleasure after the hectic time in the city. We visited our old high school friend Fred in Peekskill and stayed overnight in Kingston (where I photographed some gravestones in the old cemetery, outstanding for their sculpture and inscribed sentiments). We spent an hour or so at Schroon Lake in the Adirondacks, led there by Thomas Cole's famous painting, admiring the tranquil beauty and listening for loons. Our journey west then took us along the shore of Lake Ontario.

In Niagara Falls, we stayed at a gay-owned inn, the Rainbow House, and were happy to lug everything upstairs for the sake of the view from the bedroom balcony, complete with a swing where we could sit and smell the shredded wheat being toasted in the factory a few blocks away. It was fun to think our being there represented a much-delayed honeymoon. The furnishings and amenities of the place certainly supported the image. There was a living room downstairs with a fireplace and several comfortable armchairs. It was always empty, though; Jerry and I were the only midweek guests.

Ever economizing, we brought croissants in one night to have for breakfast the next morning with the coffee we always made in our room. I located the kitchen soon after daybreak, planning to heat the rolls in a toaster oven, but the shiny new microwave was too much of a temptation. I'd heard about these miracle ovens and thought I'd try it. I set the timer for a couple of minutes, opened the door at the sound of the pleasant ding, and removed three hard *croissants de papier-mâché* to take back and show Jerry.

Everyone had told us to go to the Canadian side—that that's where the activity is. We crossed the Rainbow Bridge and explored the busy streets, enjoying the carnival-like atmosphere. We rode to the top of a lookout tower, but Jerry stood stiff against the back wall of the elevator, relegated by his acrophobia to a long-distance view.

Our last afternoon there we spent gazing at the American Falls and exploring Goat Island. We walked through the cold drizzle to the Three Sisters Islands, laughingly remembering our apartment at the Court of Two Sisters from fifteen years ago. We lingered on the last "sister," the smallest, most remote island. The picture I made of Jerry reminds me of how cold we were; nevertheless, he stands in front of the camera holding his umbrella well to one side of his head, admitting enough light for a good photograph yet looking none too pleased at having to endure yet another picture-taking.

*
**

We celebrated our forty-third birthdays in New Mexico, where Jerry gave a concert in Santa Fe. We drove my Nova on this trip, and it was a relief not to have to worry about protecting someone else's property. Winter was imminent, and we saw snow flurries several times on our route through Las Vegas and Mora and north to Taos. Freshly cut pines lay bundled on the roadway in every small community, ready for pickup and sale as Christmas trees.

Our friend from SMU's dance department, Jane Van Sickle, had married Lonnie and moved to Taos, where they were trying to make a success of an art gallery they had purchased. Jerry and I spent a couple of nights with them in their home northeast of the plaza. La Morada, the Penitentes' shrine, is literally in their backyard, and Jerry and I made a pilgrimage there with Jane and Lonnie's dog one chilly afternoon.

The next day, we took a walking tour of Taos, stopping on our way to town to laugh at the windows D.H. Lawrence painted for Mabel Dodge Luhan, whose house stands just a little west of Jane and Lonnie's. We headed on toward the plaza, bundled up against the cold, where we visited a couple of galleries and stores and looked at Lawrence's paintings in the hotel there.

On our way back, we got lost—or, rather, I got lost, since Jerry always depended on me for directions. I liked to think I could orient myself by the light in the sky, but there was a uniform cloud cover that day, and I led us badly astray. Jerry was tired and cold and ready to be home in front of the fireplace. He'd indulged me quite enough—more of a tourist than he ever was, even waiting patiently for me at the Taos Book Shop. (He once said accompanying me to a bookstore was his idea of Hell.) And the altitude was getting to him, giving him the headache he always said it did. By the time we finally found the road back, we were no longer speaking. We didn't get over it in a hurry, either.

The Center for Contemporary Arts where Jerry was to perform in Santa Fe put us up in the Fort Marcy condominiums, a cluster of adobe buildings on a hillside within walking distance of the plaza. I swam laps in their indoor pool while Jerry made preparations for the concert he was to give that night. We took a walk to the plaza, and he made a picture of me standing in the courtyard of the Palace of the Governors, snow now steadily falling.

Later in the day, we drove up to the St. John's campus and then visited the Museum of International Folk Art nearby, where Jerry was captivated by the miniatures. (He always seemed to like very small objects, often bringing home tiny china or metal animals, cloth roses, or even plastic doll hands from the craft departments of stores.) On our way downhill, we pulled off the road and stopped to look at the sunset, a crimson glow we glimpsed between layers of dark clouds. Snow was still falling. We saw a jackrabbit dart between the piñons just a few feet from our car.

The concert that night was not very well attended, and the people who did come left early. Had we heard a weather report, we would have known why. When we finished packing, we went out to discover that the Nova had been completely covered by snow—it looked like a little hill. We dug it out, loaded it, and I drove through snow so thick that the streets had become indefinable. I was just trying to avoid trees, poles, and buildings—for all I knew, I might have been driving through parks and yards. We couldn't climb the hill to our apartment, so we had to leave the Nova and carry the largest electronic equipment up the snow-covered path to our door. I love snow and considered this my birthday present, but Jerry was less enthusiastic.

With the aid of pictures and reviews and the odd travel brochure or map, it is easy for me to recall our trips, the details of where we went and what we did. One memory recaptured lays a trap for another, and the details reemerge. The good times we had come back for me to enjoy again, and now, in my aloneness, even the unpleasant memories are welcome. But what startles me a little as I reexperience our times together on the road is that the clearest memories, the ones that engage my imagination and emotions most fully, are of those occasions when Jerry and I found ourselves alone together in remote places: on the shore of Schroon Lake among the newly fallen leaves, on the far side of the last of the Three Sisters Islands, among the foothills of Monte Sol watching a jackrabbit in the snow.

Perhaps these times are the most vivid because they summon a strong, familiar feeling and the truth I knew earliest, longest, and best: I shared a union with Jerry that was so deep and pervasive that it was easy to take for granted. But when we were alone, especially when lying in one another's arms or admiring the beauty of nature, we became conscious of this union and were humbled and uncharacteristically speechless.

The folks at the Canton feed and hardware store probably weren't too surprised to see Jerry and me come in one day and buy several hundred feet of PVC pipe and assorted elbows. They'd seen us regularly over the years, bemusedly watching as Jerry roamed the aisles, selecting the hardware he needed for whatever work we were doing on the house or for building his own equipment.

There's not a lot of turnover among the personnel of country stores, and, of course, they see the same customers again and again, so I imagine they had a pretty good fix on the fast-talking eccentric and his sidekick (the one who browsed among the housewares and always bought bird feed).

In fact, one year, a television reporter from a Dallas station came out to our house and interviewed Jerry about its unusual construction. This was part of a program on some of the "colorful" individuals living in East Texas, and for weeks after it was aired, people in the Canton stores recognized Jerry and commented on the house.

We loaded my Nova with the pipe and brought it home—not for a plumbing project, though. Jerry was going to make a frame for a freestanding room; we were to put the frame together on the deck we'd built in front of the house, label the various lengths for easy reassembly, and then take it apart and bundle like-sized pieces to transport to Houston. Jerry had been invited to participate in the New Music America '86, which was to be held there, and the PVC room was to be erected in the Museum of Fine Arts to house his installation *Birome (ZONE): Cube.*

Jerry had last performed in Houston in late 1985 at DiverseWorks. (I didn't attend, probably because I had used up all my vacation time.) In the *Public News* for November 27, Ann Walton Sieber wrote:

> I had a chance to look at performance artist Jerry Hunt's "props," which he keeps on a table centerstage during his performance. Peeking under the gauze cloth, they looked like the property of a modern-day shaman: carved sticks, straw tools, an aged tambourine, tiny bells, Tibetan bells . . . and a plastic wineglass with a purple plastic stem.
>
> Hunt used these objects as noise-makers, augmented by claps and feet-stamping, which his electronic system (reportedly built with computer chips taken from old football arcade-games) turns into an all-pervasive alive beat which remains

unbroken throughout the ninety minutes of the constantly moving show.

Perform[ing] in semi-darkness, Hunt uses the primal rhythm he generates as a setting for his dislocating performance: describing space patterns with lights, placing his objects on the end of a long pole, eerily contorting his illuminated face as he lay cadaver-like inside a wooden frame, lifting the frame so that it became a doorway, swinging his long stick out over the audience as he shouted.

When described, his actions sound absurd.

But they had a dislocating transfixing effect—as though we were witnessing an archetypal drama occurring deep in the unconscious. . . .

While watching Jerry Hunt, I found myself thinking more clearly and bravely than usual.

There had developed a following for Jerry's work in Houston, and the installation would be an opportunity for people to see another facet of his art. Houston had yet to experience its economic hard times, and the city helped support music, dance, and art events and exhibitions at various sites around town, all comprising the Houston Festival (of which New Music America was a part). The variety of the offerings and the appeal of the artists involved attracted people from all over the world. *Birome (ZONE): Cube* made quite an impact on many who saw it, and Jerry was later invited to take it to Holland and Germany. (Even the 1994 *All Music Guide* I received not long ago mentions the installation, which "Blue" Gene Tyranny refers to as a "voodoo hut.")

With Bob's and my help and the somewhat skeptical aid of the museum staff, Jerry assembled the cube and covered the frame with old sheets, quilts, and blankets that we had rounded up in Canton for the purpose. He put inside the mannequin, or homunculus, David

McManaway had designed: a sexless, or multisexed object lying on a bedlike structure and fitted with sensors that enabled it to respond to touch, movement, and sound. A video camera located in the cube conveyed images to the monitors located in the walls and ceiling.

In a 1986 interview with Bernard Brunon for *ArtsSpace*, Jerry described the installation as

> an extension of my understanding of how people actually function and behave as opposed to how they describe their actions.
>
> It is about the difference between the narrative and the action, a distance much greater than most people pay attention to.
>
> The idea was to create an isolated, thrown-together space within a public display setting, into which someone could enter momentarily and, by getting involved with an isolated object, build some change of reference. The mechanism was devised so that the participant's entry, timing, and activity within the cube enclosure would reorganize what subsequent visitors might perceive and engage. The machine accumulates information over a period of time that will determine what it can possibly do later in the day.
>
> . . . I made no effort to create a responsive environment that produces directly satisfying results. It doesn't produce a specific sound or vision for a certain action or rubbing or movement. Rather it operates on the basis of strategies of Rosicrucian chess (a multidimensional chess arrangement) in response to participant actions.

Bob and I went to the museum one afternoon to see the installation. With the old bedding that served as walls, the cube looked out of place in the sterile environment, and the weird and wild electronic sounds coming from the darkened chamber seemed to be attracting and repelling people in just about equal number.

We watched a school group approach the cube. The teacher allowed a few children to go in, at first; I can easily imagine their fascination with the spooky homunculus (which reminded me of the hermaphrodite in Fellini's *Satyricon*) as well as their startled reaction at finding such a thing in a museum in the first place. The teacher walked in but quickly emerged, somewhat agitated. "Let's go, class," she almost shouted, and those inside came out—reluctantly, it seemed to me.

*
**

After three years in Texas, Judy and Paul moved to Idaho in the summer of 1987, just after Paul received his degree from the Baptist seminary in Fort Worth. They had lived on Ferguson Road for a couple of years; Judy worked in the library down the street, and Paul supplemented his Army retirement income by working as a handyman. When he decided to enroll in the seminary, they moved to Fort Worth and rented a house across the street from the campus. Judy got a job on the school's switchboard, using the skills she had acquired over twenty years earlier while working with Daddy at Ben E. Keith.

When they left for Sandpoint, where Paul had been called to be a pastor, my nephew, Paul Michael, was eight, and his sisters, Jamie and Jenny, were ten and almost fourteen, respectively. I had grown close to these children during the three years they had lived in the area, and I frequently drove into Dallas and, later, to Fort Worth to spend the day with them—usually one child at a time. We went to movies and to the malls, to the zoo, and to amusement parks like Six Flags, White Water, and Sesame Street.

Of all the things we did together, I especially enjoyed ice skating. I had skated with Carol and Kirby years before, and I was glad to have someone to enjoy it with again. (I can't even picture Jerry on ice skates—or any kind of skates.) One afternoon stands out in particular: The rink had been decorated for Christmas, and Jamie and I skated to songs of the season beneath a Santa in his sleigh suspended from the ceiling above us.

One summer, I took Paul Michael and Jamie to Aquarena Springs, a theme park between Austin and San Antonio. We watched Ralph, the swimming pig (or one of its avatars), from a submarine chamber, rode the funicular above the park, and threw food pellets from our seats in a glass-bottomed boat to the diving ducks.

Jamie bought me a black plastic seahorse that still hangs above my desk. Paul Michael bought an ornate plastic pirate's sword that made it intact all the way to the car.

Jenny liked shopping, and we spent hours in the malls looking at clothes and, especially, earrings. As I searched for more merchandise tags to read while waiting, I understood how Jerry always felt when he waited for me in bookstores.

Judy and I had become friends. Losing our parents brought us together, and my closeness to the children strengthened the bond. We are, indeed, alike in many ways, and we choose mates that have a lot in common: energy, volatility, and a desire to set the agenda. She had the task of coming to terms with my homosexuality, and I, with her strong religious faith. I believe we appreciate one another more for the effort each of us made.

I drove over to spend a Sunday with them a few weeks before Paul's graduation. When I arrived, they hadn't gotten back from church yet, so I sat on the swing on their sunny front porch and waited. I remember thinking about a comment Judy had made a couple of months earlier about Jesus's arms, how they'd have to be strong because he was a carpenter's son. I continued swinging; it was a beautiful day, and everything was OK—except for the insects that were beating against the sides of the jar where Paul Michael had collected them for a science project. I couldn't put them out of my mind, so naturally, I let them out.

*
**

Because he didn't have associations with schools or performance groups, Jerry depended on concert offers and grant recommendations to come from friendships he had made with other composers and performers who admired his work. The very fact of his being (politically speaking) a free agent strengthened those friendships— he competed with no one, and he made no enemies. His independence was accompanied by a disarming candor about others' work and a genuine sense of modesty about his own. People liked to be with him, partaking of his enthusiasm, put at ease by his lack of pretension and his sense of humor, and being taken seriously as an artist in his or her own right.

We had many artistic guests in Canton during the 1980s and early '90s: Jim Fulkerson, a composer and trombonist living in England and then Holland (and, lamentably, allergic to Mary and Frances); Daniel Dugas, a Canadian graphic artist who wowed the checkout girls at the local grocery store with his good looks and his French accent; Joseph Celli, the composer and oboist who managed early New Music America festivals and whose label, O.O. Discs, lists a CD and a videotape Jerry made; Jane Henry, a composer and violinist (also allergic to cats) whose playing Jerry used in a piece on the CD *Ground*; Annea Lockwood, a composer who Jerry collaborated with on a New York concert in 1988; Dain Olsen, a video artist from Los Angeles; and Jack Briece, a composer Jerry had plans to collaborate with but who died of AIDS before anything concrete could happen.

As these guests and others (including Rod Stasick, who had moved back from Chicago in 1987 and met and fallen in love with Sharon) came to visit us in Canton, we enjoyed showing off the house we had built and getting the amused or amazed reactions of people who could believe neither what they saw nor that we had done it. Jerry usually took guests over to meet his mother, and the ordinariness of her house made the eccentricity of ours even more apparent. One or two guests elected to spend the night in Mrs. Hunt's spare bedroom.

Jerry and his mother continued to be good company for one another during the long periods of time when they were alone together here on the property. The three of us ate dinner at her house at least once a week; she preferred having us over there rather than coming to our house, probably simply because she was more comfortable in her own surroundings. And she didn't want to leave King, the German shepherd who had become so decrepit in his old age as to need help stepping off and onto the back porch.

Just as she had looked after Hermie and Sassie during their decline—perhaps even allowing them to live too long—so Mrs. Hunt now ministered to King, cooking and mincing chicken for him and cleaning up after his incontinence. Jerry tried to persuade her to have the poor animal put to sleep, but she just couldn't bring herself to do it. He finally died one cold day. I was not in town, but Daniel Dugas was here visiting, and he helped Jerry bury King in the little pet cemetery beside the driveway where six dogs now lie.

Mrs. Hunt seemed to change some after King's death. She gradually stopped attending her women's club meetings, with one exception, and she did less indoors and nothing at all outside. Jerry knew she kept receiving invitations to go places, but she was deaf to his encouragement to accept them. Her longtime Dallas friends, especially Maydell, could see the change in her when they came out for birthday visits, as Jerry later learned.

Part of the explanation lay in the fact that Mrs. Hunt was suffering from adult-onset diabetes, and, of course, her sedentary manner of living was only making her feel worse. The diabetic condition was not discovered until she blacked out one day while she and Jerry were coming back from Athens. And although she had the information she needed to adjust her diet, she found it almost impossible to alter a lifetime's eating habits.

It was hard for Jerry to see a growing dependency, and even a petulant quality at times, in his mother, who had always been so independent and so resourceful. The intercom he had connected between her house and ours buzzed more and more frequently: Had anyone been up to the highway to get the mail? Was anyone going to the store later? What was that loud sound? Jerry rarely showed impatience, despite the exasperation he felt. I would have to bite my lip to keep from saying anything.

I wasn't always successful. It seemed to me on occasion that her needs were gradually taking over our lives, that we were here to wait on and care for her. So many times, I saw Jerry leave the work he was in the middle of doing to go do something for her; so many times we had to change our plans, for dinner or for trips, to accommodate hers. Sometimes I felt caught in the middle, and it was then that Jerry and I argued about the direction things seemed to be headed and about what, if anything, we could—or should—do about it.

In the summer of 1986, Jerry was invited to give a concert and conduct a workshop ("on himself," as one reviewer put it) at the Sound Symposium in St. John's, Newfoundland. It was always an ordeal to pack his gear, but it was especially difficult to handle sweaters and over-coats in the middle of a hot Texas summer. However, as the few pictures of him taken there show, Jerry needed them.

There were several unexpected pleasures that Jerry enjoyed on this trip. One was being able to visit at length with Pauline Oliveros. Another was working with the comedian and performance artist Sheila Gostick (this foreshadowing, I think, Jerry's later collaboration with Karen Finley).

A lasting pleasure, though, for both Jerry and his fans and friends, particularly now, is the long interview that composer Gordon Monahan conducted with Jerry for a Canadian magazine. "Stompin' and Beatin' and Screamin'" contains "excerpts culled from extensive monologues by Mr. Hunt as he proceeded to 'talk the clouds right out of the sky' one afternoon at St. John's."

Shortly after Jerry's return from Newfoundland, we installed three air conditioners. This was no coincidence, of course. It had indeed seemed as though our summers were getting hotter, and we were getting older, too. I had continued to enlarge our vegetable garden year after year until that summer when I began to struggle against the relentless heat, drought, and insects thanklessly. We gave up on the little curry plant: we were only harvesting a few leaves each summer—even after bringing it inside for the previous two winters and keeping it under a plant light—and most recipes call for ten or twelve. I kept growing herbs, but we began buying Indian and Chinese vegetables at specialty grocery stores in Dallas and Houston, and we picked up tomatoes, corn, beans, potatoes, onions, and okra from Canton-area farmers selling their produce at roadside stands.

The new air conditioning was a mixed blessing. We were more comfortable and had more energy, but we hated the noise of the units and our growing dependency on them—though Jerry's Amiga computer was undeniably happy to be in a regulated climate.

As a direct result of meeting Paul Panhuysen at New Music America in Houston, Jerry was invited to take his *Birome (ZONE): Cube* installation to Holland. Although Jerry had received several foundation grants, the reduction of the amount of federal funding for the arts that began in the '80s meant that he, along with many other artists and composers, had to depend more and more on financial support from foreign countries. Most of Jerry's friends and colleagues traveled to Europe regularly for exhibitions and concerts of their work, and as he began to go, he'd often meet them and sometimes shared programs with them.

Paul Panhuysen and his wife, Hélène, operate Het Apollohuis (the Apollo House), a government-subsidized institution in Eindhoven (the home of Philips) that exists to promote the work of contemporary Dutch artists through both publications and events. In addition, Het Apollohuis invites artists from abroad, which gave the Dutch direct exposure to work being done outside the Netherlands. Paul is himself a composer, and he and Jerry were later to collaborate in a work.

Several years before Jerry first visited Paul and Hélène, they acquired an old warehouse not far from the city center. They converted the warehouse's office space into several apartments, occupying one with their daughter, Sappho, and making the others available to guests who came to show or perform their work. Although the Dutch government has looked closely in recent years at Het Apollohuis as a part of its effort to reduce arts subsidy in general, Paul, Hélène, and the hundreds of supporters worldwide who have written The Hague have apparently demonstrated that this institution is unique and indispensable.

Jerry was to be gone almost two months—the longest period of time we had been apart since I graduated from college. We packed the homunculus and its attendant electronics, leaving the actual construction of the cube to the exhibition halls that were to house the installation. (In addition to the exhibitions in Eindhoven and Middelburg, Jerry was to give concerts in Cologne, Berlin, Ghent, and Brussels.) He gave me copious detailed instructions for tending to things here—he always did this when he went away, even for a day or two. I think this was a manifestation of a certain distaste or unease at leaving home. He knew I would look after his mother.

What he didn't count on was getting sick in Middelburg—his first stop. At the time, we believed he was suffering from a flulike infection, but we later came to think he had pneumonia. In any case, most of Jerry's time in this picturesque Dutch town was spent in bed at his hotel.

Jerry had been very busy during the months before he left. He had given a concert in New York ("Texas's Jerry Hunt is sufficient proof for me that beings from Neptune are infiltrating new music," wrote Kyle Gann in the *Village Voice* on January 12, 1988). In February, he performed in St. Louis at the Sheldon Ballroom and, again, in New York at the Alternative Museum ("In his business suit and loosened red tie, furiously chewing gum, Jerry Hunt resembles a slightly wasted Wall Street commuter who has descended at the wrong station," according to Bernard Holland in the *New York Times*, February 19, 1988).

The gum was Nicorette. Jerry was still trying to cut down on his smoking without much success, sometimes chewing and smoking at the same time. And the "slightly wasted" comment makes me wonder whether he might not already have been ill. But back in Middelburg, he couldn't have had more considerate hosts:

> Anton & all others have been wonderful throughout the time so far—I feel better slowly, I'm not sure what it is that has caused such a slow recovery, everything at once I suppose.
>
> The alderman carried me to Domburg & West Chapelle yesterday to see the coastal dunes & to stand on the *very spots,* each

of them, where Mondrian stood & painted. In fact, the light there, & here too, is so bright & clear that it's no surprise to see the look of the old Dutch precise & clear painting.

I think most of the audience was left in a tumble of confusion from the program & the installation box. I'm trying to find some photographs of the place, de Vleeshal (the medieval meat-packers guildhall now converted into a museum, so you can see how monumental it is. My box looks like a little bit of left-over rubbish in the corner. . . . Middelburg land! all its surroundings, houses, etc., [are] all *neat as a pin*. At night, everyone's asleep by 11:00 & walking home is like being in a miniature movie set. As if that wasn't enough of the sense of *close*, they have a miniature of the area, in precise scale, in a park.

Although everyone has treated me wonderfully in every way, I've seen it, I'd come home in a shot.

As I had expected, it's like a fixed-up, set-up Canton. Once you've seen a little, you've seen a lot. I'm not designed to be a tourist. This is all something like a very high-class military service: I've got to get through it, I'd rather let someone else do it all & tell me about it, show me slides, etc. . . . This is too long to be here alone, no matter how nice, yawn—

As often seemed to happen, crises developed at home while Jerry was away. During the spring of 1988, our friends Houston and Jill both died—within twelve days of each other; their joint funeral was over by the time Jerry returned.

Jill had always had moles on her fair skin, and over the years, she had had the larger ones removed. There had never been a problem until 1986 when her doctor recommended a biopsy and discovered malignancy. Jill was diagnosed with melanoma, and she was given little encouragement about the prognosis.

The news of her condition came as a shock to her and Houston's family and friends—especially so since everyone had been more or less prepared for Houston's death to come early—hemophilia, with all the transfusions and blood products it had necessitated over the years, had affected his liver, and his knees and hips kept him in constant pain and made it difficult for him to walk.

> Your last letter came today. It made all we discussed the other day clearer.
> I'm still sorry about the situation with Jill, particularly here alone—there's just time, time, time to think about her and the problems she continues to have . . . all complicated by the fact that I felt terrible the first week here—I thought I might get into such a state as to require doctors.

After his stay in Middelburg, Jerry went to Cologne and then to Eindhoven. Worrying about transportation—ever a problem with all his equipment—and now also the need to deal with customs being concerned about Jill and Houston, and not much enjoying sightseeing ("Get a book called *Holland* and look at it—[Holland] looks just like the books show"), Jerry must have been lonely and depressed a good deal of the time he was there. What alleviated the anxiety and the boredom was his developing interest in the Dutch people and their language.

> Bob would go crazy looking at these Dutch boys: they . . . look something like what he seems to like, although I'm not sure: they're not "tough" looking, & when they get dressed up to look tough, they look "tuff."

He pored over the Dutch and English Bible in his hotel room and bought a Dutch-English dictionary. He began speaking a little Dutch.

> I've finally begun to hear Dutch so I can see the words in print. I've watched some TV also: *Miami Vice* w/Dutch subtitles: that helps. I can now read magazines, etc. Today is also Thursday—*donder-dag*—see? I know a word or twee!

In the letter, he drew Mary and Frances, their tails out straight behind them, quizzical looks on their faces, and question marks suspended above their heads.

> *Poesje slim* means "smart pussycat": try that on Frances (*No comprendo*).

He particularly missed Frances, "his" cat:

> She likes some stirring around: walk around the house some: she's not like Mary. You have to work her some.

And he wished I could be there to enjoy:

> The things you seem to like most: librar-ies, bookstores, parks (all along the canals) . . . there are concerts every few nights.

With Paul and Hélène in Eindhoven, he found warm hosts and the ideal Dutch tutors:

> Paul gave me some second-grade readers, so that has helped. I still don't get the sounds right, though. They have been very patient. . . . Because being here is like being with a family, it's a complete change from Middelburg.

Jerry loved the rich pastries found everywhere in Holland, and he visited a nearby bakery often for almond cookies filled with marzipan. One afternoon he bought:

> . . . a wonderful tart: a slightly cookie-like deep crust filled with an excellent cold cherry filling which was covered with a layer of the same pastry: on top of that was a layer of almond macaroon, cooked until crisp. That was topped with whipped cream & finally coated with light chocolate shavings.

I myself had begun to take a greater interest in preparing food during the long time Jerry was away. Jerry had always been such a superb cook that I felt outclassed in the kitchen—and usually in the way. Alone now, I began practicing basic skills (I remember how proud I was of my first roux), and I started baking muffins and breads and sharing them with Mrs. Hunt and my friends at the library. I took some okra gumbo and cornbread to Houston and Jill's home—more for the sake of the other family members than for the two of them, now too ill to eat.

Houston had been hospitalized with jaundice, and I visited him a few times in the intensive care unit. Jill was in a hospice program; she stayed at home and was no longer taking anything by mouth. She and Houston talked a time or two by phone. After Houston's death and internment, I went by to see her, to tell her how lovely the gravesite looked in the shade of the mimosa tree. She lived another couple of weeks, and when she died, a joint memorial service was held for her and her husband. A recording of her singing a movement from Brahms's *Requiem* with the SMU symphony was played.

> I was surprised to hear that Houston had died.
> I knew he was in serious trouble too. I think I've had Jill in mind so much that I'd forgotten how he looked in December. I suppose by the time you have

this letter Jill will be dead too. It
does seem like a daytime soap opera.

I fully expected never to see Jill
again, but I did forget Houston. I hope
he had my last letter. He was a sweet,
gentle & generous friend for many years.
I'd have stopped in NY years ago: he
got me to London. It's odd that I'm here
alone and he's dead.

The concerts in Belgium and, especially, in Berlin went
well. Jerry made friends there who would invite him back,
and he was planning a collaboration with a Belgian artist,
Maria Blondeel, shortly before he died. But the best part
of Jerry's long sojourn was getting to know Paul, Hélène,
Sappho, and a young man named Peter de Rooden, who
had just come to do his alternative national service at the
Apollohuis. They spent hours at Paul and Hélène's dining
table drinking coffee, enjoying the meals that Jerry was
preparing more and more often, discussing art and politics, and speaking a little elementary Dutch (Jerry had to
work hard on the difficult "g" sound).

(Paul and Hélène) are easily two of
the nicest people I've ever met. When I
returned from my shopping trip, I met
Paul at the door; a light shower seemed
about to start. He asked me to join him
on a walk since he can't stand to be
indoors during spring rains. We made
it to a sidewalk cafe table, covered,
just in time to avoid a downpour. I had
forgotten how pleasant rain was once
when I spent time in Mart. Although it
was raining very hard, it was completely
windless. The rain falls straight down.
After living in that horrible thrashing
weather (in East Texas) for so long, I
had forgotten that rain doesn't always
bring terror.

His descriptions of Holland and of the Dutch friends
he'd made excited my curiosity, and I began to hope that I

could go there with him someday. One thing, though, was certain: We never wanted to be apart again for so long a time, and we never were.

> Give the cats big sloppy kisses & some fish, give yourself a big sloppy kiss, I miss you to the point of reading your letters over & over . . .

*
**

On my weekly trips to Athens to swim, I'd become curious about the town's Trinity Valley Community College. Driving by the campus and seeing the students enter and leave the modest buildings stirred my old love of school and of teaching. I stopped one day to talk with the academic dean about the possibility of my teaching an English course in the fall of 1988. As it happened, they needed additional faculty, but the dean suggested I consider participating in the college's extension program at the state prison a few miles south. The idea appealed to me.

A few months later, I was in a college car with three other men (another English teacher, a speech teacher, and a teacher of civics) on my way to one of Texas's maximum-security facilities located about thirty minutes from Athens. We entered the building under the gaze of the guard posted in the lookout tower above, and a turnkey admitted us to the cell block. A sign above the door reminded the guards (and us) that even a moment of relaxed vigilance could result in trouble or even tragedy.

Walking down the long prison corridor—trying not to stare back as the prisoners in their white uniforms stared at us—reminded me of my night in jail years ago. I was shocked then, as now, by the sudden entry into a netherworld of despair and desperation, ineffectually camouflaged by apparent cocky defiance.

Most of these men were Black, a difference that sank the netherworld to which they were being confined a circle or two lower still from the plane of being white and being free. I felt wretched and ashamed being there, and I had to remind myself often during the semester that I had come to help.

The education wing consisted of four classrooms, two on either side of a common room that was used for waiting and smoking (this was before smoking was outlawed in state prisons). My students were already waiting for me in the classroom I had been assigned; these men had earned the right to enroll in the college extension program by good behavior (and because they had either finished high school or had earned an equivalency diploma). Twenty fellows, mostly young and Black, regarded me with suspicion and, some, evident distaste. They attempted to conceal their true feelings by showing me a respect that, for some, was the same exaggerated kind that I had so often seen since the time I worked with my father on the produce market. There were two prominent exceptions: a Black man who sat in surly indifference in the back of the room and a young white man who sat in the front and would not meet my eyes.

I had the idea of writing a paragraph with them on the board before even taking roll or issuing textbooks. I suppose I knew I had to prove myself, to show them that they'd get something out of the class they could use. We settled on a topic, a few fellows contributed ideas and sentences here and there, and we revised the rough draft into a respectable brief composition, including thesis, logical development, and conclusion. By the end of the exercise, we'd forged a workable teacher-student relationship—we were going to be able to do business together because they knew I had something to offer them.

Most of them figured out I'm gay. I expected this, even tried to facilitate it in the way I introduced myself and by not reacting at all to the macho camaraderie that sometimes emerged when women came up in discussions about assigned readings. I think I made it easier for them through my honesty—without suspicion, there wasn't much of an issue. I know I made it easier for myself, and in some strange way, I felt as though I were now putting right the sad wrong of my hypocrisy as a prep school teacher ten years earlier.

After the dropouts (some due to misrepresented qualifications), I ended up with about fifteen men in my class. The range of abilities was huge, so I tried to work as much as I could with individual students, helping them outline their essays and pointing out errors in spelling, grammar, and usage. I began each three-hour class at the blackboard, focusing on common errors (sometimes copying out sentences from papers turned in the previous week), then sketching a model of the type of essay we were going to write that week, soliciting as much input from the class as possible. Sometimes I gave them tests on grammar and usage.

The last hour or so was a workshop. As the class revised returned compositions or began the newly assigned one, I called them up individually to discuss specific writing problems. One afternoon, I was going over an essay I had corrected with my red-ink fountain pen and was startled to see a drop of blood fall onto the page. I glanced up at the face of the man sitting beside me, and I saw that he had apparently been in a fight, perhaps during the ten-minute break we had before the last hour. "It's OK. Go on," he ordered me. I did.

The warden and guards were barely tolerant of the college program, and classes were never allowed to interfere with prison routine. Students arrived late (once because they'd all been issued thongs to wear on their feet in the showers as a precaution against AIDS), and sometimes the guards showed up early to escort them to dinner. We just had to quit whatever we were doing. On two occasions, my colleagues and I arrived to find our classes canceled due to prisonwide lockdowns. There was never any chalk on the blackboard trays, so I began bringing my own. I also brought pencils and paper for those men who would sometimes come without supplies (I never asked why). The isolation cells were in an adjacent wing, and the yells of the men being punished could be heard in my classroom.

I got into trouble with the prison and the college. So that the class could retain their compositions (as well as learn from past mistakes and see their progress), I got permission from the English department chair to issue the white Trinity Valley Community College folders with the school's mascot, a red cardinal, on the front. These folders became hot items in the prison community—soon, every college program enrollee wanted one, and they began asking the other teachers for them. Having one of these folders conferred special status and, accordingly, undermined the prison hierarchy. A sudden halt was called to issuing folders by means of a memo sent to all the faculty.

It was good to be teaching again, planning lessons, and even grading tests and marking essays. I spent a lot of time working at home, and my class worked hard in response. During the second half of the semester, I distributed copies of one of the essays I had received the week before to use as a model for analysis. The men in my class got a kick out of being "published."

The surly man finally came around, and, not surprisingly, he turned out to be one of the smartest members of the class. It turns out the shy fellow who sat up front was also exceptionally smart. He later told me he was from California and had been convicted of selling drugs while passing through Texas. He had another year in prison, after which he hoped to transfer to a University of California campus. He asked me to help him arrange for him to take the Scholastic Aptitude Test for college admission, and I found out that the test was given periodically to the incarcerated at a regional testing center. The only question was if the prison would provide transportation for him. I never learned the answer.

The best writer in the group was a soft-spoken young Black man whose compositions were too good to be useful as models for the class. One of his essays described his room at home when he was a boy: the dark, airless bedroom at the back of the house, its faded floral wallpaper peeling from the upper corners, and the massive old furniture that once belonged to his grandmother and, in the twilight or early morning, looked like gods watching over him—or beasts lying in wait. This was the fellow who had bled at my desk.

Jerry never wanted me to teach in prison. He was afraid something would happen to me, and his fear was heightened by a report he heard on the radio one day about a prison librarian having been taken hostage in a facility near Houston. He always seemed relieved when I drove in, just after dark. I hadn't planned to teach the next spring because we had a couple of trips planned. As it turns out, I never went back. But I was glad to have helped over a dozen people earn college credit. And I was aware that Jerry was proud of me—that mattered almost as much.

* * *

Arriving at daybreak in an unfamiliar foreign country after a night of travel is a magical experience: with no cues for habitual behavior and the biological clock disturbed, everything looks unreal, dream-like. I'd flown from Houston (where I'd left Mary and Frances with Bob and Rany) to Amsterdam, having been held back from departing with Jerry when he left a couple of weeks earlier by my teaching duties. I was to join him now for over two weeks in Holland at Christmastime.

Jerry had been invited to participate in a new music festival in Rotterdam, where he met Karen Finley—the two of them hit it off so well, the seed for a future collaboration was planted on the spot. Then he was to give a concert at the Apollohuis in Eindhoven, where I was to join him at Paul and Hélène's third-floor guest flat.

With an odd mixture of exhilaration and fatigue, I took the subway from Schiphol Airport to the Central Station in Amsterdam, and then I rode a train south to Eindhoven. The fields of grazing dairy cattle were scored by irrigation canals that had been lined by rows of poplars; the villages, with their tile-roof dwellings, emerged from the mist as we passed by; and an occasional windmill could be spotted in the distance. All this comprised my magical landscape, and the fantasy element was only strengthened by the incomprehensible language passengers around me were speaking.

Paul and Hélène were the gracious hosts and the wonderful people Jerry had prepared me to expect. I could see right away how fond they had become of him, how much they enjoyed being in his company. Hélène's unobtrusive efficiency and ironic sense of humor and Paul's intellectual curiosity and slightly distracted manner made for a very appealing combination that assured comfortability yet promised adventure. Although the age difference between them and Jerry was not that great, the Panhuysens were a great deal like Jerry's parents. No wonder he came to love them. And just like parents, they were mentors for him, guides to a new country and a strange language.

After Jerry's concert at the Apollohuis, where I'd met and instantly liked Peter de Rooden, Jerry and I took a week for sightseeing before we were to fly home. There was some talk about planning excursions with others—with Peter and the composers Arnold Dreyblatt and Ellen Fullman—but I, privately, asserted my right to see Holland with Jerry, to discover it with him. With other people, he was a bit of a performer; I wanted him to be the relaxed companion I loved—and I wanted him to myself. I couldn't explain all of this very well, and we exchanged a few sharp words and a threat or two, but we finally compromised on a plan to visit Peter in Groningen, his home in the North, and then return south and west to Zeeland on our own. Paul and Hélène offered to keep Jerry's equipment in the flat until our flight home.

At the end of a day of sightseeing in Groningen, we booked passage on a ferry to Schiermonnikoog ("grizzled monk's cowl"), the smallest inhabited Wadden island (only residents are allowed to keep and drive cars on it). We took the *voetgangersstraat* (walkway) from the dock to the village, minding the *fietsers overtrekken* (cyclists' crossings) that are everywhere and testify to the importance of bicycles—and that can be sites of embarrassing accidents if you don't look out (*pas op*) for them.

We rambled through the village, admiring the fastidiously neat gardens and enjoying the unexpected animal encounters (dogs and cats, mostly, but also a goat tethered to a shed in the back of a house). After lunch, we walked to the lighthouse near the dunes along the isolated northern end of the island. We had read that half of all the plants that grow in Holland can be found on this island, and there were indeed many unusual-looking wildflowers and grasses, even in December. We stood and looked out to the North Sea, our heavy coats a welcome against the cold wind. We imagined what it might be like living in such a secluded spot, perhaps settling in the lighthouse.

It seemed an attractive prospect. It was fun picturing Mary and Frances racing up and down the lighthouse stairs.

We were in Amsterdam over Christmas, staying in the gay-owned Hotel Engeland (so named because of its architecture: a British-looking structure in a row of houses reflecting a variety of national styles). Our room was at the top; its windows opened onto the street, and I moved a chair there one morning to read what I could of *De Telegraaf.* I ran across the obituaries, and my attention was called to a simple black-bordered notice in the center of the page announcing a man's death; "no flowers, no memorials," it said in Dutch—and then:

> Ik heb u in mijn handpalmen gegrift. (I have you engraved in the palm of my hand.)

I was struck by the simple eloquence of the statement and committed it to memory.

On Christmas Eve, I attended a free sing-along concert of carols and hymns at the Concertgebouw, located just a few blocks away. After a few songs, I felt I had to explain to the man next to me that I wasn't singing only because I knew no Dutch. Jerry declined to accompany me ("Why would I want to go there?"), and he called his mother while I was away. When I returned, we ventured out to find a store open late (always a challenge in Holland) where we could buy something to eat. We returned to our room with some cheese, dark bread, and beer and celebrated the occasion, if not the holiday.

When we went down for breakfast, we found the small dining room freshly decorated for Christmas—there was even a big red bow on the just-filled bird feeder in the garden beyond the windows. The other guests that had come down before us were enjoying champagne (on the house) with their juice and coffee.

As it turned out, our table was located near those of two English-speaking couples: the women were over from London for the holiday, and the American men were on their way to Innsbruck for skiing. This was the first Christmas Jerry and I ever had away from our families and apart from the usual round of gift-exchanging.

We enjoyed the difference.

We visited the Rijksmuseum, toured the canals by boat, ate hot *stroopwafels* (syrup-filled wafers) on the Leidseplein, and drank beer in a "brown cafe" (pub). While Jerry met with Jim and Mary Fulkerson (the composer and his dancer wife were now living and working in Holland), I swam in the old Zwembad near the Rijksmuseum. After dressing, I took a picture of the ornate tiling around the pool; an attendant rushed up and explained to me that what I had done was not permitted ("for the privacy of our guests"), and I stumbled an apology.

An afternoon's train ride took us to Vlissingen, a city in extreme southwestern Holland with a busy harbor and ferry service to England. There, we spent a few nights in the modest Pension Golfslag ("wash of the waves"), a bed-and-breakfast that catered to the many Germans who come on holiday to the seaside town. From this home base, we took a train east to Middelburg and spent an afternoon seeing De Vleeshal, where Jerry's installation had been earlier in the year. We attended a terrible piano recital, but we had a sumptuous *rijsttafel* at a Dutch-Indonesian restaurant afterward.

The next day, we took the ferry across to Breskins, where we got a bus to Brugge (Bruges). We rode a boat through the canals of the medieval city, watched a very old lady make lace, and bought some expensive chocolate candy for dessert. (Reading Alan Hollinghurst's *The Folding Star* just a few months ago brought back a lot of the places as well as the atmosphere of this strange old town.)

On New Year's Eve, we left the Golfslag late and went out to find a little festivity. To our amazement, the town was dead: the streets were deserted, the cafes and bars all closed, and, from what we could see through the drawn lace curtains of windows, the people were all at home watching TV. We walked along the dock, in the still cold, aware that midnight was near. All of a sudden, we heard the blastings of the distant ships' horns just as the lights on their masts and rigging lit up to greet one another for the start of the New Year. It was a magical moment, and later, as we lay in our tiny room in one of the twin beds, plenty big for such a cold night, we agreed it was one we would remember always.

Our trips brought us together, renewed the intimacy we took for granted at home as we pursued our separate interests. The close quarters of the barn house intensified the need we felt for privacy: it became important for us—and for me, particularly—to have our own spaces. I was determined to make good use of the four days a week I had at home, and I got up early and spent the morning hours working on Spanish, listening to the *Puerta del Sol* tapes I received from Spain each month, reading Spanish-language newspapers and magazines, and translating a few poems and short stories. My three weeks in San Miguel de Allende, Mexico, in the summer of 1988 (where I attended concerts in the chamber music festival) had reawakened my interest in speaking Spanish, and I made weekly trips to converse in the language with Rita, a native of Monterrey, who was then living with her family in a trailer not far from Athens.

As a night person, Jerry awoke around noon each day. We'd spend the afternoon doing chores and running errands, and our only sit-down meal was in the evening, around six. I cooked for us more and more often; Jerry would go over to visit with his mother while I prepared dinner, and sometimes I would have to call him on the intercom to tell him that dinner was ready. My meals were simple ones: nut loaves and macaroni and cheese and steamed vegetables—although Rita had taught me how to make my own corn tortillas, and we'd have those with chile rellenos, stuffed with TVP-based picadillo, and Negra Modelo beer every week or two.

In the evenings, while I read or listened to music, Jerry would work at his computer and synthesizers. He had entered "the netherworld of interaction using a variety of videodisc retrieval mechanisms, with associated program changes," as he wrote Jacqueline. He also continued working on music for educational TV series. When he wasn't listening to sounds, he'd listen to TV using his earplugs, occasionally looking up from his work at the monitor to see what was going on. He especially liked horror movies, usually shown in the early morning hours.

Toward the end of his workday, he'd turn to Dutch. His conversations with Paul and Hélène and Peter in and about the language had strengthened his interest that had emerged during his long stay in Middelburg. Jerry had discovered Marten Toonder, probably through Paul, and he enjoyed reading about the adventures of the quixotic, bumbling bear Heer Bommel and his sagacious sidekick, Tom Poes (rhymes with ruse) the cat. These adventures frequently took place in a fantasy realm illustrated by the cartoon panels at the top of each page of text.

I gave Jerry a subscription to *Donald Duck* in Dutch (as a boy, Jerry had especially loved that cartoon figure). Each week, the thin magazines would arrive in their plastic bags all the way from Haarlem. Sometimes when I got up, I'd find Jerry sitting at the vanity table in the bathroom reading about the latest crisis befalling *Oom* (Uncle) Donald and his nephews *Kwik*, *Kwek*, and *Kwak*, just before going to bed. (Jerry slept only five or six hours a night.)

One week, an issue of *Donald Duck* arrived stuck to a second copy addressed to a boy in Houston (the plastic mailers had adhered to one another). Since Jerry and I were planning a trip to Houston that next week to visit Bob and Rany, we decided to take the magazine with us and deliver it by hand. Months earlier, we had discovered a Dutch grocery and gift shop in Houston, and the address label on the second issue of *Donald Duck* bore the same zip code as the Holland House. We'd already planned to visit the store to stock up on *stroopwafels*, *boterkoek* (butter cake), *Oude* (old) Amsterdam cheese, and *bosvruchten* (forest berry) tea.

We found the child's address, and I went to the door to deliver the magazine while Jerry waited in the car. There was no one home, and I returned to the car to suggest to Jerry that we just leave the magazine in the door with a note explaining how we had gotten it and why it was late. While we were looking for something to write on, three or four elementary school-age boys came walking down the street and approached the house. I jumped out of the car and asked if the comic book I was holding up might belong to one of them. Rather self-consciously, one of the fellows admitted that it did. I explained why we had it and gave it to him; he thanked me, and he and his friends went indoors.

Jerry and I had fun telling about this innocent little episode with its sinister overtones. I suggested he join the *Oom* Donald Fan Club as a way of meeting other Dutch children, and if his letter should get the *Brief* (letter) *van de Week* award, with his picture published in the magazine, he'd be sure to be popular with the *jongens*. We told Marten Bal, the owner of the Holland House, about our escapade, and he explained that there are quite a few families in the area with one or both Dutch-speaking parents, having relocated to Houston because of the oil business Shell conducts with the Netherlands. These parents, Marten told us, often try to preserve their heritage by speaking Dutch at home—where, I suspect, most kids prefer to keep it.

We began making regular trips to Tyler, about forty-five minutes east, to shop, have dinner, and sometimes go to the movies. We'd compare Spanish and Dutch linguistic notes on the beautiful drive through the pines, each of us interested in the other's interest in his adopted language, if not so much in the language itself. On our way home, driving into the sunset, we'd talk about our more serious concerns—sensing, I suppose, that it was the time to talk before we got home and allowed our habits to overtake us again. Were we really doing what we wanted to do? Was living in Europe, in Holland or Belgium, a viable alternative? What would happen to Jerry's mother? Would she be able to live independently much longer? Where was Jerry's career headed? Shouldn't it take a new direction, and if so, what would that be? And why did he feel so bad so much of the time?

*
**

Jerry gave concerts in Boston and Los Angeles in early 1989, and that summer, he participated in the Almeida Festival in London. He stayed with Jacqueline and her daughter, Emma, while he was there, and in his letter thanking them for their hospitality, he wrote:

> I returned here sick: I've had allergic reactions of increasing intensity and frequency for the past four or five years;

the allergic reaction (to some very local plant, I think a grass) works in interaction with my peculiarly designed sinuses: any mild infection along with the strain of travel, etc., leads to a major attack: I've had several terrible stretches of misery after spring or summer month airplane flights (the compression changes in the airplane seem to complicate the problem beyond some limit of immune tolerance, and I get really sick instead of having a mild cold).

I'm finally getting at the bottom of it, though:

I've made friends with the doctor here who has me on a series of investigative trials of drugs for the allergic reaction and has me next week on the latest in smoking control, a skin-patch-release nicotine system with tranquilizers, etc., etc.—an all-out war: Stephen can't stand cigarettes anymore, and my body can't take them much longer, I have early stages of emphysema already.

Jerry was caught in two cycles that he knew and admitted were self-destructive. Due to his physical addiction to nicotine, he couldn't quit smoking, and the more he smoked, the more damage he did to his already compromised lungs. As the chronic obstructive pulmonary disease worsened, he was even more susceptible to allergens—to the Bahia grass in our pasture or whatever it was that always made him feel worse here at home. The more he suffered from allergic reactions (often complaining of an intolerable pressure in his sinuses), the more irritable and depressed he became, and the more he craved tobacco, the nervous habit he had built up over three decades. Dr. Morris tried to help him break free of these cycles by prescribing tranquilizers, but that didn't work very well either because Jerry hated the way they made him feel—and in a "dopey" state, he couldn't do his work.

I, however, was at first grateful for the tranquilizers. It had become hard to get along with Jerry at times. Feeling bad, frustrated, and angry, he would throw violent fits, slamming and banging things around, and sometimes yelling abuse at me (who else?). We visited our old friend Peggy in Corpus Christi the Christmas after her husband George died, and she saw one of Jerry's outbursts up close. He wanted cigarettes (probably having put off buying more as long as he could), and I was driving. I saw a service station at a busy intersection and began trying to plan my route to it. I made a wrong turn, and we were delayed at a traffic light. He was beside himself, threatening to get out of the car and walk through traffic to the cigarette machine that was tantalizingly close. Peggy was startled, I think even a little shaken at the virulence of his angry, abusive outburst.

It happened several times that we would start out for a few days in Houston, the car packed and Mary and Frances waiting in their kennels in the back seat, and Jerry's mood was so bad that I'd nearly abort the trip—the thought of being with him in the car for over four hours was intolerable. But, as we headed east, then south, the cloud would lift, and Jerry himself would remark at how much better he had begun to feel, having left behind whatever it was here that affected him so.

Although I never seriously took his outbursts personally, I was sometimes embarrassed when they occurred in the presence of our friends. If we had words later, Jerry was always quick to apologize and I to accept, and there the matter ended. The worst times, though, were when we were alone together: he'd flare up, and I'd go off by myself (to my study, to the yard, and, once, to a rest stop on the highway four miles away), thus protracting—and magnifying—the incident.

I realize now that I had gradually developed the habit of gauging Jerry's mood whenever I returned from a day of work in Dallas:

What was he doing when I came in? What had he been doing? How did he seem? If I ever tried to cheer him up or merely distract him, he'd lash out at me or withdraw. We simply didn't have very much control over what was happening, given his illness and our natures.

Each week, I had my "day out" in Athens, swimming in the athletic center and visiting Rita and Modesto to practice my Spanish. I usually stayed late in Dallas one night a week, having dinner with my library friends Marsha, Jim, and Dick. And I had begun taking car trips with Uncle Henry and Aunt Hazel: twice to Idaho to see Judy and her family and several times to scenic areas in Texas and adjacent states. Jerry seemed happy for me to have these diversions; nothing in our relationship changed, fundamentally.

There were superficial differences, however. For one, I was doing most of the cooking now. I won't pretend that this didn't occasionally spark little explosions between us; things went better when Jerry went over to visit with his mother while I cooked. And for another—and for a change—if one of us resisted sexual overtures, it was now more often he.

*
**

Jerry's appearance with Karen Finley during the New Music America '89 held in New York was the first of several collaborations in which Jerry and another composer/ performance artist shared creative responsibility. He had many times used others in his work: Sally Bowden and Jane Van Sickle dancing; James Fulkerson on trombone, Joseph Celli on oboe, and Guy Klucevsek on accordion; and Rod Stasick and Michael Galbreth acting. Working with Karen was something different—perhaps a new direction.

Kyle Gann's review of the first Finley-Hunt collabora- tion in the *Village Voice* on December 12th reflected what a lot of Jerry's fans felt:

> I couldn't imagine how these two weir- dos would work together at Merkin Hall, but they each did what they do sepa- rately, and somehow the combination was inspired. Finley, as usual, obliterated the life/art barrier:
>
> "I don't know why they booked us on electronic music night. I wanted to play

BAM [the Brooklyn Academy of Music], but this is what I got." After throwing chocolate candy at the audience, she screamed one of her repetitive, slice-of-life poems, ending "Whenever I see a rainbow in the sky, I just see an angel being raped." Meanwhile, back at the ranch, Hunt shook rattles and bells, played with mirrors, and blew through a shofar in surreal antiphony. It was unexplainable and irreducible, like most of life's significant events.

Karen and Jerry became fast friends and began planning a future joint appearance. He was grateful, as he told me, for the chance to work with her, both because her following would increase the size of his own audience and because her creative energy stimulated his own. This latter, of course, was a common theme that ran throughout Jerry's work, as he told Gordon Monahan:

> Every performance that I do, and every compositional gimmick or technique or structure that I use, is based on [a] model of conversational interaction.

In the fall of 1991, Jerry was a resident artist and guest teacher at the Hogeschool voor de Kunsten (college of art, or conservatory) in Arnhem, Holland. The international students who attended his "workshops on himself" must have been deeply engaged by the "conversational interaction," judging by the correspondence he continued to receive from them. A young woman and man from Finland regularly wrote (and, when I informed them of Jerry's death, they sent me a beautiful card with a Finnish wildflower on the cover). Jerry was to have returned to the Hogeschool in the fall of 1993, but his health wouldn't let him. It was the first engagement he had ever had to cancel.

Had he lived longer, Jerry would have collaborated with three other artists: Joel Ryan, a composer and software designer based in Amsterdam; Maria Blondeel, an artist and composer in Ghent; and Michael Schell, a video artist in New York. He had begun making plans with each of these on interactive projects, some using optical discs. In time, a couple of these projects may be realized, using the notes and stored sounds and images that Jerry left behind.

*
**

Mrs. Hunt had always done close work. My earliest memories of her, from the late '50s, have her sitting in a chaise longue in the den doing embroidery; when I spent the night with Jerry, I noticed that she always went to bed with a book. After Mr. Hunt's death, she took up painting. As she became more and more housebound in her seventies, she watched TV a lot of the time. When she learned she had cataracts on both eyes, she was determined to have lens transplants—both because she knew she couldn't remain independent unless she could see and because she had come to realize how constricted her world had become, and she wanted to do something about it.

Jerry worried a great deal about her. It was hard to see this intelligent, gregarious lady spend her days in front of the TV. It had become just about all she could do—to prepare simple meals, do her laundry, and pay her bills. Getting ready to go anywhere had become such a chore that leaving the house rarely seemed worth the effort. So, we encouraged her to have the surgery. Jerry carried her to the doctor for the preliminary visits and to the hospital in Kaufman for the procedure on the first eye. In time, she could see so much better out of that eye that she was eager to have the other one operated on.

Her physical condition, otherwise, had worsened. She was not able to manage her diabetes, and she felt bad a great deal of the time. She went into a diabetic coma one afternoon, and after that, she began getting help at home from visiting nurses who not only monitored her diabetes but also prepared hot lunches on the days they came.

Jerry returned from giving a concert on the tenth anniversary of the Apollohuis in time to help his mother through surgery on the second eye. Although she still wanted to have the operation, she became increasingly anxious about it as the date grew nearer. The Canton doctor even prescribed a mild tranquilizer for her, but she had to stop taking it because the medicine made her so sleepy. On the morning of the day the surgery was scheduled, she awoke us—over an hour before the time she and Jerry had arranged to leave—by honking her car horn in one long blast.

Jerry had alerted the ophthalmologist to his mother's diabetic condition, and he assured us that that would not be a complication. The surgery went well, and Jerry left shortly thereafter for Vienna to participate in the music festival Tone und Gegentone in March 1991. I had agreed to take Mrs. Hunt in for a postoperative checkup in a couple of weeks, and the visiting nurses were maintaining a regular schedule. Mrs. Hunt's friends, particularly a retired school nurse, Clyta, called every few days.

One cold Sunday morning, Clyta came to my door to tell me that Mrs. Hunt wasn't doing well. The visiting nurse arrived just as I did, and we were both alarmed by Mrs. Hunt's weakened state. We were also a little surprised by her telling us that she didn't think she could make it alone any longer, even with the help she had. I knew well of her distaste for nursing homes, and that she was considering going to one startled me and made me see more clearly the condition she was in. She talked about how helpless she had become, and we could all see how anxious she was. If she could check herself into one of the Canton nursing homes for just a month and regain her strength, then she could come back home. That she hadn't given up seemed clear to me by the fact that whatever else she might have let go, she stayed on top of the eye-drop regimen the surgeon had prescribed.

We called Jerry from her bedside. I could tell he was surprised by her decision, but he thought her plan was for the best if she thought it for the best. Since I had to work in Dallas that afternoon, Clyta took her to the nursing home and helped with the paperwork.

Early in the week, she seemed to be doing a little better. A good sign was that she'd begun going to the central lounge to read at night (her roommate probably turned in early, as did most of the residents). However, when I went by Wednesday to take her to the ophthalmologist, I found her dazed-seeming and disoriented.

We had a hard time getting her dressed, and she wasn't able to tell me where the doctor's office was (in fact, she directed me to the wrong clinic).

The office staff could see how weak and confused she was, so they agreed to have the doctor examine her before her turn. I don't know why the ophthalmologist wasn't more alarmed at her condition; it was all Mrs. Hunt could do to read the letters on the chart—and for lack of the ability to concentrate, not see.

The eye had healed well, though, and we were sent on our way.

When we got back to the nursing home, I had to have help getting her out of the car.

Clyta called me after dinner that night, concerned that Mrs. Hunt seemed to be growing weaker still, and she was drifting in and out of consciousness. By the time I got there, the ambulance had arrived. When Clyta and I got to the hospital in Kaufman, we learned that she had been put in a critical care unit; an electrocardiogram revealed that she had had a heart attack—perhaps more than one. Female diabetics, we were told, are prone to "silent" heart attacks.

I called Jerry when it was morning in Vienna, and the hotel staff found him at breakfast. He had been sick, too—the usual result of the strain of travel and the pressure changes and stale air of the airplane. He was feeling better, though, and I encouraged him to go on with the concert as planned but to try to get an earlier flight home if he could. His mother's condition appeared to have been stabilized.

Bob met Jerry's plane in Houston and drove him home, and he arrived exhausted from a transatlantic flight and four-hour car ride. Bob stayed with us for a couple of days, and during our hospital visits, the three of us often stood looking out the windows at the east end of the second-floor corridor onto the green lawn and newly leafed-out trees—a view I was to have, in another season, two and a half years later.

By the time Jerry returned, they had put Mrs. Hunt in a private room; she was still on a heart monitor, however.

We left after spending the Wednesday evening with her with the expectation that she would be returning to the nursing home soon. The hospital called early the next morning with the news that she had had another heart attack. When we got there, the internist explained that the attack had seriously damaged the heart muscle, and the prognosis was poor. He went over with Jerry the living will that I had given him the previous week.

There were to be no "heroics."

When she died, they called us in and left us alone in the room with her. I held Jerry and cried with him, just as he had with me when my mother died almost twelve years earlier.

Before Jerry had gotten back from Vienna, I was at Mrs. Hunt's bedside in critical care one afternoon, moistening her lips and combing her hair. She became animated all of a sudden, opening her eyes wide, asking how Jerry's concert had gone and when he would be back. I answered her questions, and she went on to talk about Jerry in the amused, mock-impatient manner she used to employ years ago when we'd discuss his obsessive devotion to his work and his "impracticality." I felt an access of love for her then, a renewal of the feeling that she evoked in me early on when my own love for her son let me see that she and I shared something extraordinary.

There was no church service; instead, Jerry and I invited Mrs. Hunt's many friends, both from Canton and Dallas, to come to the house for a memorial gathering. The violets she had planted soon after the house was built were blooming at the front door, and her irises (most brought from the yard in Casa View) were just beginning to open. We put the text of an American Indian prayer she liked on the piano.

As she had done when Mr. Hunt died, Jerry cleaned her house from top to bottom. He spent hours examining the accumulation of her lifetime: letters and photographs; boxes of fabric remnants and buttons and craft supplies; and personal mementos, some of which meant nothing to him or to me. Jerry was never able to deal with her clothes. Several months later, I took them to Goodwill, leaving only a couple of items—a party apron and a black shawl that Mrs. Hunt had crocheted, and that Jerry had caught me bagging and rescued.

The sad time was not without its dark comedy. When we went to the Canton funeral home to make the arrangements for the cremation, an elderly employee with rheumy eyes met us at the door and commiserated with Jerry over the loss of his mother. "I used to send her my *Upper Rooms* as soon as I'd finished with them. I hope they helped her in her suffering." Jerry and I both thought it unlikely that his mother had received these devotional pamphlets, but we thanked her anyway. Then, in the funeral director's office, we were told that the expenses would be paid from a "pre-need" account that Mrs. Hunt had established years earlier. This was news to us, but we were touched by her forethought.

A week later, we went back to the funeral home to pick up the "cremains" and take them to be interred in the Mart Cemetery. It was then we learned that there had been another Mrs. Hunt (Ruth, though) who had recently died, and she was the one with the pre-need account (and the stack of *Upper Rooms*).

The funeral director in Mart had told us to bring an interment certificate along with the ashes, but no such paperwork had come from the crematorium. We stood in the office—me, Jerry, and the two clerks—examining the contents of the plastic receptacle, looking for the needed form. I pulled the plastic bag that contained the cremains out of the box, thinking the slip of paper might have been inserted at the other, sealed end. The bag was loosely closed with a piece of paper-covered wire, and it almost came open as I lifted it out. "Watch out—you'll spill her all over the floor," Jerry said—to the uneasy amusement of the office ladies. But we found no certificate, so we had to call the crematorium and have them mail one directly to the cemetery.

We made our trip to Mart with the ashes. Jerry had wrapped the receptacle in a piece of silk he had brought his mother from India in 1975. We met the undertaker (the same man who had handled Mr. Hunt's funeral arrangements: "Fish Paw," Mrs. Hunt called him for his limp handshake), and he "opened" the grave with a post hole digger. The receptacle would not go down. "It's probably the cloth—hangs it up, somehow," Fish Paw said. Jerry removed the silk.

After French fries and Cokes at the Mart Dairy Queen, Jerry led me on a sentimental (and farewell) journey to the places he had known as a boy. He showed me the house from whose second story he and his cousin Ronnie had entertained passing motorists with their spooky light show. We drove over to Waco to see the movie house where he watched the science-fiction serials he loved on Saturday mornings. We found where the ice cream parlor used to be, and we located Jerry's old school. I could so easily picture him standing curbside in his coat, waiting for his mother to come to pick him up over an hour before dismissal on the day Mrs. Quay had said, "You may go now, Jerry."

The place that most excited my imagination, however, was the radio and TV repair shop where Jerry used to get the parts he needed to finish the electronics course his grandfather had ordered and then abandoned. The tiny structure—a shack, really—had long since been boarded up. I could see Jerry going by there after school, or after the movies on a Saturday, or off and on during the long summer vacations, buying or trading for parts. I expect the repairman gave him quite a lot, tickled to see the bright boy take such a serious interest in the subject.

I went out to the storage house the other day to find a wall switch. I sat, for the first time, at Jerry's electronics workbench, taking in the piles of resistors and capacitors, the circuit boards, and the equipment that Jerry had cannibalized and left stacked in the corners. Jerry's father's golf trophies sat among the cobwebs on the windowsill, and his mother's early oil paintings stood in the corner of an open closet. They were three very different people, yet they shared a huge capacity for enthusiasm that impresses me still, in my gratitude.

*
**

Over the course of the next year, Jerry moved his study to the back bedroom of the brick house. (He kept his library in the barn house.) He made wooden shelves and work tables for his audio and videotapes and his equipment, "torching" the wood to darken it and bring out the grain. For the first time since we had begun living together, he was able to produce sound at any time of the day or night without having to worry about disturbing me. With some of the money Mrs. Hunt left, Jerry was able to buy new electronic equipment. He finally had the professional setup he needed to do his own work, as well as whatever commercial jobs might come his way.

And he rediscovered the piano, seldom played in the last years during Mrs. Hunt's illness and now in need of extensive repair to the action mechanism. A piano technician came out from Dallas and did some work, but he said to bring the instrument back to a really good condition would require several thousand dollars.

Since we were now going back and forth so much, I laid a stepping stone walkway (275 blocks!) through the post oak trees between the two houses. Often, when I'd go to get him to come over for dinner, I'd hear Jerry from a distance playing the piano. He had become interested in Zez Confrey's rags and novelty pieces from the 1920s, and I'd stop to listen to "Kitten on the Keys" or "Poor Buttermilk" or "You Tell 'Em, Ivories"—punctuated, of course, by regular outbursts of temper when he failed to execute a rough passage satisfactorily.

I had become interested in the fortepiano, and Jerry shared my enthusiasm for the music of George Frederick Pinto, a member of the London Pianoforte School of the late 1700s. Sometimes, instead of rags, Cage, or Scriabin, I'd find Jerry playing one of Pinto's sonatas; then, I'd sit for as long as he would play, in "Leto's chair" (the one with the low seat) beside the keyboard.

When the weather grew warm in the spring of '92, Jerry's allergies and attendant breathing problems really began to bother him. On occasion, the temper outbursts at the piano were due not to mistakes but to his not having the strength, or "wind," to get through a piece. He finally got to feeling so bad and so desperate that he agreed to go back to the doctor in Canton.

I knew he had lost weight, but neither of us realized he had lost so much—the clinic record was irrefutable. The doctor assumed the jocular but candid manner he had always employed with Jerry, never one to appreciate the rhetoric of medical caregiving. "You either have a viral infection aggravated by allergies and emphysema, or you have lung cancer. Since an infection is easier and cheaper to treat, let's start there."

I waited in the car while Jerry went to Eckerd's to have a prescription for antibiotics filled. "Cancer." I watched the people going in and coming out of Wal-Mart and the kids waiting for Corny Dogs at the little stand in front of the shopping strip. And I watched myself watching—and the film I was watching that was my life, broke: all that I had seen so far wound tight and flapping on the take-up reel, and all that was to come spilling off the spool in a useless pile on the floor.

When Judy called me New Year's Day 1992, she said she had something important to talk with me about. Jerry and I had just finished dinner with Bob and Rany, who had come up for a few days; I excused myself and went to the phone in a back bedroom. Judy's request came as a complete surprise: could Jamie (my younger niece) come to live with Jerry and me for a while?

Things had not worked out just as they'd hoped they would for my sister and her family. Paul had left the church that originally called him, in part due to its lack of interest in community service. At the time of the call, he was the pastor of a small congregation that met in a Grange (farmers' fraternal) building north of Sandpoint, Idaho, just a few miles from Canada. On one of my visits, I attended a church service there, and I was impressed and touched by how dedicated both Paul and Judy were to their Christian mission. Judy typed the program, taught a Sunday school class (even bringing graham crackers for those children who might not have had any breakfast), and accompanied the devotional singing. Paul made routine repairs and improvements on the building and gave generously of his time, both for the Sunday and Wednesday services and in pastoral counseling. Even my nieces and nephew helped by their chores and participation in the services.

But something happened, and Paul left this church, too. I understood at the time that the church board had expressed some dissatisfaction with Paul, complaining that he was remiss in making church visits and, perhaps, enlarging the congregation. Whatever the case, Judy and her family gradually stopped going to church altogether, and Paul began working as a clerk in a hardware store in Sandpoint (where he is today).

All three of Judy and Paul's children had some difficulty with the role the church played—and then ceased to play—in their lives. For a time, Judy and Paul were extremely zealous in the pursuit of their beliefs—even to the point of not allowing the kids to observe Halloween (because of its Satanic associations). Then they realized they might have gone too far, and they relaxed and became more permissive. This tacking must have been confusing. But, with the help of counseling and Judy and Paul's determination to make their marriage and family work, they became a mutually supporting group, and all the communication lines remain open.

When Judy called me, I didn't have all this background—and, indeed, the situation with the church hadn't yet come to a crisis. Her request that Jamie come here was based on the desire to be able to offer her a greater challenge in school. Jamie had already skipped a grade, and she still found her schoolwork easy and pointless. Near Dallas, with the variety of schools and cultural offerings available, perhaps Jamie could find some intellectual stimulation.

Jamie had come down the summer before to spend a week with us. She and I rode the narrow-gauge train between Palestine and Rusk, attended a chamber music concert in Fair Park after a picnic lunch on the grounds, and I watched her ride the Shock Wave—the upside-down roller coaster at Six Flags Amusement Park. As I always had, I enjoyed her companionship—her quick mind and gentle ways, her unpredictable sense of humor. And I saw, more than ever, how much she had in common with Jerry, from their restless inquisitiveness and nervous energy to their love for staying up late. I was fascinated by the thought of these two together—I could easily imagine the influence each might have on the other and the good company they could be for one another. It also seemed to me that by helping Jamie, Jerry and I would be sharing our bounty a little—if we could, and if he were willing. And he was, without reservation.

So we agreed to be parents, starting in mid-August. Jamie was to finish the school year in Idaho; meanwhile,

I would locate a school here for her to attend for the
eleventh grade. By the end of April, I had met with the
principal of the Ursuline Academy, and I obtained her
permission (contingent upon the school board's ratifi-
cation) for Jamie to attend as a special student. It was
during this meeting that I learned that Anne Freeman
had just joined the Ursuline faculty.

*
**

With the guest bedroom now available in the brick
house, Jerry and I were able to entertain guests more
comfortably and for longer stays. Karen Finley and her
husband and manager, Michael Overn, spent a week with
us in the spring of 1992.

Jerry had given a concert at DiverseWorks in Houston
earlier in the year, premiering *Bitom (fixture): topogram*
with the assistance of Michael Galbreth; this piece, later
taped in a studio performance in Dallas, appears on the
videotape of Jerry's *Four Video Translations*, released in
February of 1995 by O.O. Discs. Michael Schell's program
notes describe the work as follows:

> Galbreth is seated, holding a metal
> grounding plate in one hand. Jerry,
> wearing Latex examination gloves, probes
> him with a device that measures his
> skin's electrical conductivity, a tech-
> nique used in polygraphy to gauge stress.
> These measurements control the pitch of
> an intense, noisy whine that dominates
> the soundscape. In a live performance,
> Jerry would have used a host of hand
> props . . . along with a video camera and
> an array of audio equipment.
>
> Here he makes do with a probe and a
> shrill tin whistle.

Jerry described *Bitom (fixture): topogram* in terms
redolent of exorcism or healing ritual.

The score refers to his and Galbreth's roles as agent
and patient, respectively. But other dyads suggest

themselves, too: experimenter and subject, interrogator and prisoner, father and son (in a peculiar rite of passage). Some find the proceedings charged with an unresolved sexual tension, heightened by the disparity in mood between the two participants (Jerry constantly active, Galbreth calm and stationary). The exact nature of their relationship is unclear, their naive expressions belying the ominous connotations of the event.

After the concert in Houston, I met Shelley Hirsch, who, accompanied by Roulette's David Weinstein, had performed several songs in the program. She expressed her admiration for Jerry's work and her high regard for him personally. And I met Michael Peranteau, who runs DiverseWorks, while Jerry and I were packing up the next day. We told him Karen and Michael were coming for a visit later that spring, and he assured us that whatever we might have heard about her temperament would probably be irrelevant to how she behaved as a house guest.

The subject of temperament had come up because of the fit Jerry had thrown the day before. He arrived at DiverseWorks to set up and rehearse and found nothing ready. (He had sent his tech list weeks earlier.) Not only were there no preparations in evidence, but he could also find no one who even knew who was supposed to help. Whatever the nature of his explosion (it probably included a threat not to perform at all), it had the desired effect: everyone scurried to get the job done. Jerry was now apologizing to Michael for the spectacle he had made of himself.

It turned out that we had a very pleasant time with Karen and Michael indeed. They enjoyed relaxing in the country, indulging in a much-needed respite from their heavy traveling schedule.

Karen and Jerry made plans for their upcoming *Finley/Hunt Report* at the Kitchen (to be funded, in part, by the National Endowment for the Arts). We took them to the (then) "world's largest truck stop," Rip Griffin's ("Rip on In"), on the interstate halfway between Canton and Dallas. Karen enjoyed looking at the Texas souvenirs; we all stood gawking at the TV room filled with truckers in recliners. And we visited The Sixth Floor, the Kennedy museum in downtown Dallas, in the old Texas School

Book Depository building. Karen and Michael had just seen the Oliver Stone movie, and Michael was reading a new book on the assassination. Jerry and I enjoyed the memorabilia on display there because it so effectively transported us to our young-adult years when anything seemed possible.

We headed back to the library where we had parked near and got caught in a sudden rainstorm. For shelter, we ducked into the grand Adolphus Hotel and sat in the opulently furnished lobby drinking gourmet coffee and eating finger sandwiches. I was charmed by the irony of it—seeing a couple of subversive enfants terribles like Karen and Jerry in Yuppieland, Brahms's intermezzi being played unobtrusively on the grand piano across the room. Jerry collected all our rock-candy-coated coffee stirrers to take home for use in some as yet undetermined project.

The Finley/Hunt Report was to be a parody of TV talk shows, including songs sung by Karen, who wrote the texts—and music written and performed by Jerry. There were to be "remotes" as well. After Karen and Michael left, Jerry rented a camcorder and asked me to tape some footage of him standing in the crimson clover beside our road and "talking" with Karen, who was to tape her part of the planned dialogue from beside the highway between Boulder and Denver. Befitting a Texan, Jerry held a gun quite unselfconsciously while he talked about clothing styles and mock meats; at one point, just as he was insouciantly scratching his chin with the gun's barrel, a couple of men in a pickup passed, and one of them saw and yelled an incredulous "Hey!"

These fellows really would have been startled if they could have seen what I was taping down the hill. Jerry, wearing his father's paisley silk smoking jacket, took us on a tour of the property.

We showed a comparison of toilets: the one we built in the barn house and the conventional ones in the brick house—in each case, Jerry raising the lids and the seats with the ubiquitous gun. We had a lesson in horse-feeding, Jerry still in his smoking jacket but now wearing a pollen mask and berating the horses and mules and donkey for their shameful greed for trying to get the most carrots, their total lack of "Christian ethics." Jerry pointed out the weeds and the fire ant mounds and the gopher holes using the tip of his mother's parasol. Throughout it all, I was beside him, recording everything for posterity.

My favorite part of the tape was the gazebo sequence. Jerry sat in the swing and delivered a monologue through his mask about life in the country ("so here I am, allergic to my own land"). I made a slow circle around him as he talked and swung, and when I passed behind him, he launched into an inventory of the natural versus the man-made materials around him, pointing things out by means of his handy handgun: "natural . . . synthetic . . . natural . . . synthetic."

The three performances of *The Finley/Hunt Report* in June went well. Karen called Jerry to read him the *New York Times* review. People especially seemed to like the songs ("My Own Memories," about rape, and "Road Kill," about other forms of violence)—Karen's hard-driving delivery was balanced and ultimately intensified by Jerry's businesslike handling of sound sources. All three audiences were, I understand, much taken by the video footage we had made of life on the ranch.

*
**

We had another couple visit us in the summer: our young friends Peter de Rooden and Ria van Bakel, from Leiden. Peter and Jerry had kept up a steady correspondence—mostly in Dutch—since their meeting at the Apollohuis. Peter had been to New York on business, but Ria had never been to the US, and they were both curious about life in the sparsely settled Southwest. They were to spend several days with us in Canton at the beginning and end of their trip, and they planned to rent a car in Dallas and drive to New Mexico and Arizona for a week in the middle of their stay.

We met them at the airport in Houston late one hot afternoon for the drive back to Canton. Their fair complexions flushed as soon as they stepped into the nearly hundred-degree parking lot, and the whole time they were here, I never saw them in anything but shorts and the coolest shirts and tops they had. With their blond hair, European features, and Dutch accent, they drew

attention wherever they went, beginning with the Dairy
Queen midway between Houston and Canton, where you
enter at the big wooden dog ("hungry as a . . . ") and exit
at the pig ("ate like a . . . ").

Ria and I put up with a lot of talk about Ollie B.Bommel
and Tom Poes. Just as we had Karen and Michael, Jerry
and I took Peter and Ria to Rip Griffin's, where Peter
photographed the scores of eighteen-wheelers in the parking lot. One Sunday, Jerry carried them to the Kimbell
Museum in Fort Worth, leaving me to work my four hours
at the library, and when they returned to pick me up, I
gave them a short tour. After, we met Rod and Sharon
for dinner at a Tex-Mex restaurant. One morning, I aired
up the tires on my two bikes and sent them off with a
map of the county roads. We also took them for pizza and
beer at the (South Asian) Indian-owned Mr. Pizza in Gun
Barrel City ("We Shoot Straight With You") near Cedar
Creek Lake.

After their adventures in New Mexico and Arizona—
which included Ria getting into trouble with the tribal
police after hitting a traffic sign with their rented car on
an Indian reservation—we took them for a brief tour of
Central Texas before their flight home from Houston. We
stayed in an old motel in La Grange for a couple of nights,
and one evening we attended a chamber music concert
at Round Top, where a summer conservatory attracts
students and teachers from all over the world. After the
concert, we drove back to La Grange, but our young
guests were hardly ready for bed.

Since there was nothing open in town, we followed
the directions given to us by a convenience store clerk to
a country-western bar just outside city limits. Jerry and I
stood by the fellow on the sound mixer and watched Peter
and Ria dance right in there with all the cowboy boots
and hats, the big-buckled belts, and sequined blouses.
We must have been as much of an attraction for the regu-
lars as they were for us. (At one point, the man at the
mixer had to reach around the machine to make some
adjustment, and because Jerry and I were standing in
his way, he excused himself with, "Pardon me, boys—or
girls—or whatever you are." It was said just politely and
quietly enough to be ignored.)

The next night, the three of them left me to hear another concert at Round Top while they drove into San Antonio for the evening. It worried me that Jerry might have to do a lot of driving in heavy traffic, but I picked up Peter's hint that he was willing to help drive and was relieved. I know Peter and Ria were a little concerned about Jerry's health. Peter remarked at how thin Jerry had become, and they both saw several manifestations of his irritability, aggravated by the extreme heat and the allergens in the air.

We had agreed to meet at the gazebo just outside the entrance to the concert hall at about ten or so when the concert would be over. By eleven at night, I had still seen no sign of the car, and I panicked.

I called the motel in La Grange, but they hadn't been there. I was worried that they might have had an accident (neither Peter nor Ria had had much experience driving) or that Jerry had gotten sick. Would they be able to reach anyone at Round Top to get word to me? I stood there waiting helplessly another half hour or so, staring out into the darkness and straining to catch a glimpse of any distant moving light. The only relief to the void was the occasional sound of a mosquito or a cicada.

Finally, they pulled up, Peter driving. Everything was fine—they were just late, having underestimated the time it took to return and being delayed at a catfish restaurant on the way back. The concert hadn't been over long, I lied.

*
**

My nephew Paul Michael's turn finally came to spend a summer week with us in Texas. He was now thirteen, and I was eager to remake his acquaintance. The last time we'd had a day together was almost two years earlier when I took him to Spokane while visiting Judy and her family in Sandpoint. We noticed a school class on its way to a special presentation at Spokane's large Omni Theater, and one of the teachers allowed us to tag along at the end of the line and gain admission. Afterward, we took turns reading aloud chapters of Joseph Krumgold's . . . *And Now Miguel* beside the river.

Jerry and I picked Paul Michael up at the airport. We stopped at the grocery store in Kaufman on our way to Canton to give him a chance to lay in a supply of his favorite foods. He marched to the produce aisle and selected a couple of big bags of washed and trimmed salad greens, explaining that he was "eating healthy now." He also stopped by the Little Debbie display and put several kinds of cupcakes and cookies in our basket. He started on the Little Debbie snacks on the drive from Kaufman to Canton, but the salad greens languished in the refrigerator the whole week of his visit.

Although Paul Michael could have slept on the futon in the barn house, I thought he would be more comfortable in the brick house's guest bedroom. I was wrong. The first morning of his visit, I had just gotten up and was shaving when Jerry and Paul Michael came in. "Your little guest's awake," Jerry announced.

Sure enough, he had been uneasy in a strange room with everything so quiet around him (Jerry, working all night in his studio in the adjacent room, had used headphones). He hadn't slept, and he'd even grown so desperate as to go out to the car to watch the digital clock on the dashboard count down the time until morning.

It seemed it took him most of the week he was here to catch up on his sleep. We drove to Rockwall to have lunch with Aunt Hazel and Uncle Henry, and he was so lethargic—he sat on their couch and could barely take part in the conversation. On our way to lunch, we stopped by a used furniture store so Henry could make arrangements to have some filing cabinets delivered. To our amazement—and Henry's eternal delight in retelling the story—Paul Michael had found a bed on display and gone to sleep. The next day, I took him to work with me, and we agreed to meet at the library entrance at noon for lunch. When after twenty minutes or so he hadn't shown up, I had him paged. He had fallen asleep at a reading table on the seventh floor, where he had gone to look at his parents' high school yearbooks.

We made a trip to Sea World near San Antonio, and he talked me into riding one of the roller coasters. When we got to the departure point, after a long wait in line listening to the repeated warnings ("Pregnant ladies, people with heart trouble, and anyone with any reservations should not ride this ride"), Paul Michael himself was ready to back out. Remarkably, while putting my glasses safely in my shirt pocket, I encouraged him to ride. And it really wasn't so bad, thanks to my myopia helping me sustain the impression that it wasn't really happening (a kind of "virtual reality"). Neither of us, though, wanted to ride a second time.

Paul Michael and I had some good talks and renewed our friendship during our week together. One afternoon, I took him to the store to show him how to select and buy condoms with spermicide. I had become sexually active around his age, and there was no reason to assume he wouldn't soon be, too—and the risks for him were so much higher.

He also clearly enjoyed Jerry's company: they spent quite a bit of time with the synthesizers in Jerry's studio, and Jerry showed him one or two of the horror movies he had recently taped.

Since Jamie was due for school orientation in just another week, Paul Michael decided to stay on with his Aunt Ann in Dallas then ride back with his father when Paul brought Jamie and her things. I got Jamie's room ready, and Jerry and I waited with some apprehension for the adventure ahead.

It began dramatically enough. When Jamie arrived after the long car trip from North Idaho, she was obviously in trouble of some kind. Nerves had caused a rash to break out on her face, and she had chewed her fingernails down to the quick. She was considerably overweight, and she seemed to peer through her glasses (one lens of which was missing, having "blown out the window" on the trip down) with suspicion at everyone and everything. Jerry and I both were a little alarmed, but we could see how important it was going to be for us to help her make a go of things here.

We got her school uniform and books and public library card; I took a picture of her standing in front of the handsome main building of the Ursuline Academy (not far from the statue of Christ that one year had worn a brassiere, thanks to some senior girls). While I attended the orientation for new parents (where I renewed my acquaintance with Anne Freeman), Jamie visited with the school counselor in the lounge.

On the evening before the first full day of school, I took her to the home of the family she was to stay with during the school week. (Driving her in daily from Canton—almost two hours away from her school in Dallas—would have been impractical.) From the first visit I had with them to plan Jamie's stay, I had liked the Mantheiys right away. They had a daughter in Jamie's class, and they had two others who had graduated from Ursuline. And although they were a traditional Catholic family, they never gave me any reason to believe they were uncomfortable with the unusual nature of the arrangements that surrounded Jamie being here—in particular, the two "uncles" who often came together to pick Jamie up on Thursdays or Fridays and return her Sunday nights.

The Mantheiys were, I think, a little uncomfortable with Jamie, though. Although sometimes shy, Jamie can be quite outspoken, and she articulated liberally her views to the conservative Ursuline community. Most of the girls and their families supported George Bush in the 1992 election, but she (as were Jerry and me) was in favor of Bill Clinton. She told me about several angry exchanges she had with some of the girls during lunchtime.

Jamie is also an independent spirit—and a brave one, too, as her coming here certainly showed. Regular schedules and organization bedevil her, and Mrs. Mantheiy complained to her and to me about her oversleeping and her cluttered room. Jamie has a facility to lose herself in a book or music, tuning everything and everyone out—a trait that can be irritating and threatening to those who have her in their care. More than once, she left papers in Canton that she needed in school, and she'd forget to tell me about variations in her schedule until it was almost too late for me to change mine to accommodate them. What was especially hard for me to see, as an ex-teacher, was how she'd put off work until it was too late to do it well.

The more I saw of Ursuline, however, the more it reminded me of Cistercian Prep; they are schools that train for success, and they function best when that success is defined narrowly and conventionally. By the second month, Jamie was chafing under the constraints

of the school and the Mantheiys—just as she was under
the rough-textured plaid skirt of her uniform that she
immediately changed for her comfortable shorts right in
the car every time I picked her up after school.

Jerry and I often discussed Jamie's being here and
the effect that it was having on all of us. He saw earlier
than I was prepared to admit that Jamie wouldn't want
to stay at Ursuline. She began talking about going back
home at the end of the fall semester, but I encouraged
her to wait until Thanksgiving, at least, before making up
her mind.

I received proof one night that staying here was not
what she needed. We'd called Idaho to visit with everyone
there, and I left the room when Jamie was talking with
her father about the upcoming presidential election. Paul
and Judy supported Ross Perot. Jamie had tried to sway
them to Clinton several times. Jerry and I were in the
living room, and when I thought it was surely time for
Jamie to have joined us, I went back to check on her
and found her crying on her bed. "He wouldn't even listen
to my reasons," she sobbed. I had never seen her more
miserable. I called back and told Paul how inconsolable
she was; he was surprised and talked with her again and
made her feel better. But it became clear to me that, to
work things out, Jamie needed to be with her family. At
fifteen, she needed still to be in dialogue with her father
and mother.

A little before Thanksgiving, we told the school and
the Mantheiys that Jamie would be returning home at
the end of the semester. There was a relaxation of tension
all around. Jamie continued to work for good grades, and
because some of the pressure was taken off the Mantheiys,
they became friends. She had made friends already with
the staff of the children's center at the library, where she
ran the projector for Sunday films. And she made one
close friend at school, Pia, who she invited several times
to spend the weekend with her in Canton. (One afternoon,
they made gingerbread men to give as Christmas presents. Jerry said he cleaned dough off the counters and
the floor for days afterward.)

We tried to give Jamie as many opportunities as we
could to see Texas and experience the cultural events

here. Some efforts were more successful than others. We had car trouble on our way to Houston for a Saturday night concert and had to return just an hour into the trip. While my mechanic repaired the car, we ate the picnic lunch we'd prepared for the journey. By the time the car was ready, it was too late to make it to the concert.

I took Jamie to a Dallas Symphony Orchestra concert in the beautiful new Meyerson Center. We had cheap seats on the choral terrace, just above and behind the cellos and basses. During the first movement of the Brahms *Violin Concerto*, Jamie whispered to me that she wasn't feeling well. Her face was flushed, and the stage was warm. We tiptoed out to the restroom area, and I stood anxiously with an usher waiting for Jamie to come out. She did, shortly, and said she felt better after splashing water on her face. We got back to our seats just in time for the final chords of the concerto—which Jamie later told me she had found boring (nauseatingly so, perhaps).

One weekend, we took her to Austin, where we all three enjoyed Francis Ford Coppola's *Dracula*. The next day, we had lunch with David Robert Fulkerson—the son of composer Jim Fulkerson and Mary O'Donnell, the dancer who had invited Jerry to teach at the Hogeschool in Arnhem the previous fall. Jamie was quite taken with David, who had come to Austin to learn to play the guitar like Stevie Ray Vaughan. I have a picture of Jerry and the handsome, long-haired David with Jamie standing between them and looking as though she were having a very good time indeed.

However, she didn't have such a good time the weekend we took her to Edgewood, a little town just a few miles north of Canton. Edgewood created a village of restored old buildings arranged in such a way as to convey what life was like in a small Texas town in the early 1900s. One beautiful autumn day, the three of us wandered in and out of a country store, a blacksmith's shop, a barbershop, and a gift shop where a lady in a period costume was demonstrating how to weave. There weren't many young people on the grounds, and Jamie, though patient with us and indulgent of our interests, was clearly bored.

We were heading back to the car when we passed an old train on display. We walked through the passenger car and back to the caboose. Jerry's manner and mood changed suddenly, and he told us he had just realized that the car was exactly like the one he had ridden one summer forty years ago near Mart with his grandfather. He sat down in one of the trainmen's seats, and, on her cue, Jamie and I left him alone for a few minutes, giving him the space he needed to savor the memories that had so unexpectedly (and uncharacteristically) overtaken him.

This was only one of the many times during Jamie's stay with us when she demonstrated extraordinary sensitivity to the feelings of others. Jerry was having good days and bad days. Although he appeared to be free of infection during most of the fall, he complained about his allergies, suffered headaches, and had the sense of "a weight pressing down on me." He was no longer smoking (at least as far as I knew), but he had begun using chewing tobacco made in Odense, Denmark, called Oliver Twist—plugs that he would keep between his gums and cheeks and, finally, deposit in ashtrays where they piled up in great numbers. He had long since given up on tranquilizers because he couldn't "get any work done" on them.

Jamie witnessed some rather marked mood swings, and she sometimes saw what might have looked like his abuse of me. He and I had some heated exchanges in the car, and Jamie sat in the backseat with her headphones on, our flare-ups certainly audible in front of the rock and roll she was listening to. Usually, though, when Jerry felt bad, he became merely hypercritical; Jamie and I both could easily ignore this because we knew it originated in the frustration he felt at his own inability to do things.

He'd walk through the kitchen where Jamie was helping me prepare dinner and point out a better way to do something; as he left, Jamie would turn to me with just the suspicion of a sweet smirk on her face.

During the early fall, he was practicing the piano for a recital he was to give at Paul and Oz's house in November. He was planning to play some pieces prepared for piano by John Cage, the Pinto sonata we both loved, and some Zez Confrey tunes. Each was difficult in its own way: making the mechanical sounds of the Cage musical, interpreting Pinto's sometimes vague musical notation, and executing the tricky passages of the Confrey. Jamie got to hear some piano fits as well.

But she saw what all of it was for on the afternoon of the concert. She and I sat on our folding chairs in Paul and Oz's sunny home with the fifty or so other guests, all of us captivated by Jerry's conversation and mesmerized by his music. With insight and wit, Jerry introduced the pieces. After performing them, he accepted our applause with his usual humility, even apologizing for some passages that hadn't gone as well as he thought they should have.

After the recital, the guests gathered in the game room for refreshments—just as we had on so many similar afternoons over the last two decades. A few people kept Jerry at the keyboard with their questions and comments about the music. The others cornered me in the back, expressing their concern about Jerry's health, about how emaciated he looked, and how short of breath he was. By now a small crowd had gathered around me, and I told them what Canton's new family doctor, whom we had recently seen, had diagnosed: chronic obstructive pulmonary disease (COPD), a progressively debilitating condition consisting of both emphysema and bronchitis and, in Jerry's case, made worse by allergies. I tried to assure everyone, myself included, that we were on top of it—that Jerry had quit smoking, and we were taking every precaution to protect Jerry from respiratory infections that would further damage his lungs. We had just bought a book on living with COPD, and it had given us several useful suggestions about making the indoor environment more healthful and life generally easier. As I talked and sipped sherry, I caught a glimpse of Jamie standing in the next room visiting with Ron and Joan's son, Dorian. The happy (and beautiful) look on her face was exactly like the one my camera had recorded when she stood between Jerry and David in Austin.

Jerry seemed to go into a decline after the recital. He wasn't happy, he told me, with his performance—particularly the Confrey part. "It was like my brain wasn't working well enough, wasn't concentrating." Although no one in the audience I spoke with admitted noticing this, I myself had the feeling that Jerry was having a harder time playing the music than he should have, or than he usually would have. He was probably suffering from some oxygen deprivation—what he complained about was the difficulty he had "getting all the way through" the pieces.

Jamie and I would come home to find him still in his robe and slippers. More and more often, we arrived hungry and found that he had done nothing to get dinner started. She gamely pitched in to help on these occasions, as Jerry sat nearby visiting with us and playing with Mary and Frances, dangling their Cat Dancer toy (a wire with cardboard strips attached to one end) in front of them. Most days, we'd find the mail still in the box on the road. We'd get it and bring it down, and although most of it was for him, he showed little interest in it.

This was not so for the proof copy of the *Ground* CD that we brought him one day. As there had been on all the Irida records, there were a couple of typographical errors in the CD program notes that Jerry found unacceptable (including "pianforte"). It would have been prohibitively expensive to reprint the entire program booklet just to correct a couple of errors, so Jerry asked Joseph Celli to ship the lot of CDs to us, and we'd have self-adhesive labels printed to cover the mistakes.

One day, before she left for Idaho, Jamie helped me affix these labels to the hundreds of CDs that arrived by UPS. We had to remove the shrinkwrap and take the jewel case apart to get to the portions of text that needed correcting. Jerry did a few to show us how, but he didn't feel like doing many. Jamie sat for hours at the card table that we had set up for the project and systematically processed the CDs, looking up from time to time at the TV across the room.

I am grateful to Jamie for her help doing that and so much else while she was here. She gave me moral support, and she lifted Jerry's spirits and helped him pass the time—particularly during the late hours when they watched TV and movies on videotape together.

She also helped me understand a little better about what being young today means—and what being a young girl is like. She taught me to be more careful with bleach in the laundry (after I ruined a pair of her socks), and she showed me how to tie long laces in double bows to prevent tripping. And she set good examples before me,

like the day we were waiting at a traffic light and read the
marquee in front of a Baptist church that announced an
upcoming discussion of homosexuality.

"How to spot a queer," I said cynically.

She replied: "Well, at least they're talking about it."

*
**

At first, I thought it was a dream: "Stephen, Stephen"—I
kept hearing, lying in bed in the barn house, my name
not so much called as spoken—whispered almost. The
alarm jerked me from the bed toward the sound: not in
the room, nor in the next room ("Stephen"), but outside,
a few feet along the walkway between the houses. "Help
me . . . I can't . . . breathe," Jerry whispered.

I got him to the house (he had to pause after each
step), and we made it to the bathroom, where I turned on
the electric heater. Then I called an emergency medical
number for advice and was told to have him sit down,
bend slightly forward, and inhale steam.

When the breathing problem eased—and it would,
the nurse promised—I should get him to a doctor. Sure
enough, my little clothes steamer seemed to help. In a
couple of hours, we were on our way to the Canton clinic,
planning to arrive at about the time it opened.

Because that cold January morning he believed he was
near death, Jerry told me on the way to town how much
he had always loved me, what I had meant to his life. I
tried not to cry but failed. I told him how much he had
meant to me all our years together, how he had opened
up the world for me and made me a better person—but I
also said I didn't think he was dying, that we were going
to be able to get help. During the ten months he had yet
to live, we never made those speeches again—they never
seemed necessary.

The Canton doctor listened to Jerry's lungs and
explained that the wheezing, gurgling sounds we
heard were being caused by the difficulty of moving air
through diseased tissue, now further complicated by
an influenza-like infection. He arranged for Jerry to be
admitted to the Mother Frances Hospital in Tyler, and we

drove there immediately after having a tire changed on my car—we'd come out of the clinic to discover a flat.

Jerry was in the hospital for three days on an intravenous glucose drip with antibiotics and taking steroids. The pulmonologist, Dr. Gass, ordered lung function tests; he later told us that Jerry had lost over half his lungs' capacity to emphysema. "Make walking your religion," he said. Nothing could be done to reverse the deterioration (now that Jerry had stopped smoking), but Jerry could indirectly help his weakened lungs by strengthening the rest of his body, thus asking less of them.

Dr. Gass stressed that Jerry had to be extremely careful so as to avoid further infections—each one would only damage his lungs more. There were medications that dilate the bronchial passages to help keep the airway open, and a respiratory therapist would train Jerry in their use. (The blue, handheld inhalers with small bellows became commonplace in our lives. In a sad irony, over the following months, they usurped the role cigarettes had played by giving Jerry something to do with his hands and mouth.)

Jerry liked Dr. Gass—his professionalism, his candor, and his good looks. He'd come in, tweak one of Jerry's big toes, and stand at the side of the bed, listening closely and growing more and more curious about the atypical patient he had. He quickly read the nature of Jerry's and my relationship and frequently addressed me as the person looking after Jerry. (Soon after we had been admitted to the hospital's emergency room, Jerry agreed to undergo an HIV test. The hospital records reflected the negative results, and at the same time that these results allayed the staff's fear of AIDS, they announced our identity as a gay couple.)

The morning of the day he was released, Jerry had begun to feel much better. The steroids had improved his appetite: he ate the vegetarian meals the hospital provided and a good portion of what I brought from home each day for myself. Seeing his color improve and the old animation return, I realized how sick he had been and for how long. We were both encouraged that a crisis had been put behind us and that we could manage Jerry's chronic condition by prophylaxis, medication, and exercise therapy. Dr. Gass even saw no reason why Jerry could not give the concert he'd been asked to give in New York in late January if he felt like it.

However, there was one troubling element: the X-rays and CAT scan of Jerry's chest showed a spot of some kind in the upper portion of one of Jerry's lungs. The radiologist's report, which we read later, suggested that this spot be monitored. Dr. Gass believed this was probably a calcified granuloma, the result of a succession of pulmonary infections he'd had over the past several years. What we could do right away was to get Jerry enrolled in a pulmonary rehabilitation program. Because Mother Frances wasn't offering one, we signed Jerry up at the University of Texas at Tyler Health Center, a teaching hospital that used to be a tuberculosis sanatorium and thus has a large pulmonary clinic. As soon as Jerry returned from his New York trip, we'd begin the exercise therapy.

Thanks to our good friend Sally Bowden, Jerry was able to get through the New York concert—a performance of his *Bitom (fixture): topogram* (using a New York actor) for the World Music Institute. Sally arranged to have Jerry picked up at the airport, and she saw to it that he never had to carry his bags or equipment up or down the stairs to her and Ted's apartment. She also enforced rest, planning all their meals, and running all the errands. He could not have made it without her.

Shortly after he returned, we went to K-Mart and bought his exercise gear: tennis shoes, a sweatsuit, and an athletic bag to carry them. Trey, the exercise physiologist, outlined a program that combined weight lifting and aerobics, and I—as the "significant other"—was invited to join in. We made two trips a week to Tyler, having committed ourselves to an eight-week training period, after which we would be on our own (though always able to use the gym without charge).

We were both amused at what we had gotten ourselves into (we could afford to be amused because Jerry was feeling so much better). Jerry and his "trainer," Trey, hit it off at once. His cynical banter notwithstanding, Jerry was trying hard, and Trey could see it. We began to see the same faces on our regular visits, and we sometimes chatted with a couple of fellows in both the cardiac and the pulmonary rehab programs. But, above all, it was work: we both ended up sweaty and always took a shower afterward (though never together).

This was a hopeful time. We had been badly frightened, but there had been a reprieve, and we were determined to deserve it.

In his last letter to Jacqueline, Jerry wrote:

> Unless something happens to alter or interrupt the plans, I'll do a few more concerts through this season in Canada & New York, then Holland in June for a month-long installation in Rotterdam with a friend Paul Panhuysen. I'm adding a new computer system—this health problem and its expenses have actually convinced me to spend the money and do the work while I've still got the money and health to do it—if all goes well, then all goes well: if things don't go so well: you're on your way, down the path. . . .

We began to do everything together again, from making our trips to Tyler to running the simplest errands. We spent a lot of time talking. Sometimes we watched TV or movies on videotape. Things that might once have seemed a waste of time no longer did—we took rides, we went shopping, we ate out.

One early spring day after our workout at the hospital gym, we drove twenty or so miles northeast of Tyler to Gladewater, where over thirty years earlier, Helen Lee had had thousands of daffodils planted in her husband's memory. (A boxcar full of bulbs had arrived from Holland in the fall of 1960, accompanied by a representative of the Dutch exporter, to oversee the planting.)

We followed the signs along narrowing county roads until a curve revealed the sight of twenty acres of brilliant yellow and white and a small lake in the center. We were alone in the park. We walked along the path, marveling at the sight of so many flowers massed together as thickly as the tulips are in the fields we'd seen in Holland. We strolled out onto the pier where two chairs had been placed, no doubt for fishing. Jerry was a little winded, so we sat there a few minutes, admiring the daffodils' reflection in the water. What a wonderful way to remember someone, we agreed.

Jerry was never very good at being sick; he always considered illness an affront, then a bother, and he tried to go on with his usual activities, never resting enough and, perhaps, prolonging the period of recuperation. His work habits, like his conversation, were not long focused on a single project: he was up and off, on to something else, then back. Living with an ever-diminishing oxygen supply and its consequent debilities was extraordinarily frustrating for him. COPD turns energy into money: you have to save to be able to spend.

With the help of the books I brought from the library and the telephone counsel of the nurses on the Lung Line switchboard in Denver, Colorado (a service of the National Jewish Center for Immunology and Respiratory Medicine), we were gradually learning to cope with his condition. Whenever exertion brought about the shortness of breath, Jerry would snap his fingers to a steady beat to facilitate regular breathing and the return of the normal respiratory cycle. We learned to allow for periods of rest between activities: getting up could not be immediately followed by leaving the house, getting dressed was something to rest up for and from, and we couldn't make love just before dinner. The planning and patience required to live like this were contrary to Jerry's nature, and he experienced long periods of depression.

One of the requirements of participating in the pulmonary rehab program at UT Tyler was to be examined by a resident pulmonary specialist. We saw Dr. Idell, the head of the clinic, and he impressed us from the first visit with his knowledge and experience of lung conditions. Where Dr. Gass had apparently been content to release Jerry to exercise therapy and watchful waiting, Dr. Idell took a more active, interventionist role: he prescribed a variety of medications for Jerry in order to see just which ones helped his breathing the most. He also ordered more X-rays, CAT scans, and oximetry and blood gas tests to learn just where the tissue degeneration was and its exact effect on Jerry's ability to utilize oxygen. We were glad, at first, to have made the change in doctors, although the state-supported Tyler clinic was filled with sad cases: mostly elderly people in wheelchairs and on oxygen, the majority of whom began smoking as soon as they left the hospital.

Dr. Idell was particularly intent on identifying the suspicious mass in one of Jerry's lungs. He ordered still more X-rays and a localized CAT scan, and he asked Jerry to collect and mail sputum specimens. (After his hospitalization, Jerry occasionally had some blood in what he coughed up, but we understood this sometimes happened as a result of respiratory infections and their treatment.) Above all, Dr. Idell urged Jerry to undergo a bronchoscopy—only by actually looking into the lungs and extracting tissue samples for analysis would we know what was there. Jerry read about the procedure and was disturbed by its risks of causing further infection and spreading malignant cells if cancer is found. Moreover, his Amsterdam friend Joel Ryan's partner Greg, suffering from AIDS, had said having to overcome the gag reflex to swallow the bronchoscope was an especially miserable ordeal.

We made an extra trip to Tyler in March to attend classes during Pulmonary Education Day, hoping to learn even more about how we could cope with Jerry's illness and make it easier for him to get his work done. In the morning session, we were shown a variety of products, from devices used to pick up objects without having to bend over to cushions for back support. There was a session on how to correlate breathing with stooping and overcome shortness of breath by emphasizing exhalation (to expel stale air, thus making more room for fresh air to then be inhaled).

On our lunch break, we ran into Dr. Idell in the hall. "Uh oh. Dr. Death," Jerry said. Dr. Idell didn't visibly react, although he certainly heard the epithet. He had, in fact, come specifically to find us, having taken the trouble to check the class enrollment lists in the supposition that we might attend that day. He led us into his office and explained that the sputum analysis indicated the presence of a large number of squamous cells that might or might not mean cancer, but a bronchoscopy, he felt, was even more strongly indicated.

Jerry immediately asked what would happen and what could be done for him if cancer were found. Dr. Idell outlined a six-to-eight-week course of radio- and chemotherapy, requiring five treatments a week; surgical removal of a tumor or tumors would probably not be possible, although a lung might have to be collapsed to help prevent the spread of malignant cells. Jerry then asked what the quality of his life would be, how the treatments would affect him. "Well, of course, you'll be weaker—I would say the overall quality of life would be reduced, but you could handle that."

Lung function tests at this time were measured forty-three to forty-seven percent of normal capacity. Any treatments would further reduce that.

At Jerry's request, I called Paul Srere, who found a colleague on the faculty of the UT Health Science Center in Dallas who agreed to look at Jerry's test results and give us a second opinion. We took the radiologist's interpretations, along with the original films from all the tests done at both Tyler hospitals since January, to Dallas and left them. The doctor called early the next morning, and since Jerry was still asleep, I talked with him. He couldn't say definitely that there was cancer, but to rule it out, he'd recommend the bronchoscopy. If cancer were present and nothing is done about it, Jerry could still have a couple of relatively good years, he added.

All that day, we talked about what this third lung specialist had said and about what our choices might be and might mean. When I woke up the next morning, I found a long letter to me on my desk:

>   Stephen:
>   I've spent some time working tonight: mostly I've been trying to work out the . . . setup for the [new] computer, but it's also given me time to think some; because you'll be awake sooner,
>
>   I want you to read this, because you may be the first line of defence for me in correcting what I believe is a false

path . . . I do not want to continue the
visits to Tyler . . . I think it's best
for me, and for you, and ultimately for us
both, to stop all of this now and become
very selective about each new step. As
I've been working tonight, I've begun to
realize that the only way I'll be able
to have anything left of anything is
to leave this mistaken path and go on
the way I would have gone on if I had
left Mother Frances and not started up
on all of this: no new information has
been obtained since I left there: all of
the suspicions, worries, and questions
that the original information from the
hospital suggested haven't changed: only
more concentrated and [more] carefully
extracted and detailed questions about
the oddities originally noted have been
emphasized: I do understand the focus
of all of this in terms of Idell's sense
of responsibility and his professional
integrity, but whether these concerns
are accurate or not is, in my own situation, completely meaningless: there is
no way that I can tolerate continuing to
draw this out with the false expectations
that something can, in some way, be done
to avert or modify what may or may not
happen: what is happening is that this
is ruining both of our lives, both of
us becoming involved in making judge-
ments and guesses about possibilities
and outcomes, all of this is something
that I don't believe in and that can't
really help you, and that can and will
ultimately hurt us both much more than
necessary, certainly more than is desir-
able for me.

   You've heard me squeal before, you
know how to handle that.

The way I have lived up to the visit
to the hospital has been, clearly, too
destructive, but my collapse has permanently changed that, and the only part
of the past I would have wished to alter
would have been my pursuit of a narrow
dark self-destructive aspect in all my
living until now there's no way to change
that now, or to understand what caused
it; even if it could be understood it
wouldn't help: what I must do is deal with
whatever happens in a sensible but situ-
ational day-at-a-time encounter, dealing
with each circumstance and . . . situation as it occurs, not living constantly
doing one thing after another trying to
outguess nature and make something else
happen which might or might not be useful,
when both of the events are unspecified
as to outcome: this is only compounding
the problem with futile grasping in the
air. I know some people are willing to
engage in this kind of approach, but I
think it's as much self-deception as the
kind I'm willing to live with.

I called Dr. Idell's office and canceled an upcoming
appointment. He called me right back and accused me of
being "revenue neutral," encouraging me to urge Jerry to
undergo the bronchoscopy. We sent Trey a box of Aplets
and Cotlets fruit collections with a note that we'd be
putting to use all that he had taught us in the athletic
center in Athens. Jerry had already sent Dr. Idell a copy
of *Ground*.

*
**

The effect of Jerry's decision was immediate: he began
spending long hours at the new Amiga computer, and he
bought a laser printer to make fair copies of his pieces.
Because he had just received a contract to write music
for a new community college series on health (he half-

jokingly volunteered to be interviewed for the segment on emphysema), he felt he could justify the expense of a new Kurzweil synthesizer. He worked late every night.

In addition, his conversation was now more about his work than his worries. He told me about a new piece he was planning, *Hemisphere*, that would use close-up video scans of a human body that would be stored on laserdisc and then accessed in performance, along with music, by means of a computer interface.

He was preparing for concerts in New York (with Petr Kotik's S.E.M. Ensemble) and in Houston, and he and Paul Panhuysen were corresponding about their joint installation in Rotterdam. (The concert in Canada fell through; they weren't able to offer as much money as Jerry needed to cover his expenses and have any money leftover.) He also remained in touch with Karen Finley, Maria Blondeel, Michael Schell, and Laetitia Sonami, planning future work.

Above all else, though, we were both looking forward to three weeks in Holland in June. This trip became a goal and a symbol.

Together, we made two weekly visits to the Cain Center in Athens, exercising for about an hour and a half. Jerry sometimes made a third trip on Sunday afternoons (while I was at the library), and he made friends with a bright and good-looking young man working part-time as a desk clerk while studying political science at UT Tyler.

The gym at the Cain Center was an upbeat contrast to the rehab facility in Tyler. To the accompaniment of loud rock and roll, young people from the community college in Athens came in, often with friends, to pump up, slim down, and socialize. Older adults joined them occasionally, and one day I ran into a fellow who had taught at the prison the same semester I had.

Jerry and I suited up in the locker room, stuffing our street clothes, athletic bags, and valuables into one locker that I secured with a combination lock. We warmed up, walked on the treadmills, rode the exercise bikes, and lifted free weights.

While Jerry stepped onto and off an elevated platform, I used the NordicTrack and did sit-ups. We both worked hard; Jerry conscientiously added time when he had to lower resistance settings, and he always finished the number of repetitions he had set for himself, even if it meant having to take short rest breaks along the way. As things grew easier, as his strength improved, we felt more confident about being able to make the trip abroad.

In May, our friend Mark flew down from Philadelphia to spend a few days with us. He and Alan had broken up but had remained good friends. Mark was still teaching paralegal studies and enjoying it, and he was working on a textbook on the subject. Jerry and I had always felt completely at ease around Mark, and we were each able and happy to confide in him our concerns about Jerry's health and about me as well. Mark went to the gym with us one day. Another afternoon, he and I waited in the Dallas recording studio Real to Reel while Jerry used their piano to record some music for *Haramand Plane*, the new CD he was working on for Nonsequitur in Albuquerque.

Mark took a picture of Jerry and me standing at the studio's reception desk and visiting with the wife of the man who had started the business years ago. Over the years, Jerry had been a regular customer, and both his music and his manner probably made a welcome change for them from the usual clientele working on commercials or laying down tracks for what they hoped would be country-western or rhythm and blues hits. His friends at the studio noted the difference in Jerry's appearance, and the photograph clearly shows the big Ziploc bag of medicines, inhalers, masks, and tissues he now carried everywhere. The subject of health inevitably came up, and Mrs. Cunningham remarked that her father had died of emphysema. (This same studio, Real to Reel, did the audio editing for *Haramand Plane* following the instructions Jerry left and that I delivered to them after his death. Although I asked for one several times, they never sent me a bill.)

Near the end of May, Jerry's medications began to run out. Our Canton doctor was reluctant to renew some of the prescriptions, so Jerry decided to return to Dr. Gass for a checkup. Also, as a result of a couple of frightening episodes of shortness of breath, we had started to think that Jerry might need supplemental oxygen, which was available only by prescription.

Dr. Gass remembered him, remembered us. At first, I did most of the talking to save Jerry's breath, which was always a little short in stressful situations. I told him about what had happened at UT Tyler, about our cancer fears. "If the radiologist at Mother Frances had suspected cancer, he would have said so," Dr. Gass declared. Then he compared new X-rays with those on file from five months earlier and examined Jerry. Everything seemed to be in line with the usual progress of the disease. The good news was that Jerry had suffered no further loss of lung function.

Then Jerry talked. He asked Dr. Gass point-blank if he were the one with Jerry's condition and cancer was discovered, would he do anything about it. "No," Dr. Gass replied. "Treatment wouldn't affect the prognosis, and it would make you sicker. If it were me, I'd go on as long as I could, and then I'd take a bottle of Jack Daniels and some pills down to the creek bed. My kids need a daddy." I remember these words clearly.

The nurse instructed me in the techniques of chest percussion ("You now have permission to beat on him") and then brought us the prescriptions, including one for supplemental oxygen. She also gave me her card, urging me to call if I had any questions or needed help.

We had one more chore to do before we could go to Holland relatively worry-free. Our first wills had been made almost twenty years ago, and it was time for new ones. What if something happened to one or both of us—an airplane accident, maybe? What would happen to Mary and Frances and to the property? Mrs. Hunt was no longer here to take over, to see to things. We visited with our lawyer, Don McLean, the husband of a lady whom Jerry had met at SMU years earlier when she was working for the contemporary performance group Voices of Change and whom I got to know when she later came to work for the library. Since the law doesn't yet recognize gay "marriage," Jerry was especially concerned about secur-ing my right to inherit the land. Don recommended that we undertake title research and include deed descriptions in the wills. Another of Jerry's worries was that he would lose control of his life and of his manner of dying, and

Don helped us with living wills and powers of attorney to preclude that—to the extent that we could.

Nine months later, Don McLean was at my side before the county judge for the probate hearing. Everything legal worked out just as Jerry hoped it would.

*
**

Our last trip to Holland began auspiciously: from the window of our KLM flight from Houston to Amsterdam, the full moon looked so close that, for a while, it appeared to be our destination. Jerry had a copy of *De Telegraaf* in his lap, thanks to the Netherlands-based flight crew. We knew Mary and Frances would be well cared for by Bob and Rany while we were gone.

And we had made all the arrangements we could in case of accident or illness. I had been assured that there was a supply of medical oxygen on board the plane, and I had the address of a medical equipment firm in Amsterdam that would rent us a portable cylinder if Jerry needed it. In addition to the oxygen-use prescription, I had copies of our wills, powers of attorney, and living wills in my coat pocket—along with the names and telephone numbers of people in Dallas who could help in emergencies of any kind. In May, when Mark was in Canton, he had offered to take Mary and Frances if something happened to both of us; he even said he'd drive down from Philadelphia to get them.

Since we had shipped ahead of our flight all the electronics and other paraphernalia that Jerry would need for his portion of the installation with Paul, we were able to travel relatively light. The first test of how well Jerry was going to be able to manage came at Schipol, where we had to carry our luggage long distances through an area of the airport undergoing expansion; he made it fine, as long as we stopped frequently to rest. We watched the workmen on one of these stops, but we moved along as soon as Jerry translated the hand-lettered sign one of them had tied to the chain-link fence: *Aapjes kijken niet voederen* ("Watch the monkeys, but don't feed them.")

Throughout our stay in Holland, in all the trains, trams, subways, and buses we made, we never consulted the timetables displayed in the stations: Jerry couldn't rush, so it was better just to get there when we could and wait. I often thought back to our trips to New York where Jerry, like most Manhattanites, disdained to stop at cross streets, while I saw each "Don't Walk" sign as an opportunity to stand and gawk.

By the time we'd traveled south to Eindhoven, we were both exhausted, but seeing and being so warmly welcomed by Paul and Hélène again energized us. If they were disturbed by Jerry's gaunt appearance and labored breathing, their faces didn't reflect it—at first. We sat and talked for a couple of hours before going to our apartment to rest. There had been a misunderstanding about some of the arrangements for the installation in Rotterdam, and Paul was no longer inclined to do it. (As best I gathered and remember, the misunderstanding had a political element.) What would take place, if Jerry agreed, would be an installation and opening concert at the Melkfabriek in s'-Hertogenbosch; unfortunately, the opening could not be scheduled until a week after Jerry and I had planned to return home.

There was never a question of our being able to extend our stay. I had to get back to work—three weeks was plenty long for Bob and Rany to keep the cats—and any change in our advance-purchase airline tickets would have been costly. We all realized, too, that Jerry wasn't up to returning alone. The disappointment about Rotterdam was somewhat lessened by the fact that we had come, as it turned out, for a three-week vacation in Holland with a rent-free apartment and Jerry's airfare paid for, courtesy of the Apollohuis. Privately, I was relieved: the trips to and from Rotterdam to plan the installation, the eventual move there for a few days for the opening, and getting around in the city itself would all have been very difficult for Jerry. S'-Hertogenbosch is less than an hour from Eindhoven by train, and a few trips there and back near the end of our sojourn would be all that was required for Jerry's share of the collaboration.

Jerry was less sanguine. He was so tired that first night that he couldn't sleep, and he had begun to feel worse and worse. Even the chest percussion treatment didn't help as it usually did. By early daybreak (which, in

June in the Netherlands, is a little after four in the morning), he had decided he wanted to fly back to Texas the next day: "It's a total collapse: this trip, my work, my life."

I agreed to call KLM first thing in the morning.

But he felt better a few hours later, and we postponed returning (though it remained an option). How Jerry felt, physically and emotionally, seemed more and more to fluctuate between low points of despair and highs of "feeling almost good." The oxygenation of his blood was certainly a controlling factor, and rest and a good meal could sometimes affect that. Just as we had with the train timetables, we learned to avoid letting external factors set our goals: we could do what he felt like when he felt like it.

In a few days, we settled into a comfortable routine at the Apollohuis. Before Jerry awoke or got going, I wrote letters, read, or visited with Paul, who had come up to the studio adjacent to our apartment to give fresh greens to the members of his Grand Kanarie Band in their cages near the sunny windows. (Birdsong accompanied our stay there.) Later in the morning, when we saw how Jerry was doing, we'd make our plans for the day. When he felt like going with me, we went to the bookshop or to the bakery or the market; several times, we walked through the residential neighborhood near the Apollohuis, along streets with names like Nachtegaallaan and Pelikaanlaan and Koekoeklaan and Fazantlaan—to continue the ornithological theme so well begun by the resident canaries.

In the afternoons, while I took the long walk to Eindhoven's city center and back, Jerry and Paul visited and made plans for their joint work, *Marten Toonder's Studio*: an installation inspired by Ollie Bommel and Tom Poes and their adventures as much as by Toonder's old-fashioned Dutch and its grand style. Paul and Jerry read portions of a few of the Toonder books on tape, and this tape was to be played, randomly accessed, from within a double bass suspended in the center of the installation space at the Melkfabriek. Jerry's music would be heard in the space whenever it was triggered by infrared motion detectors—and the motion to be detected was that of four goats moving about in their pen on one side of the room. (We made several trips to oversee the setup of the installation toward the end of our stay; Jerry got to go to a farm near s'-Hertogenbosch to help select the guest-artist goats.) During the opening concert, which Jerry and I would have to miss, Paul would play his long-stringed instrument attached to the bass.

We usually had dinner with Paul and Hélène, sometimes contributing a dish or two that I had prepared to the meal. Several times, we ate on the roof garden overlooking the neighbors' yards. Sappho and Paul's son, Raphael, joined us on two separate occasions. I went into Eindhoven for concerts many evenings, and there were always events at the Apollohuis on weekends. We felt quite at home and kept ourselves pleasantly entertained. I always brought Dutch reading matter home to Jerry from my shopping trips, and he spent a lot of time with his dictionary, compiling questions about the language to ask Paul and Hélène. He even did a little wiring for Paul.

I could see how concerned they were about his health. Paul always tried to make certain that Jerry really felt up to whatever might be on the day's agenda. He offered, again and again, to refrain from smoking in Jerry's presence, but Jerry wouldn't hear of it; like many Dutch people, Paul loves to smoke, and it was, after all, his own house. I had bought Jerry a little battery-operated fan (with fuchsia-colored rubber blades) for use on the plane in case he had breathing problems, and he used that once or twice to blow the smoke away. Hélène brought food up several times. One morning, she knocked on our Dutch door with several pounds of fresh farmer's cheese, and she was always bringing us treats from the neighborhood bakery. She offered to wash our clothes with theirs late at night when the electricity rates dropped, but we had so few that I was able to hand wash them and hang them out to dry in a tiny courtyard behind the building. She told me once that seeing our socks, shirts, and underwear on the line each morning was a signal to her that I was up and Jerry was well enough for things to go on routinely.

We made a spectacle of ourselves on the stairway every other day. I hadn't been able to find a suitable gym in the area, so we exercised at home. We used bricks as free weights, and we did thirty minutes or so of stepping on the stairs. Guest artists, Paul and Hélène and their friends, and the young man doing alternative military service at the Apollohuis (as Peter had done) passed us as they went up and down on their errands. They were hugely entertained not so much by the sight of two odd fellows, one wearing a sweatband, stepping up and down to the ticking of a timer, but by Jerry's sardonic comments about what he had been reduced to, the pointlessness of it all, etc., etc.

*
**

Holland is such a small country, and the network of trains crisscrossing it is so well planned and efficient that traveling from city to city rarely takes more than a couple of hours (unless, of course, you take a local train—a *stop-trein*—between distant points). Jerry and I were able to visit Utrecht, Amsterdam, and Leiden, taking advantage of the *sneltreinen*, which departed often from the busy station at Eindhoven.

We spent an afternoon in Utrecht with Jane Henry, the violinist who played on "Chimanzzi (Olun): core" from *Ground*. I took a picture of him standing in front of a comic book vendor with large cutouts of Heer Bommel and Tom Poes in the display window above his head. We also traveled to Amsterdam to meet Joel Ryan for dinner.

Peter and Ria invited us to stay a few days with them in Leiden, and one rainy day, we made the longest train journey of our trip, riding comfortably through the coun-tryside and seeing more windmills than we'd ever seen. Our young Dutch friends hadn't realized how sick Jerry was until they saw how much he had declined since their visit to Texas. Peter quickly learned our pattern of frequent rests, and as he took us on walking tours of Leiden, he regularly proposed stops—for ice cream, coffee, or beer. One afternoon he suggested we take the bus to the beach, to Katwijk aan Zee on the North Sea, just a few miles north of the resort city Scheveningen. Jerry was amused by the prospect of visiting the family home of his old SMU piano teacher, Paul van Katwijk.

It was a chilly afternoon on the beach. We rested from our long walk from the bus stop at a little cafe on the sand, eating cheese sandwiches, drinking Heinekens, and looking out at the gray ocean. Peter is a photographer, and he brought his camera along, hoping to get a few interesting shots of the long expanse of shoreline and the water and the light. We resumed our stroll and followed the boardwalk down to the upper beach, studded with over a hundred individual changing houses: three-sided wooden structures fitted with benches and covered by colorful roofs, each with its own canvas door for privacy. Peter suggested, laughing, that Jerry and I sit in one of these structures for a picture. So we did—"Knabbel" and "Babbel" (Chip and Dale), as Peter called us—me with my goofy grin and Jerry with his penetrating yet distant stare, shoulder-to-shoulder beneath the mirror reflecting the photographer's right shoulder.

Toward the end of our visit, Paul and Hélène had a little more free time, and they took us to several park-like places near Eindhoven. We visited the grounds of an old castle, following an irrigation canal into the woods, where Paul pointed out various plants and birds, and we compared them to American counterparts, noting especially any interesting similarities between the Dutch and English names. One evening, they carried us to a nature area with a dessert café; we enjoyed rich pastries and dark beer and coffee, and then we took one of the well-marked paths into the woods. In the middle of one of our comparative discussions, this time on insects, Hélène, always the most wide-awake of our foursome, began shouting "*Pas op! Pas op!*" and almost too late we turned to see a cyclist coming directly toward us on the narrow path. Bicycles in the Netherlands have traditionally had the right-of-way; however, with the growing number of automobiles, that right is increasingly being threatened and not without resentment.

During the last days of our stay, Jerry and Paul were finishing up preparations for the installation in Den Bosch, and things were taking longer than they had anticipated. I wanted to see a little more of Holland, particularly of Amsterdam, so we agreed that we'd spend our last two nights near Schipol—Jerry would join me there the first night when he'd finished at the Melkfabriek. I reserved a room at one of the Dutch chain motels located just a short taxi ride away from the airport in the relatively new town of Hoofddorp. I arrived before lunch, but I decided to explore the village instead of going to Amsterdam. I ate dinner back at the motel and waited for Jerry. He had hoped to be able to arrive by six or seven o'clock, and by nine at night, I was quite worried. This was the longest period of time we'd been apart on the whole trip. I finally called Hélène, and she told me that Paul himself hadn't gotten home, so they must still be working. I sat—for another two hours—watching a tennis tournament on the lighted court just outside my motel room window, too worried to read or listen to music. I remembered waiting in the gazebo at Round Top that night, almost exactly a year ago.

The only interruption—I dove at the ringing phone—was when Jim Fulkerson called from Amsterdam (Hélène had given him the motel's number) to speak with Jerry and tell him he and Mary were looking forward to seeing him that next fall when he was to be a guest teacher again at the Hogeschool in Arnhem. When Jerry finally arrived, I tried not to let him see just how anxious I had been, but I think I was less successful than I had been at Round Top.

We decided to spend our last day in Amsterdam, a short train ride away. Pacing ourselves, we walked from the Centraal Station to the Begijnhof, a fourteenth-century garden dedicated to the memory of the laywomen of charity—the *begijnes*—and surrounded by houses dating from the sixteenth and seventeenth centuries. One entrance to this garden is the Engelse Kerk, where we heard a concert of Baroque music performed on period instruments.

We headed east to the Hortus Botanicus, where we explored the grounds and the greenhouse, taking pictures of one another. One is of me beneath a huge leaning palm; another shows Jerry beside a circular pond decorated with a large piece of iron sculpture in the shape of an overturned mushroom, the ridges of its underside and its long, curved stem suggesting an umbrella someone had carelessly dropped there. Finally, we headed west, past the new Muziektheater and the Centraal Station, on to the Brouwersgracht ("brewers' canal") and our dinner destination: De Avonden ("The Evenings"), a vegetarian restaurant named after the novel by Gerard Reve that Jerry was listening to on the CDs Joel Ryan had sent him over a year ago. By now, Jerry was tired, and the restaurant turned out to be much farther away than it had appeared on our map. We were almost there when— *"Pas op! Pas op!"* we heard from behind—a cyclist flew by, almost hitting Jerry, then hurling an epithet at him in Dutch that Jerry, unfortunately, understood: *Old fool.* Jerry was furious and tried to yell something back, but his shortness of breath allowed him to produce only a shouted whisper. Of course, he indulged himself in *l'esprit d'escalier* for several minutes to come, trying to find the most damning Dutch comeback.

*
**

We'd achieved our goal: we'd made the trip to Holland, and it had been a success (after the initial disappointment over the Rotterdam fiasco). Jerry had felt good most of the time, never even needing oxygen, and we had been able to see many of our Dutch friends as well as the Americans we knew who were living and working in the Netherlands. Our last meal at De Avonden—and the last really good meal Jerry was able to enjoy—was a celebration of our success. The young Belgian chef prepared delicious dishes using ingredients in surprising ways, and Jerry had a culinary adventure he would talk about often afterward.

After a longstanding goal has been reached, sometimes there comes a period of uncertainty, of precariousness. Neither Jerry nor I knew what was ahead or what would be reasonable to aim toward now. I was startled to see tears in Jerry's eyes as we climbed away from Schipol: "I'll never see Holland again," he said. The long flight home was miserable for him. He couldn't get comfortable, couldn't rest. Bob met us at the airport in Houston on an insufferably hot and humid afternoon, and almost as soon as we got to Bob's house, Jerry began using the oxygen we'd left there.

During the next two months, his oxygen use steadily increased. He felt like doing less and less. Every effort cost energy, and he suffered more dyspnea and, as a result, more fatigue. I bought him gadgets for use in picking up fallen objects or bringing distant ones near, and I brought in stools for both kitchens. Sometimes I'd come home from work to find him sitting on one of the stools and peeling or slicing vegetables for dinner, but he'd quickly give the chore over to me and go sit down nearby.

We resumed our gym visits, but Jerry wasn't able to do as much. He'd have to interrupt his exercising to use the inhaler, which he sat prominently beside his little packages of tissue on the desk that people put their keys on while they work out. When his breathing became especially labored, and he produced voiced sounds as he inhaled, some of the newer users of the facility would look his way in alarm. Two or three times, people asked him if he were all right, and he'd tell them he had emphysema. I had been routinely bringing a box fan in from the free weight room to plug in near the treadmills and the exercise bikes (a breeze in his face always helped Jerry breathe), and one day we arrived to find a new fan installed just where we needed it. Jerry no longer sweated and didn't have to shower, so he'd wait for me at the front desk and visit with the young man who worked there part-time while attending college.

When he felt like it, he worked at his new computer, revising and reprinting pieces. The *Village Voice* published Kyle Gann's periodic "Consumer Guide" on August 31, 1993, and Jerry's CD *Ground* was chosen as a "Pick Hit" and honored with the only A-plus given:

> Didn't expect this Texas wild man's manic genius to survive on disc, but actually, minus the distraction of his deadpan antics, his sonic originality blares louder. His noises result from electronic skrying with John Dee's angelic tables . . . ; as Hunt puts it, "congruent layers of associations of inflection-calls evoke, through a directed scanning skrying action, point specific, melody-action strings embedded in a reference context of conventions of performance." Whazzit mean? In "Chimanzzi (Olun): core," Jane Henry plays stream-of-consciousness violin while Hunt rattles jingle

bells and scrapes a hardware store of
doohickeys. "Lattice (stream): ordinal"
is a Nancarrowian barrage of nervous
piano clusters that sometimes aston-
ishes you with its prettiness. Elsewhere,
Hunt surrounds his whistling, cow-horn
blowing, and stuttering conversation
with metallic bumps and electric shim-
merings. His purism is Cagean, but the
frenetic gesture-language he's evolved is
a purposeful, undecipherable tone-magic.

This good review surely provided some impetus for
Jerry's work on the new CD that was to be issued by
Nonsequitur, although I don't remember Jerry ever saying
very much about it.

Months earlier, Uncle Henry, a veteran of World War
II, had mentioned that he'd like to attend the annual
reunion of his infantry division, The Railsplitters. I offered
to drive him and Aunt Hazel to the event, which was to
be held in late September in Cedar Rapids, Iowa. We were
to be gone for about ten days, visiting Army buddies in
South Dakota and Indiana in addition to attending the
Iowa reunion, then driving home through Kentucky,
Granny's birthplace.

As the time for our departure grew nearer, I began to
worry about leaving Jerry. He had become dependent on
me in so many ways, and I was continuing to give him the
chest percussion treatments twice daily. We discussed
my going several times, and I repeatedly offered to stay
home to arrange flights to Cedar Rapids for Henry and
Hazel. He insisted I go, and I finally decided to. I based
my decision in part on the hope that being independent
for a while might actually make Jerry feel less dependent,
more self-confident. I talked this over with Oz, who regularly called to check on Jerry; she agreed with my plan,
and she assured me that she'd stay in close touch with
Jerry while I was gone.

Due to the poor attendance, the reunion itself was a
disappointment, but our trip was a very pleasant one—
still wondering how Jerry was doing was so much on my
mind, I expect I often seemed preoccupied to Henry and

Hazel. Each night, as soon as we got to our motel, I'd call Jerry, and his report more or less determined how I felt through the next day, whether I was worried or relieved, anxious or happy. In fact, after a few rough days shortly after I left, he did begin to feel better—he even went to the gym alone one day. When I got home, we sat on the deck beneath the maple tree with Mary and Frances on their leashes beside us, and he told me that he was feeling better than he had in months. I promised myself then never to leave him again—I didn't want to miss a minute of the good times.

I began thinking about our upcoming birthdays and about their significance. That year, in 1993, we'd be fifty, and we'd have known one another for thirty-five years, a cause for celebration. My initial plan was to reserve a private room in an Indian or Thai restaurant in Dallas and invite a group of old friends to join us for dinner. It might even be a surprise for Jerry. When I talked with Oz about my idea, she insisted that we plan a dinner party at her and Paul's house with food from a Lebanese restaurant we all four liked. She even offered to mail the invitations from my list.

One of the people I very much wanted on that list was my sister. I decided to fly her down for a week in mid-November; after all, her three children had made the trip the last three years, and it was her turn. She was concerned about Jerry, and she had even offered to come down to help during his hospitalization in January. I wanted to be with her now.

Driving back from Athens late one October day, Jerry began experiencing such severe pains in his chest that he had to pull off the road. He took a couple of ibuprofen tablets that he now carried in his medicine bag. Then he told me that he'd had enough, that he couldn't go on much longer. The exercise was hurting now, not helping, and he was coughing up blood-streaked sputum again. "I don't see how anybody can feel this bad and live," he said.

So I told him about the party I'd planned. We had another goal.

*
**

Since his first hospitalization in January, I had always tried to counter Jerry's anxiety and despair about his illness with reasonable optimism. We both realized how directly his condition affected his mood—sometimes the fluctuations were swift and wide. I encouraged him to wait the bad times out, to try to hold on to a "usable" attitude. When I found him in a panicky state, it often helped if I could make a short call for outside help—to a nurse, or to the hospital emergency room staff, or to the Lung Line—for any little suggestion as to how to make things better, for any reassurance.

We learned to elevate the heads of our beds by four inches or so to facilitate drainage from Jerry's lungs and make breathing easier. As he continued to lose weight, we laid in a supply of nutritious and easy-to-eat foods, like instant breakfast and little cans of pudding and fruit cocktail. For soreness due to muscle strain, we discovered DMSO, and I rubbed it into his back and shoulders, and it gave him almost immediate relief. The electric massager we bought helped some, too.

But there were problems we couldn't solve, oddities no one could explain. Several of the arteries and veins in Jerry's chest remained swollen, and no one knew why. The sense of pressure in his head that had prompted a CAT scan of his sinuses back in January had never gone away. And his voice grew weaker—so much so that if I were around, he never answered the phone, and if a call came for him, it was by no means certain that he would be up to the effort to try and speak.

I began to worry about him being alone while I was gone, and I started calling him from work. As did others who called him regularly (Oz, Rod, Michael Schell, and Bob), I noticed that it took him some time to get his voice. He always said, though, that the effort to do so resulted in stimulation that made him feel better for a while.

He was most comfortable and could breathe most easily sitting at the small dining table that he used as a desk in his study, leaning forward and resting his head on his arms or a pillow. I began to find him in that position every time I came in. ("Howdy, Mr. Bull," he'd lift his head and say to me, alluding to an old joke that, given Jerry's weakness, had become regretfully apropos.) Eventually, he became restless everywhere else, whether sitting on a couch or in a chair. Sometimes he had to interrupt a meal for a few minutes to go lean over his desk.

It became harder for him to hold Mary and Frances for long. Because he was now staying more in the brick house, I had been bringing them over to be with us, but I came to realize that I wasn't doing him, or them, any favors. He hated that he couldn't give them the attention they were used to, and he would sit and dangle the wire cat toy for them to bat and chase, but even doing that for long started to fatigue him.

We were able to make love only when he was experiencing his best times. I watched for them—in the afternoon, before dinner, without hurrying, with no strain—it happened as a gift, bringing relief and a renewal of the old, intimate bond. But it happened less frequently as Jerry grew ashamed of his emaciated body. His last orgasm, he said, felt like someone else's.

Nothing gave me more joy than walking toward the house and began hearing him at the piano. It didn't happen often, and he never played for long. But I would stop and stand frozen on the walkway or on the porch, listening to whatever he had thought to play—a piano rag, some Scriabin or Pinto—hoping it would go on and on. He had ordered a new computer program for the generation of musical notation, and he tried it out by composing the single-page "Melody" that one day I found on the music stand.

We could see, though, that he was losing ground rapidly. He had already canceled the teaching engagement in Arnhem; not only did he feel that he was no longer up to making such a trip, he also wanted to finish up work here. For *Hemisphere*, he rented a video recorder and a camera with a small magnifying lens and scanned his body. (When we watched the tape, he told me that he thought it had more "narrative interest" than any other video work he had done.) He also continued to revise and print older pieces using the new computer and printer.

Everyone we talked with recommended that he have a flu shot to protect him against the respiratory infection he had the previous winter. He had a slightly elevated temperature the day we went for the shot, so we had to return the following week. By the end of the month (October), he was in the hospital in Kaufman with pneumonia.

One of the luckiest things that ever happened to Jerry during the course of his illness was meeting Dr. Laurie Harris. This young lady had done part of her residency at the UT Tyler Health Center, so she had considerable experience with pulmonary patients (or "lungers," as she chillingly called them). She had established a family practice in Crandall, a small town between Kaufman and Dallas. Jerry and I both were impressed by her practicality and candor. She acknowledged that the flu shot might indeed have made Jerry sick, but she also said that it would have been a mistake for Jerry not to have gotten it. She also confirmed our fear that his pneumonia had further compromised Jerry's lungs. She explained that getting over it would not be easy, and she recommended that we have a visiting nurse come by to check on Jerry twice a week during the period of recuperation. Jerry asked her if she thought he might have cancer, and she admitted that he might. She proposed another CAT scan (to compare with the ones made almost eleven months earlier), but she added that only tissue samples obtained from a bronchoscopy could conclusively establish the diagnosis. Jerry agreed to the CAT scan.

He was approaching the point where he had to know. Although he never said as much to me, I believe that he had come to feel that going on suffering would only be worth it if he could have some hope for a little more time—and that some portion of that time might be a little better than what it was now. Once, after a chest percussion treatment, he asked me how much longer I thought he had to live. "I think you probably have several pretty good years ahead," I said. He didn't comment.

I suppose I believed it. My boss and friend Frances came to see Jerry while he was still in the hospital. We stood at the foot of his bed discussing what Dr. Harris had just told us—that, yes, the CAT scan did indicate that a bronchoscopy should be done. However, she instructed that we first take Jerry home with some antibiotics and hope that they would fight the pneumonia and help him get to feeling better, then we'd see about the other later.

Jerry spoke a little about how sick he had gotten, about how little there was for him in life now. Then he told Frances that he was anxious for me, concerned about what would happen to me were he to die. "Don't worry about him, Jerry. Of course, he'll be sad a while, but he'll be alright," Frances said. At first, I wasn't sure who she was talking about. Then I was startled—alarmed—to realize it was me. *Sad a while.* Eighteen months ago, I had first imagined losing Jerry, but I had not yet imagined myself going on alone. Could I? And would I, beginning now, have to reassure Jerry that I could?

*
**

As Jerry frequently pointed out, I've always been adept at seeing what I want to see. This "selective inattention" may have served us well during Jerry's illness: he sometimes had to prove to me he couldn't do what I thought he could, and, on occasion, he happily failed. After his hospital stay in Kaufman, I began to see more clearly, more honestly, how sick he was, and the way other people reacted to his appearance helped me—forced me—to bring his condition into focus.

The visiting nurse came four or five times to monitor Jerry's vital signs and listen to his chest. He was eager for her visits, and she always managed to allay some of his anxiety by reminding him that recuperating from pneumonia takes a long time, especially for people with COPD. Each time she came, she said she thought he was moving air more efficiently in his lungs.

Her calls would begin with my telling her, as we walked to the house from her car, how anxious and despondent Jerry was, and her visits would end along the same route, with my thanking her for her encouragement and concern and for how generous she had been with her time (she always had to telephone her next client to tell them she'd be a little late). I couldn't help notice, however, on these trips to the driveway, that she wasn't as encouraging to me as she had been to Jerry. She later told me that she knew he was dying the first time she came.

Jerry made a trip to the library with me one Sunday afternoon. We had taken full advantage of the medical research materials there over the years: the physicians' drug manuals and the accompanying CDs, which included articles from medical journals and reference sources, had helped us learn about the side effects of some of the medicine Jerry was taking. We also gained a fuller understanding of the nature and likely course of Jerry's disease.

I don't know everything Jerry investigated that day, but he did read extensively about antibiotics. Several times during the afternoon, he came to my floor to have some coffee and rest at the table in the staff area. As always, my colleagues and friends got a kick out of seeing him; they'd all told me again and again that they'd never met anyone like him. Even as ill as he was, he was outrageous, ranting on about doing his own bronchoscopy and about having Dr. Jack Kevorkian (notorious at the time for having helped terminally ill patients commit suicide) as his "personal physician." When he came out to the service desk area, he would so command all our attention that the library patrons just had to stand and wait their turn.

After the hilarity would come the questions: Is he serious? Is he getting better? Everyone was obviously concerned, and I look back now on a year filled with the kindnesses of every type that they showed me, from volunteering on short notice to work in my place when I had to be with Jerry to knowing just when to ask about him and when not to.

One expression of thoughtfulness especially touched me. Yolanda was on her way to work one day and spotted a chair on wheels someone had left on the side of the road. She had her husband pull over, and they loaded it into their pickup and brought it in to offer to me. I had been talking about how hard it was to find a chair for Jerry that was both comfortable and would allow him, without getting up, to roll from the computer or the synthesizer to his desk and back. Our needs were on her mind.

The Humanities Division gave me a surprise birthday party: a complete lunch and a birthday cake, all beautifully served on two large tables. Shortly after we'd sat down to eat, Jerry called from Canton to tell me that he had unexpectedly run out of the medicine he used in his breathing machine and that he was going to Canton (seven miles from our house) to get the prescription refilled. He would call me again, he said, when he got back, so I would know he'd made the trip all right. I begged him to call our neighbor, Garland, who I assured him would be glad to run the errand for him. *No*, he insisted; he'd be careful, he'd take his time. I was extremely upset. Jerry hadn't driven alone in weeks. In addition to his shortness of breath and overall weakness, he was taking powerful antibiotics and an array of analgesics.

My panic was such that I don't remember how much, if anything, I told my friends about the nature of the call, although everyone knew it had been from Jerry. Brian had devised a birthday scavenger hunt for me, and I went off to follow his witty clues from book to book until I located the treasure: a box of Indian sweets that Tarlika had brought. Shortly after I returned, Jerry called to tell me that he was home and had made the trip fine; he had only gone off the road once. Whether or not I had been able to disguise my anxiety, I am sure I made no attempt to conceal my giddy relief.

Having Judy here was a joy and a comfort, although it hurt to see how shocked she was when she saw Jerry. She fell into our simple routine, helping with chores in such unobtrusive ways that I only realized all she had done much later. The best thing was the three of us to sit and visit, reminiscing about the adolescence we shared while watching *The X-Files*, *Mad About You*, and the British sitcoms that gave Jerry some diversion during the last weeks. Judy listened to what Jerry had to say about his illness and what it was stealing from his life and his future, and she offered her loving sympathy without a trace of false optimism. She knew then as I do now that he often told her things in order for me to hear them.

As our joint birthday party approached, Jerry began to doubt that he would be up to attending. Certainly, everyone would understand if he were not able to make it, but I pressured him a little because I believed going would be good for his spirits. It was to be a happy evening, a celebration—almost twenty longtime friends would be there.

Weeks earlier, I had written the poet Mark Doty to ask if he would record his poem "The Wings" from *My Alexandria* so that I could play it at the party as my gift to

Jerry. He agreed, and he sent me a tape of a reading of the poem in Provincetown—a reading he dedicated to Jerry and me. Before the tape arrived, however, I had decided not to use it that night. As I watched Jerry grow worse, I began to feel that the poem would be too wrenching for an occasion that I wanted, above all, to be a joyous one. I did read the poem to Jerry myself one night after Judy had left, and I listened to Mark's tape, alone, on Jerry's birthday.

Dressing and leaving the house had become very difficult for Jerry; he wore robes around the clock unless he had to go out. I could see we were going to be late for the party, so I called ahead. As soon as we entered Paul and Oz's home, Jerry was led into the living room and seated beside Judy, and Oz asked me to accompany her to the dining room to assign places at the long table. I shuffled the name cards she'd made and placed them in such a way as to separate couples while she followed along behind me and made a reference list to post at the door. As I worked, I became aware of how quiet the living room had grown as everyone took in the change they'd seen in Jerry and strained to hear him.

Jerry and I were seated at the head of the table, in front of the beveled windows that I'd looked through for so many years—they were behind the piano that had been moved in for the Sunday afternoon concerts. The Lebanese food was delicious: thyme pie, baba ganoush, falafel, and various meat dishes with white wine. My matchmaking must have been successful because everyone seemed to be engaged in lively conversation.

When we'd all just about finished eating, Jerry began to speak to the group. (He himself hadn't eaten much, and even I was too nervous, too distracted, to be able to concentrate on the food.) He talked a little about what a good life we'd had, how lucky we'd been in one another (in spite of my "meanness"), and in our friends. And then, he made his way around the table, addressing remarks first to one person and then another, recalling events from years back or mentioning special traits that he had always appreciated about the individual. He regretted that Houston and Jill weren't with us. It was as though, in his steady gaze at each guest, he shone a light on the uniqueness—and value to him—of each relationship. Because his voice was so weak and his breathing difficulty forced him to speak so slowly, we all hushed any table noises to be able to hear.

There was a moment of relief and laughter when Jerry described a certain period of time and happened to mention lava lamps. "Jerry—wait just a minute," Paul interrupted, jumping up from his seat and rushing out of the room. And he returned with one, a gift for us from Oz and him and David and Norma McManaway.

When I talked with some of these friends later about the monologue Jerry delivered that night, several of them characterized it as a "piece," as Jerry's last performance. It had been extraordinary, the way it wove together sentiments, ideas, and personalities in the most unpredictable and yet exactly right manner. As I listened to him, looking into the beams of his eyes and stealing occasional glimpses at their targets down the table, I felt again that familiar excitement that had always come from the way he could heighten my perception of the world, enthralling me by his extraordinary way of seeing it. Just as he'd done this for me for thirty-five years, from that day on the blacktop outside the junior high school cafeteria when he demanded to know the secret the green door was keeping, so had he done it for almost as long for most of those people listening to him now.

There could have been no better celebration—and no more fitting memorial because Jerry himself led it.

Dessert was served in the game room, but Jerry soon came up to me to say that he had begun to feel bad and that he thought we should leave. Oz packed some food for us to take along, and Judy and others gathered up the gifts we'd received and loaded the car out front. We got Jerry settled in the front seat, and I noticed Toni standing on the front lawn staring at Jerry with tears in her eyes. I went over to her and told her something I had wanted to tell her for years: that Jerry had told me her appreciation of his talent and her support of his work at SMU, almost thirty years ago, had helped his parents accept the fact that they had a homosexual son because they saw from the way she regarded him that his sexual orientation would not be an obstacle to success.

*
**

We had reached our second goal, but just barely. Jerry continued to feel worse as the evening wore on, and around midnight he asked me to take him to the emergency room of the Kaufman hospital. We supposed that the antibiotics he was taking for the pneumonia weren't working, and the young doctor on duty that night agreed that that might be the case. After examining Jerry's records, however, he talked very frankly with Jerry about the possibility that there was more making him feel bad than just pneumonia. He changed the prescription for antibiotics and released Jerry to return home shortly after daybreak.

I began to see a change in Jerry's emotional state after the party. Where he had been despondent, even depressed, before, he was now often agitated and sometimes desperate. He could not sleep in the bed at all, and he got what little rest he did by putting his head down on his desk. The nights were long for him, and he seemed to want to keep me with him late. The last few mornings Judy was here, he called me on the intercom at dawn to ask me to come over. After she left, I set up a cot in the living room of the brick house and slept there to be close to him, leaving the bed available to him whenever he might feel like trying to lie down.

He wanted me to take him to Dr. Harris's office the day before Judy's departure, and she repeated what the resident at Kaufman had told him. Jerry had been taking antibiotics so long that he had developed a bad case of thrush, and he was feeling worse and worse in spite of all the medication. Dr. Harris asked him if he would let her set up an appointment with a pulmonary specialist in Mesquite to discuss a bronchoscopy, and Jerry agreed. He had to know now, he said, if he had cancer.

I took Judy to the airport the next day. She had done so much for us during the week she was here, and I was able to work a day or two more than I would otherwise have been because she offered to stay with Jerry. I know it meant a lot to him to see how concerned she was for me and how close we are. And it was good for me to see the two of them renew their friendship as they sat talking or watching TV—just as they had when we were all teenagers, and I left them to spend a couple of weeks with my aunt in Kilgore. I waited for Judy in the car while she told Jerry goodbye. When she got in, she said, "Well, that was hard."

We saw Dr. Zevallos the next week, on the day before Thanksgiving. He told us pretty much what the other two specialists had, but he admitted that what he saw on the X-rays did look like a tumor. Jerry asked if it were cancer, what could be done. Dr. Zevallos told us that there was some chance that the tumor (or tumors) might respond to radiation and chemotherapy—we could talk about that after the bronchoscopy—but that such treatments wouldn't make Jerry feel better and might not even prolong his life by much.

Jerry was very frank with Dr. Zevallos, as he had been with all the other doctors he had seen. He was interested in the quality of life—merely adding days was without meaning if his life was without meaning. "We've had a wonderful life together," I said. To avoid a long delay from the upcoming holidays, the bronchoscopy was scheduled and performed that afternoon. Dr. Zevallos came to the waiting room and told me that yes, it was cancer. He said it was in both lungs as well as in the esophagus, and there was some involvement with the vocal cords. "Well, that's it, then," I said. He mentioned again that some radiation might help, but I got the feeling that he didn't really believe it would.

When they let me into Jerry's room, he was sitting up straight in his paisley hospital gown, the color good in his cheeks and his eyes unusually wide open and bright. The nurse asked him if he wanted a soft drink, and he replied he'd split a Coke with me. "It wasn't so bad. Actually, I don't remember much about it," he said. It was a pleasure sitting there with him, drinking our drink, and enjoying the illusion the drugs loaned us that everything was OK.

It wasn't until we were halfway home that he asked me what the doctor had said. I told him everything.

We had an ice storm that night, and the lights were off for eight hours. Jerry was frantic, even though I had brought over a large kerosene stove from the barn house,

and we had plenty of kerosene lamps, candles, and flashlights. He had me call the electric cooperative every hour
or so, and I was told each time that all their crews were
out and working as fast as they could.

On Thanksgiving Day, he dictated a letter to Steve
Peters, the producer of the Nonsequitur album. He went
over with me the notes he had made earlier about how to
edit the audiotapes for that CD as well as the videotape for
the *Hemisphere* laserdisc. I helped him set up two mikes
in the bedroom, and we put an assortment of sound-making devices on a card table at the foot of the bed: bells,
rattles, metal and plastic objects, and sticks to beat them
with. While I monitored the audio levels in the study,
Jerry created one of the soundtracks for *Haramand Plane*.
Later that afternoon, he showed me a list he'd made of
the composers and performers he believed would promote
his work. That night, we called Judy and her family and
told them about the results of the bronchoscopy. I heard
Jerry tell my older niece, Jenny, that he only had a few
more days and that they should all help me because I'd
need them for the next few months. (Jamie later offered to
come back to live with me.)

We decided it was time to call Bob, and we asked him
to come up the next day. He had a hard time believing the
bronchoscopy results; he didn't think Jerry was that sick.
But when he arrived Friday afternoon and saw Jerry, he
was convinced. The three of us talked a long time Friday
night, sitting in the living room and looking over at the TV
from time to time. "These last few days, Stephen's been
like steel," Jerry said.

Saturday morning, Jerry needed more oxygen, so
Bob and I made a quick trip to Athens to get a full cylinder. When we got back, we found him anxious—worried
because we'd been gone so long. For lunch, I fixed a
Mexican cheese omelet, and Jerry ate well.

After lunch, we talked a while. At one point, Jerry
caught me staring at him, and he smirked. Then he got
up to get dressed. He called me, needing help. I guided
the belt around his waist, loop through the loop, my
arms encircling him—and then I lost control: "If you ever
needed proof how much I love you, this is it," I cried,

kneeling before him with the side of my face against the front of his trousers.

"I never needed any proof," he replied. I noticed that he was steadying himself by holding onto the edge of the lavatory. "Stephen," he said quietly, "this sentimentality leads nowhere."

I stood up to help him finish the job. Bob and I were going to Wal-Mart to return some slippers I had bought for Jerry that turned out to be too small. Jerry walked with us out to Bob's car.

"Bye-bye, Stephen," I heard Jerry say.

I turned around and looked him in the eye.

"Bye-bye, Jerry," I replied.

Then Bob drove me away.

After

Kyle Gann's obituary of Jerry appeared in the *Village Voice*, December 21, 1993:

> When John Cage performed in Dallas in 1975, the private reception afterward was dominated by a thin, intense-looking guy whose spindly limbs swept the air as he spoke. He was comparing episodes of *I Love Lucy* to the Beethoven sonatas as varied manifestations of a recurring structural formula. I thought he was brilliant and nuts at the same time, and those two words have come back to me every time I've seen Jerry Hunt perform. I had no idea he was anybody significant, but five years later, I saw him again at New Music America, making high-tech electronic music by hitting a suitcase with a stick.
>
> Hunt was a bundle of nervous energy, never boiling over but eternally simmering. His doctor made him cut down on his forty cups of coffee a day, and after he gave up chain-smoking—not early enough, tragically, to prevent him from dying of lung cancer three days before his fiftieth birthday—he chewed nicotine gum vigorously, even onstage.
>
> He was the fastest talker I've ever interviewed.

His music was a personal, hermetic religion. His works, with titles like *Chimanzzi (Olun): core* and *Bitom (stream): link* were based on a private geography of Texas towns meshed with the angelic tables of the sixteenth-century magus John Dee. Bells on his wrists jingled as he banged endless tremolos on the piano. Electronic sounds would burble, video images would flip as he whipped fishing poles toward the audience. Every gesture in his repertoire seethed with inscrutable meaning. When I told a friend Hunt had died and that I wished I understood his music enough to describe how it worked, she said, "No one knew what Jerry was doing. Make up something."

Hunt lived in a barn on his mother's property, somewhere northeast of Dallas. When you called up, his mother would answer and switch the call to the barn. He's survived by his lover, Stephen Housewright. Unfortunately, his primary exposure outside new-music circles came from a pointless controversy. He had collaborated with Karen Finley (even *she* couldn't upstage him), and when he was later on a panel that gave her a grant, right-wingers trying to discredit the NEA trumped up a conflict-of-interest complaint. Even had they investigated Hunt personally, they wouldn't have comprehended his level of artistic purity. Luckily, before he died, he got one fantastically characteristic audio document of his work onto a disc: *Ground: Five Mechanic Convention Streams* on the O.O. label.

His death on November 27 makes no more sense than his music did, but the

latter was an astonishing feat of manic
intensity.

Several concerts of Jerry's works and pieces composed
in tribute to him were performed during the first six
months of 1994. This is my description of the first:

> The memorial concert for Jerry in
> Houston was given in the Rothko Chapel on
> January 29 by DiverseWorks, the contem-
> porary arts organization for which Jerry
> had performed several times over the
> years and that had invited him to give
> a concert on the 29th in connection with
> the John Cage exhibition at the Menil
> Collection. The octagonal Rothko Chapel
> is located on the grounds of the Menil,
> a park-like area near the University of
> St. Thomas and the Montrose district of
> Houston. The Chapel contains the huge,
> almost solidly black paintings of Mark
> Rothko; as one walks about the space
> or sits on the benches, each of these
> somber works becomes a window opening
> inward to the darkness that we usually
> decline to see—a darkness both of a
> personal dimension and of the world. The
> tiny square of light at the very top of
> the ceiling invites the gaze upward and
> beyond, but it is hard to keep the head
> back for very long.
> On the 29th, that gaze was, instead,
> led forward to the stage and its video
> monitor, microphones, and various nonde-
> script objects cluttering the performance
> space. There was little sound as the 150
> or so people assembled on the benches.
> Michael Parenteau began by reading
> a tribute to Jerry that described his
> career and his art and the influence Cage
> had on him and that he himself has on
> artists and audiences. For a minute,

nothing happened. Then Michael Galbreth
started a videotape of Jerry performing
on a stool, gesturing and waving some of
the objects he made to a background of
his music.

No one would have been less likely
than Jerry to invite people anywhere
for "canned" entertainment, and the
Art Guys, Ellen Fullman, and Pauline
Oliveros tacitly acknowledged that fact
as they very slowly and deliberately
opened the live portion of the concert
by making sounds and gestures that had
come to be associated with Jerry's own
work. Michael began reading quotes from
Jerry's letters and interviews by taking
cards at random from a paper sack on the
floor. The quotes pertained to music and
religion, primarily, but several were
anecdotal and of a personal nature. Many
were funny. Sometimes Michael lay down
to read them, like a little boy doing his
homework. And sometimes he drew a card
only to read it to himself; Jerry would
have liked that touch.

Meanwhile, Ellen began assembling
several objects on the other side of the
performance space. She dragged a metal
folding chair across the stone floor, then
brought in a man's sports coat and a pair
of shoes. She carried a picture of Jerry,
one that had been taken in performance,
through the audience, illuminating it
with the flashlight that Jerry himself so
often used.

Jack Massing accompanied the words and
movement by making a variety of sounds.
He held a yards-long glass tube filled
with BB pellets, allowing them to roll
first one way and then the other, producing a rushing, oscillating sound like
ocean waves or heavy, eerie breathing.

Then he put on plastic gloves (another of Jerry's trademarks) and shook tiny bells and other metallic objects—often quite close to Michael's face and body as he read. Most of these small instruments were taken from a suitcase sitting in full view of the audience, yet another of Hunt's practices.

And through it all, from the sides and back of the Chapel, and sometimes from places on the benches themselves, came the notes from Pauline's accordion—plaintive, distant, occasionally angry-sounding, moving here and there. At one dramatic moment, she appeared in a side doorway holding a black umbrella over herself as she played.

Within a few minutes, Ellen had completed her tableau: the chair now with the coat on the back, the shoes placed together in front of it, Jerry's picture in the seat lit by the flashlight lying in front of it, and the tilde (~) that Jerry always signed his letters with reproduced on a card and positioned just above the photograph. Then Ellen walked to her mike and read Jerry's words in a loud, strong voice: "If I don't get there, just put my picture in a chair."

The final minutes of the concert were devoted to a portion of another videotape Jerry made. We see only his head above a broad, white Elizabethan collar. He whistles, blows, and breathes, all the while making a series of facial expressions that suggest, alternately, a magus and a clown; sometimes, it appears that he has, in fact, been possessed. The lamps used to light the video recording are bright in Jerry's eyes as he looks directly out at us. The white brightness that had emanated from the center of the

Chapel ceiling seemed to have moved to those eyes.

One by one, the performers left the stage.

Pauline's accordion stopped playing. Then there was a loud noise offstage, like a paper sack being burst. And Michael Galbreth walked out, looked at the audience, and said (as had Jerry so many times at the ends of concerts), "Well, I guess that's it."

The Dallas performance group Voices of Change dedicated their February 7, 1994 concert at SMU to Jerry's memory. Pianist Jo Boatright played "Melody," Jerry's last composition. Laurie Shulman described the work in the concert program:

> "Melody" is not nearly so simple as its title.
>
> Hunt builds the piece above a static open fourth in the left hand that functions as an ostinato.
>
> The right hand has all the activity, alternating shorter notes with long, wide intervals with an occasional melisma. The effect is an appealing mix, rather like chant crossed with new-age jazz . . . "Piano was always Jerry's first love," says Housewright. "It's appropriate that his last piece should be for piano."

On March 12, Voices of Change presented a memorial concert at the Contemporary Culture Gallery. In addition to the video works *Birome [zone]: plane (fixture)* and *Transform (stream): core*, some footage from an interview with Jerry filmed by Paul Bosner was shown. Jo Boatright again performed "Melody," and the chamber ensemble, assisted by Ron and Joan Snider, offered an interpretation of *Chimanzzi (Olun): double*. Various audience members were asked to read some of Jerry's quotes.

There were three events in New York City in March remembering Jerry. Petr Kotik's S.E.M. Ensemble performed "Melody" in two instrumental versions and showed three video works (including *Bitom (fixture): topogram*) on March 15 at the Paula Cooper Gallery. On the 16th, Roulette hosted an informal "video shivoo," showing interview footage, a videotape of a 1977 recital given at Paul and Oz Sreres', and title music sequences from programs Jerry worked on for the Dallas County Community College District (with Paul Bosner).

A memorial concert was held at Phill Niblock's Experimental Intermedia Foundation on March 19. Jane Henry performed a version of *Chimanzzi* on violin, and Laetitia Sonami presented a piece employing an electronic glove; both artists used some of Jerry's music. Joseph Celli offered *Phalba (Revisited)*, a piece "loosely based on materials, mimetic gestures, sounds, and notations from the original *PHALBA (stream): extractive* that Jerry composed for me in 1983." The electronic arts ensemble 77Hz/REV 2 created a multimedia work, *Telephone Calls to the Dead*, based in part on an unfinished collaboration between Jerry and Michael Schell. And Karen Finley sent a videotape in which she read excerpts from letters Jerry had sent her through the years.

Two memorial concerts took place in the summer. One was coordinated by Steve Key and was held in San Diego. Some of Jerry's as yet unrecorded songs were played, accompanied by slides, and a couple of his video works were shown.

The last concert was given at the Outpost Performance Space in Albuquerque on June 18. Pauline Oliveros performed, using several of Jerry's video works; she was assisted by Ione, Margrit Schenker, and Joanna Whitney. The evening was sponsored by the Nonsequitur Foundation, whose music gallery on Fifth Street concurrently displayed several hundred of the artifacts Jerry used in his video work and in performance. (Steve Peters had come to Canton the previous weekend to select these objects and take them back to Albuquerque for the exhibition.)

I described that last concert as follows:

Steve Peters welcomed the audience and talked a little about Jerry's work, pointing out that Jerry's interest in the occult had a playful dimension that adds a special element of pleasure to the usual bafflement audiences feel when exposed to the pieces. He then introduced Pauline Oliveros, whose remarks emphasized Jerry's originality; she made the comment that although Jerry might have been considered a "marginal" composer by the music establishment, "margins always surround the text."

Jerry's video work *Birome [zone]: plane (fixture)* was shown. Then Pauline led a meditation while playing the accordion in accompaniment to a videotape Jerry had made of his performance artifacts moving through space (he used this tape as an adjunct in performance). Margrit, Ione, and Joanna meditated alongside Pauline, whose accordion sounds were sparse—tones played from the keyboard, sometimes short, sometimes sustained, low notes from the bass buttons, some "scratching" of the bellows themselves.

After an intermission, the final piece, a quintet, was performed. Margrit appeared in black with her face swathed in gauze. She remained a ghostly presence at the grand piano, plucking the strings, striking the wood of the instrument, from time to time playing a few notes on the keyboard, and groaning, sighing, and even screaming intermittently. Ione, dressed in a gold and black sari, wandered around the performance space carrying a candle on a dish; her face, like Margrit's, was concealed.

Joanna approached the microphone dressed in a tight gold lamé gown, sleeveless to reveal the extensive tattoos on her arms. As she gently gyrated her hips and undulated her right arm and hand, she read excerpts from quotations taken from published interviews with Jerry in an exaggerated declamatory style, widely varying pitch and volume levels, sustaining and clipping phrases, and yet maintaining an expression on her face that suggested a vast distance from the content of the texts. She never stopped the regular motions of her body throughout the reading.

Pauline stood at one side of the space and blew on a conch, producing both staccato sounds and sustained, sometimes tremulous sequences. The video monitors showed Jerry's *Transform (stream): core*, the piece he made wearing an Elizabethan collar, tonelessly whistling and blowing, making a variety of facial expressions, and accompanied by a percussive soundtrack using rattles, bells, and drums.

What was especially moving about the "quintet" was this inclusion of Jerry as a participant throughout the piece. The sounds on the videotape, but mostly his facial expressions (ranging from delight to incredulity to shock), made a kind of commentary on everything else that was happening, and there were some remarkable *frissons* when coincidences involving the quotes occurred.

Everything melded together, through a climactic moment and to the final words about the experience of being "reborn to sound" that Joanna read after the videotape had concluded. Pauline had directed the entire piece, it seemed, blowing into the shell; her last, breath-like sound lingered in the quiet room a while after the tribute was done.

Partners

Originally self-published, 1995.

ISBN 978-1-953691-04-0 (paperback)
ISBN 978-1-953691-08-8 (hardcover)

Published by Blank Forms Editions in Brooklyn, New York

Designed by Alec Mapes-Frances
Printed by Ofset Yapımevi in Istanbul, Turkey

Blank Forms Editions
468 Grand Avenue #3D
Brooklyn NY 11238
blankforms.org